The 360 Degrees
of the Zodiac

Adriano Carelli

First Printing 1977
Sixth Printing 2004

ISBN: 0-86690-063-2

Published by:
American Federation of Astrologers, Inc.
6535 S. Rural Road
Tempe, Arizona 85283

Printed in the United States of America

Dedication

This book is dedicated to my unintentional benefactors
To misery, which made me free
To hunger, which taught me to work
To my enemies, who accustomed me to fight
and awakened me to my own abilities

With the help of God I hope to see the da y when I can
dedicate a greater work to those who have benefitted
me intentionally though I did not deserve it.

Contents

Foreword

This book is not meant for profane hands. It began as a monograph I wrote for my own exclusive use, before thinking it might come in handy to other astrologers. Then I rearranged my personal notes and drew them up in book form.

Since the times of Hipparchus and Ptolemaeus, traditional astrology has known the twelve signs of the zodiac, the twelve corresponding houses (or sectors), and the seven classical planets. There is a vast literature on Neptune and Uranus; Brunhubner has devoted the whole of his intelligent activity to Pluto, with results that can be termed satisfactory. Less has been written on the incorporeal planet Lilith, and still less on the lunar Nodes, though what is strictly indispensable is known about both. In all these subjects opinions may differ on details, but the essentials are out of discussion. There are more relevant divergences as to the planetary aspects, though no one has ever dreamed of questioning their foundations and denying that a quadrature is dissonant, or that the exact conjunction of two planets is more powerful than their trigonal aspect.

Every astrologer keeps some American, English, German or even French publication at hand as a reference where memory fails; and as far as signs and sectors, planets and aspects are concerned, incontestable and unchallenged facts are available. As to the fixed stars, we usually refer to Robson,[1] who has brought different opinions into a measure of agreement. Trouble begins when one tries to interpret the degrees, which has been astrology's heel of Achilles until now. My aim in this book is to render this delicate point less vulnerable.

What does anybody know about the degrees? In some treatises of scientific astrology and in all those of onomantics, the so-called Theban Calendar is reported, which is generally attributed to P. Christian; there is a short sentence for each day of the year in onomantics and for each degree in scientific astrology.

More interesting is the work of the Italian philosopher Pietro d'Abano (1250-1315), a professor of medicine and a martyr of science, as he fell a victim to the "holy" Inquisition. The chapter about the degrees in his work was reprinted at Venice two centuries later; i.e., at the very beginning of the art of typography, by Johannes Angelus,[2] and inserted in his later *Astrolabium.*[3]

This work is further carried over, but without its typical drawings, in a French compilation published about one-and-a-half centuries ago.[4] Both this and the work of Johannes Angelus supply one symbolic image for every degree, which this latter also illustrates with an etching, whereas the French author describes it only in Latin. They use hardly more than half a dozen words to describe and explain (as, for instance, *aqua profluens = nascetur instabilis).* The two Latin versions differ a little in their form, but mostly agree in their sense. Their translation is found inserted in many a recent treatise.

There is furthermore a modern work, *The Degrees of the Zodiac Symbolized* (Chicago: Aries Press, 1943) comprising two smaller treatises, the former written by the seer Charubel at the end of the last century, the latter by the great astrologer Sepharial as a revised edition of an older work, not available nowadays, by an Italian clairvoyant who wrote under the *nom de plume* of Volasfera and is quoted once by Sepharial (p. 48) as one Antonio Borelli, and another time (p. 54) with the surname of Belloni. I could not find his real name. These two describe one symbolic image for each degree and explain its meaning as well; but at somewhat greater length than previous authors, the more diffuse of the two being Sepharial.

The famous British astrologer, Alan Leo, in his *Astrological Textbooks*[5] defines the influence of each degree with a sentence as short as those of the Theban Calendar. Finally, E. C. Matthews has recently published a book on the degrees under the title *Fixed Stars and Degrees of the Zodiac Analyzed* (St. Louis: New Era Press) where the author does not quote any symbolic image and goes so far as to exhibit pride therein. That is why I have not laid any store by his conclusions. As to Alan Leo, I could persuade myself that, at least in this specific matter, he is entirely misled.

[Editor's Note: There are two other individual degree publications with which the author apparently was unfamiliar. *Zodiacal Symbology and Its Planetary Power* by Isidore Kosminsky (London: William Rider & Son), and a work largely translated from some European manuscripts published by Henry J. Gordon, entitled *Rectification of Uncertain Birth Hours with the Aid of the Individual Delineation of the Rising Degree and Mid-Heaven Degree*. There is also a more recent title by Donna Walter Henson: *Degrees of the Zodiac* (Tempe: AFA, 2004)].

Tot capita tot sententiao. According to classical tradition (which Charubel rightly follows) for every arc of the circle, as from 0°00'00" to 1°00'00", and so on, there is a spiritual Power radiating its influence down here. According to Sepharial's and Alan Leo's revolutionary school of thought, instead, from the furthest point of every one of the 360 arcs into which the zodiac, or rather the ecliptic, is divided, an influence streams forth and finds its limits where it meets the two other influences radiating from the two next points on its right and left; thus one center of influence would be localized in the geometric point 1°00'00"; another one in 2°00'00", whereas the two influences would become mutually neutralized at 1°30'00". Therefore, according to the classical authors and Charubel, the first degree corresponds to the arc between 0°00'00" and 1°00'00", and for the moderns to the arc between 0°30'00" and 1°00'00".

Moreover, one can count on one's fingertips the degrees on

which, out of the 360, the authors give similar—never alike—symbols, and even in those very few cases, each writer seems to be alive to only one of their meanings, so that, also where no contradiction is apparent, there is variety of interpretation.

Under such circumstances, the poor scholar is bound to be thoroughly puzzled, and the most obvious solution would be to stick to the points on which all five authors (Alan Leo included) agree and do away with the rest, which is exactly what I began by doing. But I soon realized that, had I pursued such a course to the end, I should have come out of it empty-handed; as in some cases the views were so glaringly conflicting as to bar any point in common. I shall give two examples of this below. Then it dawned upon me that each controversial degree—in other words all of them—called for a process of thought and meditation on spiritual lines, the only course enabling me to rise above the clash of jarring opinions. On such a plane, I thought, the whole prism of truth must be. The different scholars must have caught but a glimpse of one of its facets at a time. But, as soon as I set about my task, I saw that even where the texts under consideration seemed to agree, my meditation led me to entirely independent and unexpected results. This is how this book came into being.

And now here are two instances of how widely the four texts I studied (Alan Leo's work having finally been put aside) differ:

4° Virgo

Symbols:

Pietro d'Abano: *vir bobus arans.*

Charubel: A square patch of ground, resembling what might be set apart for lawn tennis, covered with red cloth, or what resembles such.

Volasfera: A field of corn standing high and ripe.

Interpretations:

Pietro d'Abano: *nasceture agricola.*

Theban Calendar: Sense of truth; love of nature; an intelligence bent on metaphysics.

Charubel: Whoever may have this degree on his Ascendant is born to enjoy the luxuries of this life; plenty follows him; but willful waste and useless expenditure on what pertains to matters conventional, superficial and the artificial, these prove his leading characteristics. Whilst he is intensely devoted to art, he will ignore the beauties of nature.

Sepharial: It denotes a person of simple and rural habits, who will succeed in the cultivation of natural products, and in husbandry and farming. The mind, although simple, is full of the essential elements of right thinking, and the nature is ripe with well-directed aspirations and endeavors. Such a one will live a useful and successful life, and will come to the length of his days in competence and peace. It is a degree of produce.

As can be seen, Charubel, by stressing love of luxury and artificial things and denying understanding of things of nature, says exactly the opposite of what the others imply. But even these do not entirely agree as to the rest. Sepharial endows the native with a mind which, if not downright weak, is at any rate simple, whereas the Theban Calendar foresees a philosophical mind. My personal meditations have led me far away from all four texts considered and to grasp the essence of this degree as not consisting in either a tiller's or a craftsman's or a thinker's work, but in the planning of the work itself. Thus the image I have conceived is at variance with all three symbols reported above.

5° Virgo

Symbols:

Pietro d'Abano: *aquila quiescena.*

Charubel: A very long, straight road, the terminus of which I do not see.

Velasfera: A soldier prepared for battle.

Interpretations:

Pietro d'Abano: *sine labore mercator.*

Theban Calendar: A sharp, practical mind.

Charubel: This life is uneventful, there is little or no ambition, nor is there much in such a life to stimulate such a feeling. This life being uniformly even, there is but little calculated to put caution on the alert. Hence the native is liable, after the prime of life, to become poor, as adequate provision for future contingencies has not been thought of. Thus a quiet life is not always to be desired where provision depends on one's exertions.

Sepharial: It defines a man of ready spirit, quick to respond to the calls of duty and honor; a man of noble instincts and well-disciplined habits. Such will prove a ready and willing friend and a redoubtable opponent. He will succeed in life through his own executive powers, and the credit which falls to him will be earned. It is a degree of efficiency.

An even wider discrepancy confronts us here. Two of the authors considered are in open contrast with the other two, and Sepharial and Charubel seem to hold diametrically divergent opinions.

A real question of right and wrong does not however arise. Meditation has shown me a symbol outwardly resembling the one of Pietro d'Abano, yet in a profounder sense far different. Not the free, lordly eagle is the image fitting this degree, but the gerfalcon, a bird tamed by man and obedient to him.

As this may have shown, the symbol is the key to everything. Lucky is the astrologer who can discern it clearly for each degree. I am still far from such clairvoyance.

Meditation on the 360 degrees has taken up one year of my life, but this has not been the worst. The hardest work has been the quest for fitting historic examples. I said purposely "the quest" and not "the collection," as unfortunately most of the texts available are imprecise, often wrong, and I had to cast all horoscopes concerned all over again.

Obviously some misprints are, so to speak, inevitable; lack of precision is, up to a certain point, excusable, as astrologers are not always alive to the importance of degrees and many supply us with only planetary positions within one degree, either by excess or by defect, of the correct one.

This would still be comparatively little trouble. But in some cases misprints are so thick that, in one of the texts I went through, an otherwise excellent one, Goethe's horoscope has become altogether unrecognizable, as such ideagrams as Virgo and Scorpio are mixed up, and the like. Much of this muddle is due to many an astrologer's habit of having their graphs copied by draughtsmen who, though skilled at their work, have not the slightest idea of astrology and look for an easy way out when they fail to decipher the author's curlicues, and on his side this latter never takes the trouble to check up how far the copyist's fantasy ran away with him. Once I stumbled upon a mysterious figure 25 which, on closer scrutiny, proved to be the Dragon's Tail.

Nor is this the worst, as for many mistakes the astrologers themselves are to be blamed. *Errare humanum* and all books, whether astrological or otherwise, contain blunders, but there is a limit to everything. There are people who style themselves astrologers, write and publish books expounding new theories, and in the end prove not to know even when the Gregorian reform of the calendar was carried out. I once saw a horoscope of Richelieu which resembled the great Frenchman as closely as I resemble the inhabitant of another planet. What had happened was simply that the author had found it proper to add ten days to the Cardinal's birth date, as if the Gregorian Calendar had not been in use in France since

December 1582,[6] This makes me wonder sometimes what right we have to complain of disbelief on the part of the public, if we astrologers ourselves have no self-respect.

I am very much afraid that, in spite of the editor's efforts and my own, some misprints and mistakes have crept into my book also, for which I apologize beforehand. May I humbly entreat all readers stumbling upon any inaccuracy to be kind enough to let me know, that I may do away with it in the next edition, for which I thank all in advance. It would show even greater kindness to express freely to me one's personal and unbiased opinion of my work; and the highest proof of friendliness would be to supply me with precise data on the birth of some interesting figure to be added to my collection of historical examples.

With these thanks in advance, I take leave of those readers who have been sensible enough to read the foreword as well.

Adriano Carelli
Rome, September 1950

Endnotes
1. *The Fixed Stars and Constellations in Astrology* by Vivien E. Robson (London: J. B. Lippincott).

2. Some modern authors dealing with the degrees have credited Johannes Angelus with this monograph on the zodiacal degrees, the oldest work known on the subject. But Johannes Angelus is not to blame, as on the reverse of leaf e8 of his work he plainly states that the part of his book dealing with the degrees is due to Pietro d'Abano: *graduumque omnium signorum imagines—ab excellentissimo viro medicine* (sic) *facultatis doctore experto Petro de Abano elaboratas—in medio figuarum celi* (sic), *proprietate earundem imaginumaque figuratio = ne appositis, locantur.*

3. *Astrolabium planum in tabulis ascendens . . . cum quodam*

tractatu nativitatum utili ac omato . . .— *Venetiis, Anno Salutis MDII.* The part concerning the degrees goes from the front of leaf f to the reverse of leaf r4.

4. *Origine de tous les cultes, ou Religion Universelle—par Dupuis, citoyen francois—a Paris, l'an III de la Republique une et indivisible: tome septieme* (p. 129-150).

5. See pages 241 to 246 of *Astrology for All,* the first volume of the work quoted.

6. Richelieu was born on September 9, 1585.

Instructions for Use of this Handbook

1. A general premise for the reader is the Latin proverb *Opportent studuisse*. This book is meant neither for the profane nor for the one intending to profane it. To make use of it one must have delved deep into astrology. Even before that, one has to have a culture. To the layman who, for example, has no inkling as to the meaning of the abbreviations Asc. MC, etc., the text itself would hardly make sense. To the routinist who, deaf to the real meaning of words, murders his own language, and to the quack who reviles his art by selling prefabricated horoscopes off the assembly line, the author's ideas would be equally incomprehensible.

I am firmly of the opinion that, in order to study any spiritual science, the scholar ought to have at least the background of a very good pupil about to graduate from high school. On this point I set lower requirements than Marquis DeGuaita,[1] who would not admit to his school anybody who, apart from the rest, knew no Hebrew.

The truth is that occultism is the most arduous among philosophical methods. Spiritualism is, among philosophical systems, the one demanding the utmost exactitude of expression. Readers who would miss the hair's breadth difference between caution and prudence; or worse, who would not tell pride from haughtiness; or worst of all, who would mix up sexual and sensual as if they were synonymous, are not in a position to use this book.[2] I have striven to write it in such a way that routinists and quacks may not do any harm.

2. The zodiac's degrees are reckoned like the houses, the years, etc. In such languages as the classical Slavonic or Teutonic ones, this is more evident than in English or Italian, as they use ordinal numbers and say, e.g., "half of the four(th) hour" for half past three. As to the years, other languages also agree on the general basis of ordinal numbers. At its face value, the expression sounds like a cardinal number.

The first house is the one going from zero hour (00:00) to 01:00 hour; the second from 01:00 to 02:00, etc. Zero year, on the other hand, has never existed; the twelve months after Jesus Christ's birth constitute the year A.D. 1. Though we use grammatically cardinal numbers to make the years following or preceding (e.g., Augustus died in the year A.D. 14) nevertheless each number is logically the ordinal one, the year 14 being really the fourteenth, as there is no such thing as a zero year.

Likewise there is no zero degree. The graphic expression 0°00'00" Aries is but an abstraction indicating the limit between Pisces' last degree (from 359° to 360°, viz. to 0°) and Aries' first (between 00°00'00" and 1°00'00").

3. In astrology the respective influence of each spatial unit—be it large or small—gradually decreases from beginning to end. Take for instance the zodiac's subdivision into twelve units (signs). We shall find that Aries' maximum influence lies in the vernal point. At 29°59'59" this influence is reduced to its minimum, but still exists. At 30° it fails suddenly and is instantly replaced by Taurus with maximum intensity. The same applies to the houses or sectors of a horoscope. Nor do the single degrees escape this rule.

If I were allowed to express in figures the intensity of a purely spiritual force, and to represent with a graph the wane of a degree's (or a sign's or a sector's) influence, the result would be a conic line of the second degree, with a course like hyperbole. That is to say that the typical features of a given influence stand out as conspicuously as ever at the initial point of the unit considered. At any further point these features are remarkably blunted out; still further this weakening makes itself less and less felt; toward the end of the unit there is a tendency for the influence to stay constant, till it suddenly vanishes as soon as the final point is reached.

4. What has been said in the previous paragraph raises practically no problem for those celestial bodies which material astronomy calls planets. If measured in sexagesimal seconds, their diameter is negligible, and, at any rate, very much less than the approximation degree marked on the tables and ephemerides in general use. The problem arises instead for the Luminaries.

The Sun and the Moon have a slightly variable apparent diameter which, on the average, exceeds by little over half a degree, skirting thirty-two minutes.[3] When, therefore, the middle point of a luminary occupied—e.g., 18°44'—(viz. is within the nineteenth degree) the edge of the orb usually already skims over the following degree (the twentieth). With the center at 18°45', a tiny (if compared with the whole) rim has already overlapped into the twentieth; still with reference to an average diameter of thirty-two minutes, it would be a fraction corresponding to 689/100,000 of the whole orb. Nevertheless, this .689 percent of the twentieth degree is located just where the degree's intensity is at its utmost. On the other hand the rest of the orb, still in the nineteenth degree, is, so to speak, in twilight, namely where the influence is reduced to its minimum.

Therefore it can be said on the average that the following degree's influence begins to interfere with the preceding one's from the very instant when the luminary's middle point has traveled forty-four minutes of the former degree.

5. Geometrically speaking, each degree is part (1/30) of the arc embraced by each zodiacal sign. On the contrary, astrologically speaking, the influx of the degree is hardly a part of the sign's influence. Elliptically expressed: the geometrical degree is a part of the sign. The astrological degree is not.

This will strike even a superficial reader, to whom it will suffice to cast a glance on the symbolical images to notice how far they differ from, or even contrast with, the symbolic image of the sign encompassing them. A degree is hardly part of its sign. The same applies to the decans.

These three influences—the one of the sign, the one of the decan and the one of the degree—must be combined with one another and with the rest of the astrologic factors. Signs and decans; houses; planets; their Nodes and aspects; fixed stars; degrees of the zodiac: all these go to make up the birth pattern. The result is what usually (and not too properly at that) is called "horoscope," which etymologically would mean "time observer" where the word "time" is to be taken to mean the time of birth, foundation of the astrologic pattern.

6. But unfortunately one cannot rely upon the time recorded at the registrar's and entered in the birth certificate, on some of which I could detect mistakes of whole hours! On the most hopeful view, he who reports a birth does not know the hour fraction and, if he knows it, the registrar will neglect it.[4] This still assuming the best. Should the worst come to the worst, the entries will be deliberately falsified, with a view to postponing military service,[5] to eluding the fine for delayed report, or out of even stranger motives.

I for one would swear that Giuseppe Garibaldi was born a couple of days before the alleged date and that Girolemo Savonarola was born one day earlier. I am registered myself as born sixteen days later than I was. Once I met parents who admitted having antedated by one day their daughter's birth, happened on a thirteenth, to avoid this ill-renowned number's baneful effects. This far can superstition lead those unacquainted with occult sciences.[6]

7. However, in the few cases where the accomplished astrologer's or the astrology scholar's work has been booked in advance before a subject's birth, and where the specialist knows he can rely on the cooperation of intelligent parents, those interested have to

be warned that the instant of birth is the one when the child begins breathing through its own lungs, and breathing through the navel string is interrupted. Virtually this instant nearly always falls in with the severing of the navel string. Yet it may happen that the child already leads an independent life and that for some reason the midwife delays severing the string, already hanging limply ;[7] or on the contrary that the foetus, though materially already separated from its mother, delays by some instants after the string's excision the absorption of external air into its lungs.[8]

Likewise the horoscope of a ship is usually cast at her launching. This corresponds to birth, as the laying corresponds to conception. Only after her launching does the ship begin to lead an independent life, though her building is not completed, as the newborn human body's development is not completed at birth.

In the horoscope of any juridical act, the moment when the transaction comes into being is when the signatures are attached to it, not the time marking the beginning of the preliminaries, or when the contracting parties start writing the text, and least of all the moment when the preliminary term before enforcement of the act itself expires.

On the other hand, in order to cast the horoscope of a new state or of any new form of government, the Sun's culmination time is considered for the day the new state is proclaimed or the new government comes into power. As a state, however, comes into being usually through a solemn juridical act, be it a bilateral treaty or the unilateral proclamation of independence or unity, the question arises whether the moment such an act is signed ought not to count.

The Sun's culmination is taken to figure out the character of the state or of the form of government concerned; to foresee its victories and reverses, its political crises and public calamities, its progress and fortunes. On the other hand, the astrologic theme of the juridical act instrumental to the state's or government's birth points out the psychological features and the future of the act itself, as an international treaty may be called off or expire without the expiry of the state born of it being involved. Thus the Philadelphia proclamation of July 4, 1776 (nearly 3^h04^m): Gemini rising, Mars on the Ascendant, has such a warlike aggressive horoscope as the one of the United States Libra rising is easy-going and peacefully fond of comfort. This latter refers to the midday noon immediately following the declaration of independence.[10]

8. The importance of the Ascendant sign and degree in proportion to the other factors varies according to cases. The Ascendant's close conjunction with a jarring planet results in something widely diverging from the typical features of that sign and degree. The ruler of the Ascendant's position and aspects bring in more variety and changes. But the Ascendant still is the most significant element in any given astrological pattern.

It is therefore clear that the degree of the Ascendant is the one that, if possible, ought to be taken into consideration first, before all other degrees appearing on a given pattern.

Closely follow in order of importance the degrees occupied by the luminaries and the bisector of their angle (point of equidistance between the Sun's and Moon's centers.[11] Third come the degree of the Midheaven and of the Ascendant's ruler.

From this one can easily conclude that if the Ascendant is in Cancer, the Moon's degree will carry much weight even in a man's horoscope; and I need not stress the importance of the Sun's degree where the Ascendant is in Leo.

9. The Ascendant and the Point of Equidistance between the Sun's and Moon's centers make up the personally exclusive contents of a horoscope.

The Ascendant expresses a synthesis of the forces connected with the three vehicles given by karma to one's spirit (astral, etheric and, above all, physical), viz. the quantum of energy and the direction of the impulses and tendencies: in other words one's abilities and limits. The Point of Equidistance's influence is subtler, more hidden and intimate. I should define it as an underground impulse, an expression where a psychoanalyst would recognize the subconscious or unconscious forces.

Neither Ascendant nor Point of Equidistance means anything or anybody but the native himself.[12]

10. All other factors in one's pattern show at the same time the ego and the non-ego.[13] Among these the outwardly most conspicuous is the Midheaven (MC), the most personal and the ruler of the Ascendant. But the purport of the corresponding zodiacal degree is outshone by the brighter though less individualized one expressed by the luminaries' degrees.

I think it is true that the degree of the ruler of the Ascendant is an element directly influencing the meaning of the Ascendant.

The degrees occupied by the other planets, by the two Moon's Nodes, by the cusps of the various sectors, all bear upon the whole. Sometimes, between the horoscopes of two people born nearly at the same time in the same place, there is no other difference but the one between the degrees of two diametrically opposed cusps.

11. Unfortunately the tables of the houses employed in neo-Latin and English-speaking countries are the so-called "Placidian tables," viz. the ones set up according to the principles laid down by Fr. Placido Titi (a name usually latinized as *Placidus de Titus),* a professor of astrology at the Pavia University in the Seventeenth Century. This Italian was no doubt one of the greatest masters astrology ever had, and the discovery of secondary directions is due to him. But it must be plainly stated that his housing system is wrong.

The right system is the one of Johann Müller of Königsberg (called in Latin *Johannes Regiomontanus),* whose tables are nowadays in use again in Germany. Whether this is due to a nationalist socialist motive carries no weight with me. What matters in my eyes is that those tables are the right ones, whereas ours are of no use in interpreting the degrees of the cusps of the succeedent and cadent houses.

Nevertheless, whatever the system employed, the MC does not change, and the four angles of the horoscope—Asc., MC, IC, Desc.—are at least safe. The astrologer knows to whom and to what to refer the elements thus pointed at.

12. May I humbly apologize to the occultist reader for the fact that the series of symbols corresponding to the degrees is far from being complete. I am no clairvoyant, and the symbolic image takes shape, when it does, very slowly in my mind, through a laborious and indirect process of rational appearance. I should have shown off better if I had published no symbols at all instead of publishing some. But showing off is not in my line; and on the other hand I know that the symbol is nearly all that matters for the occultist, who will therefore acknowledge my effort, even if a partially successful one. From a strictly astrological point of view the reasoned explanation of the influence of each degree serves our purpose, and whoever aims only at casting horoscopes can exact no more.

As a counterpart to the symbolic images, I have quoted some historical examples. And here a further remark is necessary. Often when speaking in public I happened to collate data of spiritual science with sacred texts. It occurred to me that the public did not understand that I quoted the Scripture in order to illustrate and emphasize its truth in the light of mysteriosophy, but thought on the contrary that I tried to support secret lore with the help of the Bible. As a result I had to give up quoting the Bible. I should not like a similar misunderstanding to arise here.

I want to emphasize that, when outlining the features of any given degree, I paid no heed to the characters in flesh and blood born in that same degree during this or any past century. It is never made sufficiently clear that astrology is a spiritual science and that such disciplines have nothing in common with the methods of material sciences, and that the statistic inductive method is the one farthest remote from Spirit.

Between statistics and astrology there is absolute incompatibility. It is not an opinion of mine, but something subject to mathematical proof and therefore above any opinion. How many figures would be needed to write the number of possible combinations between the only known planets,[14] the signs and the houses, on any given point of the Earth's surface? Please note that my question is restricted to the combinations regarding one geographic locality only; and that it embraces only combinations between planets, signs and houses, abstracting from the 360 degrees, the 36 decans, the fixed stars, and above all, the aspects.

The answer is that in order to write that number, fifteen figures are needed;[15] that is to say, the really possible combinations range above 735 million million or, in plain words, nearly 735 thousand billion for any given point of the Earth's surface. As it is common knowledge that a spheroid surface holds infinite points, anyone may conclude that the possible combinations in astrology are infinite in number.

After what I have said, all readers capable of reasoning will realize that statistical astrology is an absurdity. But he who calls himself an astrologer ought not to need proof to know this. Any astrologer worthy of the name will hold to an exclusion on principle: the method proper of spiritual sciences is occult meditation, and nothing is so far remote from the occult as what is abstract, mechanical and quantitative.

But to return. The concrete figure of an historic personage completes the imaginative figure of the symbol insofar as it helps the mind to conceive something human and alive and to see how the supersensible power of the ideal archetype is realized, and to what changes it is subject, in the world of senses.

Endnotes

1. A cabbalist and a student of secret lore of the 19th century, he led a Rosicrucian movement within the fold ofMartinez de Pasqually's followers. Most of his activity was devoted to the struggle against black magic and satanism, whose secrets he laid

bare in his works *Satan's Temple* and *The Key to Black Magic*. Such a struggle is assumed to have cost him his life.

2. To avoid misunderstandings I have said-and I repeat-that possible desecrators would not be in a position to understand. I have not written that they are unworthy, as unworthiness is tacitly understood in quacks.

3. Sun's minimum 31'30", maximum 32'36". The Moon's average is slightly less, and its changes slightly more noticeable.

4. A physician friend of mine was going to have a child. He would have its horoscope; I emphasized that the exact moment was necessary. The child having been born, its father and I went to the registrar's office and reported its birth. "Time?" asked the clerk. "Fourteen hours three minutes." The whole office burst into laughter. There was, of course, nothing to laugh about (except perhaps themselves). But this goes to show that one cannot expect precise data from the civil records.

5. Obviously, if the child was born in December.

6. My efforts to rectify my clients' birth hour by having recourse to so-called "radio-aesthesy" have been stubborn and prolonged. I have experimented with specialists who had, so to speak, proven themselves through a series of clamorous successes, diagnosed latent illnesses, discovered water sources, mineral ores, etc. The result was failure. I know of only one radio-aesthetist who does not fail, but he is too far above me in years and wisdom for me to dare molest him. As a matter of fact, the pendulum swinger ought to be an Astrologer as well to get what we call "mental orientation," as physical radio-aesthesy is of no use here. On the other hand, if he were an astrologer, he would be likely to work on his own and to waste no time rectifying a colleague's findings. In our profession as well, the prevailing slogan seems unfortunately to be "everybody for himself and, fortunately, "God for all."

7. The Count of Chambord's (the so-called "son of the wonder's") birth is a remarkable case in point. On the eve of old age he

stood a fair chance of becoming King Henry V. The excision of his navel string was delayed a great deal as it was deemed necessary to have people gathered around him to witness that the string still bound the son's navel to his mother's womb, in order to dispel suspicion of the child's suppositiousness, which, however, stayed on.

8. When the baby is affected by asphyxia.

9. Noon of real, not civil, nor local mean time.

10. To avoid misunderstandings I mentioned states, not nations. On this point constitutional law and Astrology agree in discriminating between the two. The question under what influence a nation is placed is harder to solve than it appears, and out of place here.

11. It is well known that in a horoscope one may calculate equidistances between all the points that one intends to consider, but no one will deny that the midpoint between the Sun and the Moon is the most important and foremost equidistance.

12. The degree of the Point of Equidistance can sometimes help to rectify retrospectively the birth hour of someone well-known. The degrees covered by the Point of Equidistance during twenty-four hours seldom reaches nine, being usually seven to eight, only some of which coincide in time with the one of the two solar degrees depicting the native's character. Each of these Equidistance degrees corresponds in its turn to two or three lunar degrees. By exclusion, the birth hour can be induced with a certain degree of approximation but without danger of error. Particularly sensitive astrologers can spot the Ascendant with absolute certainty, but this implies laborious calculation in retracing step by step through the landmarks of one's life, the slow planets' transits on the Ascendant or aspected with it.

All of which is part and parcel of our art; and art, according to the Italian philosopher Benedetto Croce, is primarily a result of intuition.

13. The surroundings in which we live spread and unfold before our eyes our own failings and offer us at the same time examples of the virtues we ought to develop in ourselves.

14. Enclosing the immaterial planet Lilith.

15. Such a result is easy to check. Let me explain roughly the reasoning upon which such a calculation rests.

At any given moment the Sun can be in any of the twelve signs; viz., the possible combinations of the Sun with the zodiacal signs are twelve. But for each position of the Sun there are three possible positions of Mercury: in the same sign as the Sun, in the sign preceding it, and in the one following it. The possible combinations of the Sun and Mercury with the twelve signs are, therefore $12 \times 3 = 36$. For each of these, five possible stations of Venus are to be reckoned with: either in the same sign as the Sun, in any of the two preceding ones, or in any of the following two ($36 \times 5 = 180$). The Moon, Lilith, Mars, Jupiter, Saturn, Uranus, Neptune, Pluto, may have each of twelve different co-locations for any among the one hundred eighty combinations previously considered ($12^8 \times 180 = 77,396,705,280$).

Let us now take in the positions of the six couples of houses (they cannot be taken singly, as each house is tied to the diametrically opposite one, and the respective cusps move symmetrically) and consider their positions both insolation to the signs and to the planets.

Spatially all points on Earth's surface with equal latitude have the same system of housing, but in time the position of the cusps varies every instant of the twenty-four hours of the sidereal day. How many are the possible combinations during those twenty-four hours?

In relation to the signs, the six couples of houses move twelve times each during the twenty-four hours from one to the other couple of opposite signs: $12 \times 6 = 72$ possible combinations between houses and zodiacal signs.

In relation to the planets, each of these moves from house to house twelve times a day. We mention eleven planets, for any single geographic locality there are 12 X 11 = 132 possible combinations between houses and planets.

Now let us multiply 77,396,705,280 X 72 X 32; the total is 735,578,280, 981,120. Should we consider the immaterial planet, Vulcanus, the number of possible combinations would rise to 105,923,273,325,281,280. With the Moon's Nodes they would amount to 15,252,951,358,840,504,320, and taking in the trans-plutonian planet whose existence is about to be ascertained, the result ought to be multiplied by 144 again, which would imply a number of twenty-two digits.

All this disregarding the fixed stars, the thirty-six decans, the three hundred sixty degrees of the zodiac and the aspects of the planets among themselves and with the cusps, each of which aspects offers an endless variety of hues. Above all, I have narrowed the problem down to one single geographic spot, though the tightest crammed human hive holds hardly 1/250 of the whole of mankind.

ARIES

1° Aries

*Symbol: An armed warrior of herculean
build tilling the soil*

An outstanding, original, independent personality. His ambitions and aims are beyond the common mark. He is up to great undertakings and can stand the hardest tests, not so much with the forces supplied by a spiritual faith (which the native may or may not have, according to the other features of his horoscope), as with the inborn energy of his own character; not only in the name of an ideal (which he may or may not feel) but especially with a tangible result in sight.

Here are the marks of endurance, positivism or at any rate practical sense. Such a nature will do everything passionately (even the most passionless, self-denying deeds), will be led by natural aggressiveness, seldom by human solidarity, and prompted by a spirit of contest, which in less noble beings may drift into base envy.

Example: Nationalist Socialist Germany, the so-called Third Reich (Sun's degree).

02° Aries

Remarkable powers of concentration, of close, steady, well-planned work (as, for instance, laboratory research), with chances of good results for science. There is faith in oneself and in one's forces, with the attendant danger of haughtiness, overbearingness, ostentation of one's own abilities. One's ideas are challengingly asserted, one's own way of life is pursued with a tendency to full self-sufficiency. At the same time, there will be hardly any ability to personally exploit the scientific results obtained.

Few friendships; an unsocial, perhaps even grouchy character. The native may let his envy of his neighbor run away with himself.

Examples: Paul Doumer, president of the French Republic (Sun's degree); Lloyd George, British prime minister from 1916 to 1922 (degree of Neptune, ruler of the sign intercepted in the house of personality).

03° Aries

A great heart, inborn kindness, courage and love of peace and concord; smoothness and spontaneity; no afterthoughts or mental reservations; hospitality and broad-mindedness; many true friendships; love of art.

The corresponding defects are thoughtlessness, impulsiveness, reckless decisions; an unguarded and yet violent passion, lack of self-control; a lack of inhibitions. The native may run into danger through his own foolhardiness.

04° Aries

Symbol: A forest

A rich, impulsive, naturally exuberant and thoroughly prodigal human being, always directly drawing on nature's reserves. Other pointers in the horoscope must show whether he will be educated or ignorant, clever or foolish, lucky or unfortunate. Even if well-bred and educated, the native will retain something rough and uncouth about himself, a wild energy, as it were. Should he on the other hand (as is more likely) be uncultured, he will show a greater wisdom than purported by the rest of his pattern. In luck he will

2

take the blind goddess's gifts for granted and is not likely to exploit them in heaping up wealth. Bad luck, on the other hand, will be unable to teach him moderation in lavishing his own on others and giving himself up entirely in whatever he does. He is extremely kindhearted and yet very irascible; he is fond of the country—nay, of his own country—has compassion on all living beings and may nevertheless be a passionate sportsman; he is careless in dress and yet vain. Instinct prevails on logic, the heart on reason; his only consistency lies in his being perfectly natural, as he sucks from Mother Nature's breasts the hoary wisdom enabling him to give advice to people who ought to know more than he does.

Examples: Louis Pasteur (degree of the Point of Equidistance between Sun and Moon); Arturo Toscanini (Sun's degree); Luigi Einaudi, first president of the Italian Republic (Sun's degree).

N.B. Here is also the Soviet Union's Lilith (theme of January 18, 1918).

05° Aries

The subject will lead all his life or most of it in obscurity. He will be either bodily disabled by blindness, deafness or otherwise; morally or intellectually adrift; or steeped in the darkest misery. Whatever his plight, he will have to face a long and hard ordeal. If he emerges at all from his gloom, that can be ascribed only to a powerful, stalwart, plucky character (which this degree certainly grants) and certainly not to any favorable circumstances (excluded by this degree, unless other influences are at work). Once he has the "dark night of the soul" and the obscurity of misery behind his back, the native, hardened by the struggle, may assert himself and even rise very high and reap a plentiful crop to reward his nearly superhuman effort. He will then enjoy liberally what he conquered and will exert imperiously but with a fatherly spirit the authority to which he acquired the right.

Examples: General DeGaulle (Moon's degree); the City of Rome (degree of the Sun, whose middle, however, is placed nearly at the end of the degree, so that almost half of the orb is in the following degree).

N.B. The conventional date of Rome's foundation is April 21, tallying, after the classical texts, with the one of the old Roman festival termed *Palilia.* Even the date on which Christmas, the Savior's nativity, is held, coincides with the ancient heathen celebrations in honor of Saturn *(Saturnalia)* and of the unconquerable Sun *(Sol Invictus)* on December 25, but no histories will induce from it that Jesus was born exactly on that day.

From Rome's foundation to the beginning of an historical age, five centuries elapsed during which the town went up in flames at the hands of the Gauls; Rome's first calendar was lunar, and one month had to be inserted now and then in order to restore the seasons, etc. It would be childish, to put it mildly, to believe that the springtime recurrence of *Palilia* never has been affected by changes as far as the Sun's position is concerned! That would be tantamount to mistaking our own springtime festival (Easter) for an immovable feast.

One need but study history to see that whenever the slower planets touched some particular points of the zodiac something happened to Rome, such points being between 05° and 06° Aries and about 24° Cancer. Assuming that the city was founded about the middle of the 8th century B.C., we should have the fixed star Regulus in conjunction with the Ascendant. For the date 754 B.C. we should have Uranus in Aries near the MC and therefore in conjunction with the Sun.

On account of the precession of equinoxes, Rome's Ascendant entered Leo shortly before the Punic Wars, and Regulus shortly before their end. Today, since World War I or shortly before it, Rome's MC is placed in 13° Taurus; its Ascendant has overstepped 01° Virgo and, since World War II, is placed within two degrees. What can be said of Rome can be said of Italy, as it is shown clearly by the pattern of Italy's unity (Turin, March 17, 1861).

4

06° Aries

No element of gravity in or around the native will be present to pull him down to earth. His ascent, both materially and figuratively, will be easy and smooth. Looking from above, or looking down, at the teeming bustle of human masses will come natural to him. Placed high through political authority, wealth or any other kind of power, a simple airman or a mountaineer, or a scientist given to researches into the imponderable or the abstract (anyway, remote from humble earth). Riches and honors will be easily within his reach, though the very nature of his pursuits has in itself the threat and the danger of his fall.

The lightness of those without burdens is apt to drift into foolhardy light-headedness; too-easy luck is likely to make one fling caution to the four winds; those who indulge in daydreaming risk to build castles in the air. However it is, according to the Italian couplet:

He who rises too high, will often fall
as quick as, when kicked up, down flops a ball.

Example: Palmiro Togliatti, Italian Communist leader (Sun's degree).

07° Aries

Symbol: A feudal lord wearing his armor, the headgear over his eyes, holding a bow and an arrow

A wary and cautious conservative, sometimes sluggishly fond of his own groove, often watchful, always endowed with great presence of mind, the native goes out of his way to shirk clashes and dodge risks, and may go so far as to run away altogether from them. Should the worst come to the worst, he knows how to come out of a scrape by a sudden brainwave or a lightning-like makeshift.

He loves the country and rural life and is a great sportsman. Yet he hates violence and is a subtle diplomat. His success in life is

5

assured provided he can stay in his natural abode and avoid the hated novelties. Marriage will be lucky, unless other influences point to the contrary.

08° Aries

Symbol: A mangy dog

In neoplatonic parlance, the subject's "irascible soul" is incontinent: Dante would have doomed him to his Stygian swamp (according to interpretations of Dante by Luigi Valli and Giovanni Pascoli). In other words, he does not know will's golden mean; he is either high-handed or subdued, either an infamous executioner or a contemptible victim of life, according to the whole of his pattern pointing to the one or the other form of incontinence.

If overbearing, he will be a quarrelsome daredevil, devoid of self-control, inclined to the most arbitrary violence; his recklessness will be his own undoing.

If cowardly, his life will be a grey one, dully monotonous in its boundless misery and endless gloom. Luckily enough, he is not apt to live long.

09° Aries

The native has such faith in himself as to border on heedlessness, but will be assisted in danger by that cool-bloodedness which usually is the mark of true courage. Too proud to serve, he can fulfil himself as a leader or a cultist of the free arts; he is hardly a bearable subordinate, as his lack of modesty will let his inborn pride drift into conceit, haughtiness and misplaced touchiness.

Yet his never-failing, positive sense of reality always will lead him back to the right path if vanity has led him astray, and will enable him to show it to anyone willing to follow him.

Luckier than he deserves, he has a noble sense of friendship, which he feels strongly. He is on the other hand a dangerous foe.

All human activities based on the written or spoken word-political and forensic rhetoric, philosophy, writing-are congenial to him. He speaks well, even too well, and is bent on listening to himself rather than to others.

Examples: Richard Wagner (degree of the Point of Equidistance between Sun and Moon); Warren G. Harding, twenty-ninth president of the United States (degree of Neptune, ruler of his Ascendant).

10° Aries

Symbol: Saint George slays the dragon

Courage, nay daring; here too, as in the foregoing degree, the borders of recklessness are skirted.

Led by a successful ambition, barring signs to the contrary, the native is likely to beat his foes, to reach the highest standing, to attain peerless distinction. His career will be at any rate exceptional or uncommon.

The native will be blessed with an inborn righteousness and with a mind open to truth. Should he be gifted for mental work, natural sciences would be his branch; should he be particularly sensitive to spiritual forces, he would have the gift of clairvoyance, perhaps of prophecy. Initiation is not excluded.

The other aspects of the horoscope will show. A great fondness for hunting is to be expected.

Examples: Cardinal Richelieu (degree of Pluto, ruler of Ascendant); Elizabeth Delavigne, a clairvoyant of the eighteenth century (Sun's degree).

11° Aries

This degree apparently can produce diametrically opposed effects, which are, however, to be traced back to the same cause—lack of balance between rights and duties, between one's own and the others' dues. If, therefore, the native is by the rest of his horoscope predisposed to selfishness, his self-conceit will go so far as to make him extravagant and ridiculous. Should he, on the contrary, tend toward altruism, he would be done for. The rest of the pattern will show in which of the two senses there will be exaggeration. Potentially both excesses are present, and their expression may sometimes alternate (as in people who are in some things childishly boastful, and who forget themselves in all the rest).

The egotist born under this star may act in a grotesque and harmless way, as well as prove really evil and slander all others. The altruist will be so yielding and subservient as to verge on absolute want of will power; he will indiscriminately please his neighbor, and all will exploit this to his harm. For a woman, this would mean she might be an easy prey to seduction and even to corruption.

To the mild-natured people born under this sign, the warning can be given that indiscriminate generosity is not goodness, but weakness; that to yield to the first comer and to resign one's own duties toward, oneself is to resign one's human dignity. Weakness and submissiveness are vices as great as the virtues they pervert.

The lopsidedness and misproportion of this eleventh degree may extend their influence to the body and render it crippled or misshapen. Apart from this, the features will be fine and delicate, beauty being not at all excluded; on the contrary, a beautiful face often can go with faulty limbs.

Example: The Duke of Maine, legitimized bastard of Louis XIV (Sun's degree); Otto von Bismarck (Sun's degree).

12° Aries

Symbol: An eagle on its nest

It is a degree of "sacred selfishness' in a familiar or national sense. It gives a strong fatherly or motherly instinct, a high conception of one's standing as *pater familias* or *mater familias,* a keen sense of one's "I", of personal initiative, of the free individual property; and leads to the attendant danger of clashing against the established order in more or less collectivistic sense, or against the economics of the so-called modern democracies.

If this danger is not borne out by other threads in the astrologic pattern, the native's steady effort to rise higher and to improve his condition may bear honor and distinctions in the social and civic fields.

The native's rugged individualism may let his or her generous and lordly nature appear extravagant.

Example: Elizabeth Tudor, queen of England (Moon's degree).

13° Aries

Symbol: A crucible in its oven

The native's character will be subjected to exceptional tests; his or her youth will be such a furnace of grief as to blast anyone not made of the sterner stuff. Should there be any real gold in the crucible, the furnace might purify and purge it of any dross. Ripe age would then reward the native for his youthful ordeals and would lead his inborn superiority to universal recognition. When the rest of the horoscope shows other signs in support of this, the highest steps of the social ladder can be reached.

In less noble patterns the temperament will be harsher, warlike, even destructive; the tests will be less frightening, but courage will not be unrewarded.

Last, the theme may point only to a particular fondness for gold and gilt fittings; the horoscope taken as a whole will have, as usual, to decide.

The sturdier the mind, the frailer will be the body, and the limbs often will be puny and sickly.

Examples: Emile Zola (Sun's degree); Mme. Curie (degree of Neptune, as ruler of the sign intercepted in the house of personality).

N.B. In Mme. Curie's case the Symbol has two meanings, a material and a moral one. Here a metal much more precious than gold is concerned, and radium exactly corresponds to Neptune.

14° Aries

The native is an uncommon being; whether above or below the average will have to be left to other pointers to show. No doubt there is something forceful about him, either his passions or his wishes or his more or less noble aims.

In a way he is a solar being, as he stands alone, cannot count on personal friendships, and his career tends to trace a parable. Where most of the other features hint at success, the native is certainly destined to lead and sway. In questions regarding the whole community or the masses, success awaits him.

Where other pointers do not help, he will be utterly poor and lonely, an outcast, or worse, an outlaw heading for an obscure end, for exile and perhaps even jail.

Whether a winner or a loser, he always will be an isolated, strange being.

Examples: Tamerlane (Timur-Lenk), emperor of the Mongols (degree of the Point of Equidistance between Sun and Moon); Alcide De Gasperi, clerical leader, president of the Council of Ministers of the beginning of the Italian Republic (Sun's degree); Charles Maurras, French writer and political theorist (degree of the Point of Equidistance).

15° Aries

Symbol: A warrior whose iron armor covers him from his toes to his chin, his head staying bare and unshielded

The native is one whose idea of safety consists of shutting all windows, without worrying in the least about the door left wide open. You cannot say whether he is more likely to be a gentleman or a sharper. He is certain to be reckless and to think he is high and dry when on the contrary he is between the devil and the deep blue sea. He may often have a faint heart and not a spark of faith in himself, and yet seek shelter in the bosom of the most unreliable beings. Whether a man of honor or a knave, he always will be taken in and left in the lurch by those upon whom he relied. Should he by ill luck try his hand at stockjobbing, he would get into a mess headfirst.

To the honest-minded, whose thread of life has not been prematurely snapped in childhood or early youth (as always can happen under this influence) three pieces of advice can be given: (1) make a habit of keeping both your eyes open and leave nothing to chance, (2) have faith in yourself first if you want others to rely upon you, (3) do not lean on others for anything; listen courteously, but follow no advice. Further experience will show you how far wrong your first impressions of people were.

16° Aries

Symbols: (1) A man pouring water from an ewer.
(2) A reaper at his work.

The seaside dwellers who both till the soil and rake the sea are often under this influence. By itself this degree does bestow luck, but not exclusively in farming; it does not ensure renown to one dealing with agriculture from a scientific viewpoint, like botany, agricultural economics, statistics, etc.

As a tiller, an agronomist or a naturalist, as a seaman or a fisherman, the native is fond of nature and tends to a contemplative life, which may lead him to passivity or even idleness. Hard working as he may be, he will, however, love what the French call *ecole buissonniere* and like roving outside the four walls of school. As a boy, he will play truant, or will rather do his "homework" in the open; as a grownup, he will have no ambition and will not care two hoots about academic laurels.

Neither contemplative love of nature nor work (whether material or scholarly) will hinder the native's eloquence. If the other aspects favor it, he may very well take to teaching.

17° Aries

More gaudy than elegant, precious rather than refined, sooner worldly than lordly, very fond of luxury and display; the native may outwardly appear a gorgeous personage, imposing in spite of his inward misery. Inwardly he is torn by the ever-recurring clash between his craving for pleasure and his sense of duty, without being able to give up to either one.

This degree by itself gives no love for work; however, if this should be borne out by other aspects in his horoscope, the native would become what I define as a laborious adventurer who might strike oil during his industrious adventures, be they journeys or financial gambles; he may even become famous. Gain, however, comes to him easier than thrift. He can smell luck, but cannot spend with a pinch of salt what he laid hands on.

Example: Gabriele D'Annunzio, Italian novelist and poet (degree of his Ascendant).

18° Aries

Symbol: Wedding night in the king's palace. The queen, still in bride's attire, waits for the prince consort, seated oh the marriage bed in a queenly yet modest attitude.

This degree will give a keen intelligence, a very sociable and hearty nature, a talkative disposition without a shadow of wantonness, a peaceful yet courageous and resolute character. Such a personality will be worshiped by some, envied or slandered by many, feared or respected by all.

For all his love of peace and concord the native is by some karmic law compelled to face some decisive fight, for which destiny exacts the strictest self-control. Any rash act may lead to trouble, any show of light-headedness may have fatal results owing to the plots of the envious

In a man's horoscope, such an influence will make the native's success in some way dependent on a female friend's support, either in the smart set, financial world, or elsewhere.

Examples: Cardinal Mazarin (Moon's degree). Also in this degree are placed Cardinal Richelieu's Saturn, and Queen Victoria's Mars.

N.B. Cardinal Mazarin was a lay cardinal. During Anne of Austria's regency he played a king's role and took his abode near the queen's suite. Some still deny he had wed her in lawful, though not public, marriage; some even deny he ever had intercourse with her. The reality of such a *marriage de conscience* is proved by (1) the Princess Palatinne's (Anne of Austria's daughter-in-law) letters, where the thing is outspokenly and repeatedly stated; (2) a confidence by the queen's confessor to Fouquet; (3) the queen's letters to Cardinal Mazarin, wherein, rather than affection, wedded love is revealed. These were published by Cherubel, Walkenner and Roch; the originals are to be seen in the Clairmbault collection, 1144, leaves 88 to 101.

As far as Richelieu is concerned, in whose horoscope this degree plays a secondary role, he owes his luck to Queen Mother Maria de' Medici's protection, whom he later requited with exile (but this is another story).

19° Aries

Symbol: A gold digger at work in his mine, a satchel of nuggets slung from his belt. His face and attire betray a harsh, stunted life.

The native will have an eye on only gain; his life seems to have no other aim. His soul may not be utterly devoid of feelings, but his craze and the ensuing need of being constantly on the lookout will stifle them. He may, therefore, become selfish, stingy, suspicious, hidebound, misanthropic, and often unscrupulous. Whether driven toward the noble metal, as the Symbol has it, or toward other gains, the subject is more than likely to work on a mine—and to kick the bucket there, too.

20° Aries

Symbol: Ulysses in Polyphemus' cave

Few moral scruples, if any at all. An original mind, inexhaustible in resources, never at a loss.

An extremely active and daring temper with a pioneer's or an adventurer's craving inquisitiveness. A life of travel, exploration, of scientific discoveries, perhaps of more or less reckless adventures. There will be some renown and possibly a violent death.

The native ought to remember Dante's warning *(Inf.* 26, 119-20): *You were not born to vegetate like beasts, but to follow the path of truth and virtue.*

Examples: French King Henry II (Sun's degree); Charles Baudelaire, French poet (Sun's degree).

21° Aries

The native will be an elementarily active, generous, loyal, truthful being. Unfortunately, his virtue is too self-conscious and seeks outward recognition, which on the other hand is not withheld. His or her faithfulness in affections and hospitable ways will win many friends, and success will reward hard work. Respected by all, the native will be able to say in truth, "I have what I have given." (D'Annunzio's slogan).

There may be some adventurous journey or voyage.

Charubel holds that this degree gives birth to grave diggers and undertakers. To him I leave the authority of this statement.

Example: Giuseppe Verdi (Moon's degree).

22° Aries

By itself this degree will not bring the native ill luck, but it is not ruled out that his persistent shilly-shallying may attract a hail of misfortunes onto him. He is likely to live in a muddle of laziness, bewilderment and suspense, leaving him powerless and puzzled; he will make a bad partner and be beset by gloom. A bohemian's untidiness will hold sway in him and about him. An untalented musician, he prefers decadent authors, loves the artificial life of modern towns and finds his congenial atmosphere in dance halls, comic shows, etc.

What threatens him, his property and credit is much more an inborn weakness than ill luck; the native will get more luck than he deserves. Little as he exerts himself to conquer his slackness, his ambitions will be satisfied, if other stars help.

Example: Here is Neptune in the pattern of France's Third Republic. As Neptune's usual astrological meaning is "the crowds," and as it rules the IC (the nation) in the above-mentioned pattern, it ought to signify here the French people under the Third Republic.

23° Aries

Symbol: The medical pharmaceutical emblem of the snake and the chalice, the reptile's tail being wound round the stem and its head overhanging the bowl, its cleft tongue nearly skimming the contents.

It is a degree of fatality. An instrument of collective karma or the victim of his own, either a healer or a great invalid; aggressive and warlike, yet in some things or under certain aspects exposed to man's and fate's ambushes and attacks; the native is wise and capable of having immense following, yet liable to fall under the influence of ill advisors.

What this native is, what his skill, where his power and his shortcomings lie, how far he is apt to influence others and others him, which evils he is likely to work, which to heal, which to suffer—all this can be shown only by the rest of the birth pattern. Only through its whole can we establish whether his pugnacity is a sign of force or weakness; i.e., whether the subject's bite, or the one of his foes, is venomous, or both; whether his is a real following or a drunken rabble in arms; whether the cup he reaches out to mankind is brimming with wholesome drugs, with dope, or poison; whether he is really original or rather eccentric, an imaginative being or rather a daydreamer, an enthusiast or a man perverted by fallacies. One thing is certain: the mark of fatality.

Initiation is not ruled out.

Examples: Frederic Nietzsche (degree of Pluto, ruler of his Ascendant); Francesco Crispi (degree of the Moon); D. J. P. Sartre (degree of the Point of Equidistance). In this degree are also Giuseppe Garibaldi's MC and the Third Reich's Uranus, ruler of the house of war and death. According to Raphael, this is Lord Kitchener's Ascendant.

24° Aries

Symbol: An almost naked woman

No explanation, but rather a commentary is needed. This is a hard truth to my countrymen's ears: the habit, nearly everywhere accepted by now, to marry several years after the provocative forces' full development is tantamount to condemning to public infamy or hysterical folly the woman who, in my country, has been born under this degree. In Anglo-Saxon or Teutonic countries things are different. There, instead of that old austerity of custom which seems, for the time being, too hard to reestablish, a campaign for the reinstatement of equal rights between the two sexes has been successfully carried out. Instead of an equal purity of life, an equal freedom; instead of Jesus Christ's moral, a purely human justice. Should a man want to be free, he must let the woman be free as well, who may become his wife tomorrow.

16

But to return. The vulgar expression "sexual need" never has fitted so well as in this degree. It is more than a need; it is an inescapable necessity, something fatal. Any attempt to repress will end in a female native's perversion or hysteria. Nothing doing; she either marries or satisfies otherwise her irresistible need. Cooler people may well judge and condemn. But whoever judges will be judged. Nobody is in a position to know what takes place in a different being's nervous system. No further comment is needed, as those who have ears may well have understood; as to the others, none is so deaf as the voluntarily deaf hypocrite.

To such hypocrisy we owe the institution of the *demivierge,* a typical infamy of the so-called modern civilization.

As to the other features of this degree, we may point out that the subject will not strive too high, and will be content with eking out a living, which will not be denied to him.

The native is obviously fond of fun and is rather wanton and carefree. Male subjects may have trouble with the other sex; female ones have been even too clearly described.

Example: The government come to power in Syria through the *coup d'etat* of August 14, 1949.

25° and 26° Aries

Symbols: 25°—A crisp-haired man riding a huge ram, which he holds by his horns. 26°—The mediaeval ceremony of investiture. A king bestows high orders of nobility on one of his subjects, entitling him to one of the kingdom's largest feuds.

Both degrees awaken an ambition to rise very high, and they supply the power to do so.

The twenty-fifth makes one more active, fierce and independent, but restless and selfish as well. The power it vouchsafes tends to drift into whimsical and intolerant tyranny. There is no sense of justice, not the least trace of chivalry toward foe or opponent. Hence the danger of being repelled into the nameless herd after having taken the first steps toward power and glory.

The twenty-sixth degree, on the other hand, grants a nobler, a more spiritual (or artistic, scientific, or otherwise) kind of talent, but allows loss of independence. At any rate, where no other aspects are in the way, the native's success is assured on the bright path he wants to follow. The support of the powerful will be more than deserved, but the recognition and the official consecration of the native's merits, whatever they are, can be expected only from that source.

Examples: 25°—Henry II, King of France (degree of the Point of Equidistance between Sun and Moon); 26°—Pope Urban VIII (degree of the Sun).

27° Aries

Symbol: A high-grown tree under the blast of a hurricane

Le vent redouble ses efforts
et fait si bien qu 'il deracine
celui de qui la tete au del etait voisine
et don't less pieds touchaient a l'empire des morts.—La Fontaine, "Le chêne et le roseau"

Whether the native is pushed upward by his noble household's fortunes or by his own luck, he is likely to climb unhindered the ladder of honor and power. Should he have chosen a clergyman's career, prelacy expects him and nearly belongs to him by birthright.

But the very circumstance of his high birth and obvious ascent will weigh down the subject's distinctive pride with lack of experience in life's storms and, barring pointers to the contrary elsewhere, will deprive him of the power of recoil and of the art of passive resistance. He is more than sturdy and powerful, but not enough broken in to man's and destiny's dirty tricks, and will skittishly rear and prance rather than adopt the elastic resistance tactics of those who had to conquer their territory step by step.

Little as the stars may show the sign of drawbacks or reverses being more probable than steady luck, the tree may crash and be uprooted, the native may lose his brilliant position, and his family's star may dim and set forever.

Example: Queen Victoria (degree of Venus, ruler of the Ascendant).

28° Aries

Symbol: A good-looking and beautifully attired wet nurse

A spontaneously vain and showy nature, whose body will brim over with vitality; an unruffled temper coupled with a sound and fruitful sensuousness; a character high in optimism and heartiness, bountiful and free-handed. There is a gift of serious ponderation, an unruffled and bright mood, and a pinch of stubbornness.

The native will win people's hearts through her own goodness and will get plenty of useful advice and precious support from good friends. Especially one (seldom more) female friend will supply most of the material help needed.

The symbol may be taken literally when the horoscope leads to the picture of a wet nurse. Should the native be male, industry and trade of milk products could be expected.

29° Aries

Symbol: A heavy war tank

Whatever his social rank or his inherited means, the subject will have to break painfully his path upwards in order to reach his aim. Where the rest of the horoscope admits of luck, he will attain his goal through his deliberate will to break through and his resistance to prolonged effort. Low born, he may one day be called a self-made man. Of high birth and well-to-do, he may well set his aim far beyond his inherited-not despicable-level, but not beyond his reach, horse sense being one of the native's foremost gifts.

Should the rest of the picture show a vulgar being of low extraction, he would be employed in heavy and well-rewarded work. Where pointers of notoriety crop up, he will be a wrestling champion, a prizefighter or something of the kind. On a somewhat higher level, we shall have Vergo's Mastro Don Gesualdo or, in an aristocratic family, a cadet son who will work his way up with his sword and end by conquering a kingdom or founding a dynasty.

A tough fighter, whether in real war or in the struggle for life, whose first weapon is the steadfast doggedness with which he goes toward his aim, shattering and crushing any hindrance that may bar his way, making it into a further stepping stone for his climb.

Should the native have spiritual blinkers, this would result in a greater concentration of effort.

He is simple and true to the core; hesitation and wavering are unknown to him. He knows what he wants and likes to pay his price. He balks at no problems but sees his job ahead and gets down to it.

Example: Tamerlane (Timur-Lenk), emperor of the Mongols (Sun's degree).

30° Aries

Symbol: A virago leading by the bridle a horse entirely covered with iron plate

An imperious, selfish, and unpleasant temper. The native's ambition to sway his neighbor for personal interest is even too conspicuous. This estranges his friends and relatives but does not deter the native from his pursuits, which will lead him in the end to face unassisted some too-heavy task exceeding his forces.

In a man's horoscope, a woman may be feared to be his undoing, so as to dash him headlong into misery or to make a criminal out of him (if the theme as a whole admits of such an extremity).

Another feature is proficiency in riding. In times past such a skill would have led to jousting—an indispensable accomplishment in a knight.

Examples: Henry II, King of France (Moon's degree); Napoleon III (degree of Sun and Mars conjunct here). The Point of Equidistance of Italy's unity is to be found in this same degree.

N.B. Both the above-mentioned rulers were highly skilled horse riders, and Henry II was mortally wounded jousting; their wives are even too well-known for it to be necessary to point to Catherine de Medici's bloodthirsty despotism and Eugene de Montijo's reckless intrusiveness.

I think it was this degree's influence that spoiled the Italian women's character after the achievement of national unity, in 1861.

TAURUS

01° Taurus

The native will have to stand forever on the lockout ready to parry unforeseen attacks, as his destiny has fierce struggles in store. But in struggles he surely will thrive and revel as if it were his own element, and he will engage himself in them to his utmost. He has a great will power, is versed in tricks and makeshifts, and can be very reserved in spite of his liking for arguments and polemics. Churlish and insensitive to pain, he seems born to have things his own way in spite of the war furiously waged against him on all sides. He may even be endowed with magic powers.

This hard character's failing is ungenerosity; it may even become cruelty.

Examples: Charles Maurras (Sun's degree); General Douglas MacArthur (degree of Point of Equidistance). In this degree Saturn and Mars were unluckily joined when England declared war on Germany on September 3, 1939. If the registrar's book has not been falsified, here is Adolf Hitler's Sun.

02° Taurus

Symbol: A man dying on the ground. Clouds hide the Sun.

It is a degree of impotence; the karma of one who in a previous life was driven to murder in a fit of despair. Therefore, in the present life the native will be loath to insert himself as a living being into the moving flux of time and space. The present repels him, human society holds no attraction for him. If he, therefore, does

23

not find an outlet in the pursuit of nature's secrets or in historical studies and the like, he will lapse into a dull idleness, root of all evils.

He must break the ominous spell isolating him spiritually from his kind if he is not to find realized in himself the biblical threat, *Vae soli* (Woe to him that is alone—Eccl. 4:11). He must draw a wholesome lesson from his disappointments and realize that he has produced them himself with his wrong attitude of estrangement from life. Life must be loved if she is to present us with her gifts; these are not to be frowned upon in comparison with the unattainable day-dreams, toyed with by cloud-dwellers apt to slump defeated to the ground if they cannot reach their aim.

Any vital force that does not find a proper outlet will cease to flow. The greater one's inborn vitality, the more quickly idleness will blight it.

Example: Sir John French, British commander-in-chief at the outset of World War I (degree of Pluto, ruler of the Ascendant).

N.B. Compare this with 07° Cancer, where his Point of Equidistance is.

03° Taurus

Symbol: Old Silenus gathers in the grapes

This influence points somehow to untimely love. The native may have older people propose to her in her youth, or vice versa, will insist on marrying a younger partner in her elderly age. The planned match risks to come off whether the younger partner looks at it as a sincere and generous gift of his or her youth, or is driven to it by base interest-where the one alternative does not altogether shut off the other.

Aside from the question of love or marriage, the native will be luckier in later years and will reap tardily the fruit of his days of labor.

Examples: Catherine de Medici, Queen of France (Sun's degree). The Moon was here when France declared war on Germany on September 3, 1939.

04° Taurus

Symbol: A stronghold built siller fashion, crumbling and decayed; on its ramparts, warrior awkwardly handling dangerous Greek Ore contraptions.

An exacting, disdainful, short-tempered being, destined to remain, so to speak, raw stuff throughout his life, who cannot possibly keep in harmony with the ones he loves. The native has, however, a nearly military sense of discipline as something absolutely necessary for himself and for others.

The keynote of this character is its lack of that indispensable minimum of feminine fluidity needed to melt and blend any spiritual alloy; therefore, both the native and his never sufficiently plastered buildings tend to harden and collapse. A male every inch of his boorish being, an irksome grumbler, easily roused to a fury, the native will not be able to put up with anyone; he will handle things and people awkwardly and clumsily and will be peeved and disgusted at any show of weakness in his neighbors. Hence a tendency to isolation and ultimately to self-destruction, as in Dante's figure of Pier della Vigna *(Inf.* 13, 70) who, embittered and nearly crushed by all his fellow courtiers' envy and slander, ended by committing suicide. Unless no other features balance this influence, the male native never will be able to appreciate feminine charm. The female native should never marry.

This degree shows sometimes a remarkable feature: a special fondness for fireworks, which may well become a passion if the rest of the pattern helps (the fire element). The native's body will be subject to decalcifying.

Examples: Warren G. Harding, twenty-ninth president of the United States (Moon's degree). I personally incline to believe that

25

this was George Clemenceau's Ascendant (according to Alan Leo, it ought to be Gemini).

05° Taurus

Symbol: An ox lying quietly in a field

The native will worship nature and at the same time be cordially hospitable and open to mental intercourse with his fellow beings. A quiet, unambitious hard worker, satisfied with what he earns, happy to have earned it himself with the sweat of his brow; he has a good aptitude for contemplative life and meditation.

It is not to be ruled out that such a smooth, inwardly rich and outwardly even temper may harbor an unsuspected longing for travel and adventure.

06° Taurus

Symbol: A three-headed man holding a sheaf of papers and showing on it to others the way to follow.

An innovator's mind of exceptional force, also hovers on different subjects at the same time. A manifold intelligence with diverse aptitudes; the native can leave a mark in history through his intelligence (or genius, as other pointers may bear out).

The native's weakness is inability to hold the golden middle with regard to sex. A passionate admirer of beauty, he may easily incur criticism owing to his excesses; or on the contrary, withdraw into a nearly cloister-like asceticism and forget life in order to pursue the incorruptible beauty of art or to contemplate the cold gleam of science's abstract truths.

Example: Gugliermo Marconi (Sun's degree).

07° Taurus

Symbol: A slaughtered pig hanging in a butcher's show-window.

A woman's hair will draw more than a hundred yokes of oxen.—Italian proverb

This influence neither promises nor excludes intelligence by itself, but it secures exceptional gifts elsewhere, like an uncommon beauty, surplus of vigor, or both of them together. The native will gloat on such gifts and, in particularly vulgar horoscopes, boast and display them, going out of his own way to exhibit the innermost, and not always the most attractive, sides of his or her person.

Unless other aspects point to a strong will power and high feelings, the native will be a shallow-brained and cowardly being, in whom only lust is deep-rooted. Though unfit for any long-winded, consequent and methodical effort, the native's charm may, however, give a powerful and resolute heave to undertakings which humbler and better suited performers will or would be able to carry out without the native's help. Fortune (at least for awhile) will shamelessly lavish her favors on him, and make him, as long as luck lasts, the cynosure of all eyes. But woe betide the day when luck leaves him in the lurch. He will be in for either mental or bodily tortures.

Example: In his work *Astrologia Gallica*, Morin de Villefranche puts Jerome Cardano's Ascendant here (06°15').

N.B. It is a case in point. This great scientist has left behind some rather ticklish autobiographic passages which would suit an antedated psychoanalyst. His son John, found guilty of his wife's murder, was sentenced to death. Here is a case where the subject is only partially struck himself by his pattern's negative influence. The rest of the evil forces hit him indirectly, discharging themselves on the head of a dear one, to whom the stars had foreboded the same evil (John's Sun was here too). And who would deny that the father felt in his own flesh the torture human justice inflicted upon his son, a miserable murderer, but his own offspring?

08° Taurus

If the other stars do not point to a watchful mind and a power-ful intelligence, the native's wits will be blunt. Should he be driven by an intense religious feeling, faith in God will set his heart in peace; but if all his aims are earthly, he may be unhappy, unless other astrological features correct this degree's bad luck. To such a dull being as this, man's natural ambition to improve his lot as far as possible with the minimum effort can bring only failure.

Only a concrete religious sense, training him to a really Christian way of life, can restore his balance. Should a lack of Fire in his birth chart discourage this endeavor, he could resort to an incentive to hard and passionate work, inwardly felt as something refreshing and uplifting, regardless of material gain. In a word, he can find his way if he learns not to shun work and not to turn away from life, an old man in his young years, before even getting started in it. He ought to be taught the story of the dog that left its real prey to pursue its reflected image, in order to harden him against life's treacherous mirages and the ambushes of his fretful lust, apt to deliver him into the hands of scheming harlots.

09° Taurus

Symbol: A shepherd leading his cattle to graze

The very figure of *pater familias,* or of the good housewife; love for one's home and large family, careful upbringing of one's children and well-meaning strictness toward one's dependents. A humane, honest, peaceful yet energetic nature, such as to attract the young and inspire confidence in all. Love of nature and country life; good sense rather than common sense? efficient running of affairs rather than mere routine.

The native will do his utmost for his children's happiness, but is not in the least certain to reach happiness for himself; on the contrary, when particularly badly aspected elsewhere, he could look forward to death as a release, though no attempt at self-inflicted death can be foreseen; the good shepherd will not leave his flock.

This degree may produce corpulence if other factors concur.

Examples: Catherine de Medici, Queen of France (degree of Venus, ruler of the Ascendant); Alexander II (the Liberator), tsar of Russia (Sun's degree); Hirohito, emperor of Japan (Sun's degree); Alcide De Gasperi, clerical leader, Italian premier at the beginning of the Republic (degree of Point of Equidistance). In this degree the ruler of the Ascendant of General Armando Diaz, Italian commander-in-chief (1917-18) is to be found. To this warrior, who won the final battle of the Italo-Austrian War in 1918 and was later awarded the title of Duke of Victory, this influence assured the unquenchable hatred of that part of the Italian public administration which goes in other countries under the name of brass hats. True, Diaz took command after one of the ugliest defeats and led his army to complete victory; but this cannot acquit him of the blame of having been born in Naples, nor can it wipe away the shame of his having dared to treat the soldiers like human beings. The well-rooted Piedmontese tradition of the small military bourgeoisie has instead always treated the rank and file impersonally, like numbers. For Marshal Tito's and the Negus Negesti's good luck, tradition and the old spirit got the upper hand again later, with well-known results. Diaz was but an interlude, which is now definitely closed. Here also is Pandit Jawaharlai Nehru's Midheaven.

10° Taurus

The native may have two love affairs at the same time and handle them with an artlessness bordering on foolishness and with an unrefined simplicity verging on coarseness. He loves pleasure and enjoyments, is self-indulgent and always worried about his own welfare, which does not prevent his reaching an intellectual level above the average, his mind being as supple in abstract things as it is clumsy in leading concrete action, and this theoretic intelligence as sharp as his practical outlook is blurred and blunted by his heavy sensualism. Mathematics is the most suitable field for his mental capacities.

11° Taurus

If born poor, the native may manage to rise higher; if rich, he may become famous. He is, however, likely to sell the bearskin before having bagged it.

One thing is certain: his yearning to climb. Whether success or failure is in store depends on the measure in which the native really can carry out his ambitious plans and can steer clear of the misjudgments induced by his own enthusiasm.

This same alternative applies to the moral field. Will he be stingy or generous? A fair-minded man or a scheming upstart? It can well be said that, save modesty, resignation and self-effacement (which are thoroughly foreign to this influence) nearly always lie open to this forty-first degree of the zodiac; it is up to the other astral factors to pave one or the other, and to the native's free will to follow any of them.

12° Taurus

A soul full of good will; a hard working, modest, patient nature; a feminine daintiness; a precision free from fussiness; a sociable, likeable, lovable character, helpful without servility, bent on pleasing others. The native will rely greatly on the future and easily put up with her present share; will act fairly and will be able to radiate harmony, hope and faith in life, around herself. The native has the makings of an ideal partner and co-operator, and will like it, though preferring, of course, to be in society with congenial people. Devoid of earthly ambitions, here may be the seventh blessing of the Sermon on the Mount: "Blessed are the peacemakers, for they shall be called the children of God." (Matt. 5:9).

Example: James I, king of England (degree of Point of Equidistance).

N.B. Compare this with the other main aspects of his horoscope, especially with 08° Cancer, where his Sun is.

13° Taurus

Rational logic will be hard put to explain why an envious, anarchic nature is nearly an inseparable companion of artistic gifts. This native will sometimes be an artist, often a refined aesthetist, but invariably, unless checked by other influences, an envious, quarrelsome being, ready to sow discord around himself.

As to all envious people, others' luck will prevent his own. Moreover, one may well say that he is looking for trouble. Should the rest of the horoscope sharpen this feature, the native would be fond of trespassing against penal law, not out of any real wish for dishonest gain, but out of spiteful fancy for what has been denied to him, which will prevent his keeping and enjoying greater gains within reach and easily attained with honest labor. More than fooling and damaging the others, such people end by digging their own graves. But, as the proverb has it, forbidden fruits taste better.

14° Taurus

The native seems born to compose quarrels. His straight, peaceful, fair mind has a smooth force in itself which is likely to compel respect effortlessly and to inspire love of justice.

This is his showier side. Not less worthy of attention is the other one: a way of getting down to his work and keeping fondly at it without fuss and display, a feature which, if supported by other influences, may at times lead the native to withdraw into himself, shutting him out of other people's company. This may temporarily blot out—never stifle—the native's instinct for human brotherhood.

The native is not unlikely to become a mystic—a seeker after hidden knowledge—but his need of seclusion will not make a misanthrope out of him, nor will contemplative life dry up the source of his charitableness. Should he become an initiate, he would silently use his occult powers in service to others.

Whether or not on the secret path, he will be comforted in his old age by the fruits of his efficient work and his good actions.

15° Taurus

Symbol: A hoary, venerable looking augur looks up at a flight of seven birds. Desert around.

The native possesses the gift of inspiring unconsciously and nearly unintentionally, a sudden and durable liking, and to make others trust him as much as he himself. Whether the field of researches he keenly pursues is material or spiritual, his ideas will be original, daring, uncommon; his intuition may even foreshadow the future.

In heathen ages he would have been an oracle, a *fulguriator,* a Sybil. In this materialistic age, he may get the hang of scientific or material truths as if by inspiration, but his mind will ever run to the hidden causes and the living root of phenomena. A deeply religious being, he will, short of any confessional faith, worship the scientific line he has embraced. Should the horoscope bear it out, his life would have an ascetical outlook.

This degree tends co give a bold, icy temper if the fire element is absent from the rest of the pattern. Nevertheless, this somewhat uncouth being, lost in his mighty visions and more or less indifferent to love, may have a following of utterly devoted friends and of disciples not likely to forget his teachings. In unusual and remarkable patterns, such a being may well end by being looked at as a forerunner or a prophet by posterity, and his doctrine may become an article of blind faith.

Examples: Kari Marx (Sun's degree); Oliver Cromwell (Sun's degree).

16° Taurus

Symbol: A man riding an ass

Stubborn rather than steady, slow and often sluggish in everything; groundlessly cocksure, incapable of abstract thinking, the native will not carry his headstrong efforts to any successful end.

He will not be liked by many, and will have to go through life nearly alone. Whatever amount of luck Fate has in store for him, it will run low in his life's former half. Bad luck will set in later, owing to his foolish self-assurance. Neither exile nor forceful segregation can be ruled out. Marriage may be lucky.

Example: Emperor Charles V (degree of Saturn, ruler of the Ascendant).

17° Taurus

Symbol: The vision St. Thomas of Aquino had while trying to fathom the mystery of God's unity and trinity; a child trying to drain the ocean with a pitcher.

(I do not know who the author of the perfect squelch was—"I do not need your advice, I can make mistakes myself!"—but he may have been born under this star.)

The native's habit of thinking with his own head is apt to make him unpopular; his failings will bring about his misfortune. His intelligence is like a river liable to flood the barren sands of Utopia instead of fertilizing the happy valley of originality. He is in for unceasing, often wasted, labors, which will not make him move a step forward. There is a guilty light-mindedness; the native will believe that he can solve single-handed and in his own way certain problems which repose on natural laws, as those of economics, dynamics and the like. On the other hand, such a being can easily rely on Divine Providence and reach that absolute faith which moves mountains and goes so far as to give personal success in spite of rationalistic logic and science's "infallibility."

Examples: Robert Browning (Sun's degree); Peter Chaikovski (Tchaikovsky, according to the English transcription) (Sun's degree). The Moon of the *coup d'etat* of July 25, 1943 (General Badoglio's dictatorship) and the Sun of the armistice of May 7, 1945, are both in this degree.

18° Taurus

Symbol: Two furious bulls goring each other

The native will easily fly off the handle and quickly work himself up to a climax of frenzied and bloodthirsty rage, even if his own peevish and quarrelsome temper has sown the seed of discord. According to his background and breeding, he can make a *sabreur* of a ruffian, and can reap the hatred of many, running the risk of wounds or death in duels or brawls.

19° Taurus

*Symbol: A maid of dazzling beauty pouring water
from a jug into a pitcher.*

An exquisitely feminine nature. The native may go so far as to be a genius, but even in normal cases she will have some very bright gift which she is not likely to exploit in full and will at least partially leave untapped.

A gentle and sweet character, even too little self-assertive, which will tend to flabbiness, indecision, passivity and gloom. A certain typically feminine futility will accompany an equally feminine skill in getting things done. A voice of pure musical pitch, an unconstrained speech, a naturally smart and graceful demeanor.

Her main virtues will be self-possession and cleanliness. In a mystic sense, the Symbol may be taken to mean the Sacrament of Baptism.

Destiny may have in store travel or emigration to the New World. Teaching may be a congenial profession, if the pattern contains such elements as to give the necessary authority for this.

20° Taurus

This degree's positive side may well be said to consist in a great moral or material strength at the service of ambition, which may, when other aspects help, lift the native into eminence.

The negative side consists in envy and lack of moderation. The native will nearly invariably be an impulsive rashling, or a lowly meddler, but in any case an envious being. He cannot find a middle course between those two extremes. When he does not plot mean ambushes, he will show off arrogantly and bully people about. In either case, his stumbling stone is his envy, a vice that, as Sannazzaro puts it, gnaws at itself, or, as exemplified in Dante's figure of embodied envy, Filippo Argenti, tears its own flesh with its own teeth. While stabbing somebody else in murderous frenzy, one may well injure self, as happened to Caesar's murderers.

21° Taurus

A frugal, cautious, watchful, silent and close character bearing the hallmark of individuality, a deep mind, a pitiless logic, a precise and methodic intelligence, more suited for analysis than synthesis. The native will rely but on himself, yet destiny will baffle him with gleeful spite and take a cruel delight in hitting him just where rational logic would rule out failure or even danger. The collapse of his most accurately prearranged plans will tell on the native's temper, whose guardedness may drift into suspiciousness, and misanthropy into wickedness. Example: Mahatma Gandhi (degree of Jupiter, ruler of the Ascendant).

22° Taurus

Skill in handiwork, craftsmanship or surgical ability, according to the other bearings. Sparing and industrious habits. There might be some disablement due to illness or wound, if borne out by the rest of the horoscope.

Surrounded by loving relatives and friends, the native will see his hard work crowned by success in the end.

Examples: Dante Gabriele Rossetti (Sun's degree); Winston Churchill (degree of Pluto, ruler of the Ascendant).

23° Taurus

A great spiritual force, a generous, passionate character whose mind, compared to a large heart, may appear limited. Faith in one's power is excessive, hence a tendency to overreach oneself by a display of arrogance, weakness, light-headedness and fool-hardiness which may head the native for a dangerous fall. This may be taken in the literal sense of bodily falls, as well as in the metaphorical one (financial, social, moral, or spiritual).

Examples: Alphonse Daudet, french writer (Sun's degree); Albert I, king of Belgium, who died shattered in a mountaineering accident (Moon's degree); Paul Doumer, thirteenth president of the French Republic, who fell victim to an attempt on his life (degree of Uranus, ruler of the sign intercepted in the house of personality).

24° Taurus

Symbol: The Moon in its first quarter. The thin, bright crescent, encompassing the planet's lower rim, seems to hold the dimly looming orb as an earthly offer to Heaven.

Assuming as we did that no degree of the zodiac can convey any meaning if not looked at in the light of the horoscope as a whole, this rule does not fit any degree so thoroughly as this fifty-fourth degree which has something mysterious, or transcendant, in itself. Should the rest of the pattern be of a spiritual nature, an intense but hidden inner life would be the result. If the other features concur into a majestic picture, the native may have been assigned a mission reaching beyond his country and his age. "At the limit," to borrow a mathematical expression; that is, in such a cosmically vast and sublime horoscope as can be drawn in the heavens only once in mankind's history, this degree becomes one among many other components from which, written in star characters, the announcement of the Redemptor's birth was given.

This can be stated fearlessly. Here is one of the many astro-

36

logical clues which revealed to the three Magi from the East that God had taken human shape.

Especially the words of the biblical seer Isaiah—later called the fifth evangelist—fall in with the influence of this degree. Foreseeing the godman's destiny, the prophet defined him as a being despised and rejected of men *(Is.* 53:57; Luke 4:24).

And now, let us look at the destiny of a common being marked by this degree. He will be an honest worker, pure in heart, full of a candid faith in mankind, and therefore, in danger of being shamelessly cheated and exploited. An humble and meek being, he will refrain from maltreating his neighbors and showing his fist to defend himself or his own interests. His inner nobility will hardly be discerned by those dealing with him; people will usually despise him and not think twice before taking advantage of a good heart, too feeble in the eyes of the world.

The advice to give to the native (another mystical quotation) is an extra-canonical saying attributed to Jesus Christ: "Let thy alms sweat in thy hand till thou hast found a righteous one to whom you may give it" (Didache 1:6. The *logion* is quoted also by St. Augustine—P.L. 37, 1326-27—*desudet eleemosyna in manu tua donec invenias justum, cui eam tradas).*

Example: Will it strike as strange, in the light of what precedes, that the State of Israel's Sun is right on this degree?

25° Taurus

The subject's inner world will stay closed and unknown to all. Yet this is no cowardly nature, rather an arrogant one; the native is inwardly proud, haughty, overbearing, but not vain. As he is spiritually isolated among his fellow beings, he will have justice done to himself, if necessary, by having recourse to arms. As he is misunderstood, he will endeavor to have his own way even by resorting to violence; as long as his strength does not fail him, he will see subdued servants around himself, never friends.

He will risk either to die a stray dog's death or to be kicked and spat upon on his death bed, like the lion in the fable.

Examples: The Count of Cavour (Ascendant's degree); Pierre Laval, Vichy premier during World War II (degree of Point of Equidistance).

N.B. Cavour's Jupiter in 29° Taurus is in close connection with the Ascendant and is trine the MC and Venus. This planet, in 26° Virgo is trine the Ascendant. Here are the luck and the mostly feminine support that accompanied the great statesman's ascent and permanence in power. Here is the jovial touch as well, blotting out this degree's worst feature (never friends).

P. Laval, whose horoscope does not show any such silver lining, saw the worst come true, and what Taurus' twenty-sixth foreboded came to pass in the most tragic way.

26° Taurus

Symbol: A lonely lady wandering about singing and picking flowers one by one. (The image of Matelda in Dante Purg. 28, 40-41.)

A personality to which nature, not ambition, lends authority; a steady reserved, self-assured being; a mild character agreeable to all; one who sees the right spiritual angle of problems and the poetic side of life, understands beings and things; gathers effortlessly whatever the world around him offers of beauty; loves peace and spreads harmony and comfort around himself. He needs to live in the open air.

Example: Giovanni Pascoli (Ascendant's degree).

27° Taurus

Should other items in the horoscope point toward aptitudes and propensities for the occult, this degree could spell danger; though leading toward magic, it does not assure the native absolute freedom from worldly interests or cravings. The Wise Ones have, however, ruled that no operations should be undertaken if the atmosphere is not perfectly clear; by which they mean, of course, the spiritual atmosphere. Let one whose soul is still benighted by worldly passions or, worse, by greed of power (which is less coarse and therefore more dangerous) not set his hand to the Great Work. The alchemist, instead of transforming into a spiritual Sun the Mercury and the Moon of his inner mirror (soul) would be tempted to transmute the metals of the outer world and to make real gold out of quicksilver ore. Were he not driven to this by a thirst for enjoyment, but by a yearning for power, the native would, run an even worse risk, as this is one of the ugliest kinds of black magic.

On the other hand, should the native's pattern exclude magic and any tendency to the acquisition of occult power, this degree could be of the greatest use to anyone striving after success in the usual sense, as it bestows eloquence, a knack of running things efficiently, a liking for hard work, and an inventive mind (not necessarily in the field of practical application), a sparing temperament, something intriguing which is certainly not made to alienate people, and does not hinder conquest of wealth or power. Which one it is going to be ought to be decided by the horoscope viewed as a whole.

28° Taurus

Someone has said that heaven is for the unsatisfied. Sometimes this may be true, but not in this case.

If the native has a perfect mental balance, he can enjoy happiness. But he is likely to be tormented by ambitions and dreams of power past realization. On the other hand, he does not lack steadfastness, but his day dreams are widely different from real life. The more he can put up with this latter (drab and dull as it can be), the better for him; his life may be long and peaceful. If unsatisfied and craving more, he would be but a castle-builder.

Happiness is bred of contentment.

Example: Nicholas II, Russia's emperor 1894-1917 (Sun's degree).

29° Taurus

Symbol: A woman leading a beast of burden by its halter

The female will order and bully the husband. Should other features bear out a hard and domineering temper, with an outer display of bluster, we have a regular Xanthippe who will not see anything in her husband but a burden-bearing and brooding animal, exclusively reserved to herself, and at the limit will martyrize him systematically and go so far as to drive him to murder her, unless he has a Socrates' endurance.

Things are worse in a male horoscope. The other components ought, however, to be carefully weighed, and it has to be decided whether the omen refers to his mate or to himself. In the former case, the man, of course, is the victim. Should contrary features of overbearingness be at hand, which could not possibly regard others, he is then certainly himself the tyrant looking at his dependents as pack mules, ignoring their human dignity, or taking a great delight in trampling upon it. The one hypothesis does not altogether exclude the other.

Whether a woman or a man, the native would assuredly be in for a great many unforeseen events. He may well be cowardly as all real bullies are; but he is unlikely to have true foresight. Someone may thrash him within an inch of his life, or even shoot him as a dog. Vulgarity and bigotry usually complete the picture of such a character.

Examples: Catherine de Medici, queen of Henry II of France (Ascendant's degree); Mary Stuart, queen of Scotland and, for one year, of France (Ascendant's degree); Victoria Regina (Ascendant's degree).

N.B. Mary Stuart had her second husband, Lord Darnley, murdered. As to Queen Victoria, compare 03° and 04° Gemini, 18° and 27° Aries, where the Queen's Mars is found, a planet indicating marriage in any feminine pattern.

30° Taurus

Symbol: A beautiful house, splendidly fitted out

Look around yourself for one with whom you may eat and drink, before you choose your food and beverage, for a dining table without a friend is what lions and wolves have.—from Epicurus' fragments

Suave mari magno turbentibus aoquora ventis
E terre magnum alterius spectare laborem;
Non quia vexari quemquam est jucunda voluptas,
Sed, quibus ipso malis careas, quie cernero suave est.—Lucretius, "De Rerum Natura," 2, 1-4

A refined utilitarianism. An out and out self-centeredness, which however admits of a sincere love of mankind; a dignified and well-meaning sensuousness, an indispensable need of luxury; a love of finely built houses, equipped comfortably according to the latest technical devices. A lenient destiny will grant wealth together with a sizable and profitable estate, provided the native does not throw caution to the four winds in pursuit of pleasure, and that other factors do not oppose this. The native is likely to win prestige and a certain ascendance over his neighbors and even outside his own circle precisely through his mastery in drawing mental enjoyment from sensual motives. A certain amount of distinction will befall his lot.

Examples: Richard Wagner (degree of Venus, ruler of the Ascendant); Dumas père (Moon's degree); Willy Ferrero, orchestra conductor (Sun's degree).

41

GEMINI

01° Gemini

Friendship has a lion's share in the native's life. Prompted by his unprejudiced, merry, kind, confident nature, he will lay open his heart and his hearth to his friends and will expect them to do the same to him. Influential and highly placed people may take a sincere liking to him, obliging him with their protection and such favors as may greatly help him in his private life and public career.

All of which is likely to happen, but the other astrologic aspects must not be lost sight of. Friendship may be interesting and purposeful, and the unconditional surrender of one's home may lead to family strife and married unhappiness on the side of the more confiding and naively faithful partner. Or worse, should the horoscope point to lack of dignity and self-respect, it could be assumed that favors and protection have been curried by conniving to one's own wife's misbehavior and support for her lover from the betrayed husband and friend. Even if such a point is not reached, the friendship's moral influence may prove harmful to self-respect.

In female charts this degree may portend laborious and even deadly deliveries.

Example: Richard Wagner (Sun's degree).

02° Gemini

A writer friend of mine, whose birth degree is this, has devised as *Ex Libris* a man armed with an ice axe looking from the bottom at a mountain top, and the motto Why not? As I cannot think of a better one, let me quote this *Ex Libris,* whose image and slogan both are as suitable as any to illustrate the typical attitude of this second degree of Gemini. One could add the Latin proverbs *audaces fortuna juvat* and *memento audere semper.*

A great ambition ruling over a great courage, which is in turn rewarded by a great fortune.

The rest of the pattern must, as usual, suggest how to interpret this correctly. Whatever the share of mental gifts the stars have meted out to him, the native has the power of concentration and can, as the case may be, discover, innovate or find original practical applications, as the other components show.

He may be a daring and gifted reformer of a natural science (physics, chemistry, etc.) whom the misoeists will oppose violently and the rivals try to rob of his discoveries; but he will triumph over both. Where the astrologic pointers are all of a spiritual nature, the innovation and the attending fights may refer to spiritual sciences and to religious reform. In the case of an artist they may refer to till-then-untried techniques, or the like. In a less bright horoscope and with police pointers, the native will be a new Sherlock Holmes breaking new ways open to investigation and fearlessly hand-shackling the criminals; and getting the truth from them without having recourse to violence. Or he may be a criminal of genius, like unscrupulous Aresene Lupin versus Sherlock Holmes, a bright plagiarist, etc.

Example: Gabriel D'Annuzzio (degree of Mars, ruler of the Ascendant). It is a typical example; a leader of new and daring war adventures, bright plagiaries, literary daring, useless slander by his rivals, etc.

In this degree is the Moon of Italy's unity (pattern of March 17, 1861, Turin.)

44

03° Gemini

Symbol: Orpheus, playing his lyre, moves the stones to build a town

Poetry and music, a great imaginative power, love of the marvelous. The native's personality shows two features that will seem irreconcilable to anyone wishing to apply the iron rules of logic to human psychology.

On one hand the subject is a daydreamer who cannot keep in order what concerns his own person. A whimsical being, whose mind is forever pursuing dreams of beauty, he cannot stem the rush of his private expenses; he is in love with everything beautiful, luxurious and refined and will have it, cost what it may. This produces a chaotic disorder in his household, and goes together with a merry sprightliness and a happy inconscience of some practical duties.

On the other hand, destiny may have saddled him with the burden of a society of which he is the founder, the head, or the leader. It would seem to stand to reason that he should be unequal to such a task. Yet this bohemian shoulders such responsibility with a swing and a smile and will prove as wise, as eloquent and efficient in setting in motion gigantic things as he proved unfit and helpless in running his own estate.

In a word, the native is a true artist, even if he does not write poetry or music, and will prove more at home in flying than in treading hard ground.

He will be endowed also with a sturdy physical build and a powerful character, though he will be open to influence and worried about public opinion.

Examples: Victoria, Queen of England (degree of the Sun and of the Point of Equidistance); Arrigo Boito, Italian opera composer and poet (degree of Point of Equidistance).

45

04° Gemini

A lucky destiny, confidential political appointments, an eminent position due to personal merits await the native. An inborn sense of dignity will exert a magnetic attraction on others and will call for their respect. The intelligence is lively and piercing, the faculty of observation precise and minute. There is a great deal of practical sense, a generous, friendly and hospitable spirit. Marriage will be happy.

Examples: Victoria, queen of England (Moon's degree); Alcide De Gasperi, clerical leader and premier at the outset of the Italian Republic (Moon's degree).

05° Gemini

Symbol: An arbalister

As the symbol clearly shows, this degree has an influence like the first of Sagittarius, namely a courage verging on daring, an adventurer's temperament; a lightning-like, jerky and jumpy way of acting; a gift for polemics, a dialectic zest; a stinging sarcasm; an orderly, methodical, precise, ruthless intelligence. The ability to earn money is remarkable, but below the native's unappeasable thirst for money. An unbridled ambition fills the native with envy and drives him into quarrels where he foolhardily stakes everything, burning the bridges behind him in order to attain his aim at all costs. Whether the attempt is to be successful will be shown by the horoscope as a whole.

Distant travel is probable. This degree tends to confer beauty, especially to the eyes, which will be dark but bright.

Examples: Cardinal Mazarin (degree of Point of Equidistance); Frederick II, king of Prussia, named the Great (Ascendant's degree).

46

06° Gemini

Symbol: A book and a plumb line

There is the greatest adherence to and the greatest detachment from, reality. A great sensitivity to which no inner feeling corresponds. The native is righteous, clever, has a juridical mentality, a faculty of unbiased judgment, and is aloof from the impact of passions. He is outwardly smart and inwardly cold-hearted.

The native's mind is adorned with an education above his social status, but with no trace of cerebralism, as his fundamental sanity and poise would not admit of anything morbid. The subject will be lucky as his legal or business activity will grant him riches, welfare, perhaps renown. Lack of feeling will, however, make him unpopular. He will shrink from the limelight into the coziness of home and will prefer the company of animals to that of his fellow beings, which will bless the end of his long life.

Example: George Bernard Shaw (Moon's degree).

07° Gemini

He is well paid who is well satisfied.—Shakespeare

A steady, smooth, quiet existence expects here a native of a peaceful, kind and affable disposition. He will be graceful and good-looking, well bred and clever, but his retentive mind will lack originality.

Life has few and moderate sufferings in store, and they will be easily borne, as the subject's unimaginative nature will not be capable of deep-seated grief. There will be luck in love. Marriage is likely to be happy.

08° Gemini

This degree's influence can hardly be depicted with sharp outline. Its dualistic and self-contradictory nature will bestow two opposite features, which could, however, even co-exist in the same native; but interference by other radical influences or the effects of breeding may well let one side fade out of view.

One side of the character is rough, irascible, reckless, often breeding strife and contention; anyhow well-equipped for prompt action and violent activity, as the military career, surgery, arts and crafts connected with iron and fire (fireman, smith and the like).

On the other hand, the native has commercial aptitudes, loves comfort, desk activities and administrative jobs, leaving others to do the hard work; he is fond of home and family even if his character's other side may lead to domestic strife. Destiny threatens the home with the omen of a sudden, fiery outburst apt to upset it from its foundations or to shatter its very core.

Other astrological traits must say whether this is inevitable and whether the native's destructive features or other causes are to blame.

Example: Alfred Dreyfus (degree of Uranus, ruler of the Ascendant).

09° Gemini

*Symbol: An enthroned queen holding in one
hand he Earth's gold surmounted by the cross;
in the other, her scepter*

It points to a nature conscious and confident of its power and harboring a dignified and exquisite kindness, together with a noble pride. A sharp intelligence, apt to catch at once the point of difficult problems, which it will then patiently unravel. The native is a ruler born, and fortune may help his lordly character to conquer power should this not have fallen to him by birthright, so that his position may consolidate in later years. A peculiar feature of this mind is its fondness for conundrums and riddles, chess and pastimes involving mental effort; should the native have a garden, he will have a maze in it. There is a daintiness in cleanliness and food choice.

Examples: Wolfgang von Goethe (degree of the Point of Equidistance); Charlotte, Empress of Mexico (degree of Mars, ruler of the Ascendant).

N.B. In this degree there is now the fixed star Aldebaran.

10° Gemini

Symbol: The good Samaritan succors the Jew
whom the highwaymen have beaten to within an
inch of his life (Luke 10:30-35).

A great heart fired and inspired with the wish to help mankind, to whose service a great store of energy is placed with somewhat childish enthusiasm. Sympathy for the poor and the sick is apt to take concrete shape, and there is a sincere wish to succor and heal social misery.

The reverse of the coin consists in the delusion of reaching such aims with merely material means. Should the horoscope not bear the imprint of a deeply religious spirit, the native will stick to the faddish concept that vice and crime can be fought by spreading well-being and strengthening the police forces. In a word, a well-meaning, well-fed, well-bred, humdrum middle-class fellow, whose limited mental powers will not prevent delving deep into medicine and political economics, to pursue his ambitious but charitable aims.

Luck may smile on this good fellow and lavish him the means to carry out his beneficent plans.

Examples: Those who hate absolute government may be stung to the quick to learn that Benito Mussolini's Moon and the Soviet regime's Jupiter, lord of the Ascendant, are in this degree. Dictatorships are objectionable, but what about the emasculated constitutional monarchies? And what about some clerical republics? In Jesus Christ's parable, the good Samaritan is an idolatrist, but he helps the oppressed; the priest and the Levite know God's law, but gives the fallen a wide berth. Jesus Christ's words are still true.

11° Gemini

Symbol: An eagle feeding her three eaglets

In some senses a superior, but in any event an uncommon, being gifted with a mystifying and nearly prophetic insight. A commanding person, apt to take advantage of his strength, very fond of his family, but sensuous, despotical, unscrupulous, craving travel and adventure and forever unsatisfied with surroundings he deems unworthy of himself.

He may make a great deal of money, especially in the field of arbitrage on a large scale, but luck is not steady, and his restless urge to be ever off and out will let many a good chance, passing close to him, escape his notice altogether in spite of his grasping nature. Exile cannot be ruled out.

Example: Louis of Bourbon, Duke of Maine (degree of the Point of Equidistance).

12° Gemini

An honest being, brimming over with plans and faith in the future. Others may be wrongly led, by some lack of decision on his part, to mistrust his purposes. Anyhow some hitch will hinder or delay the ripening of his plans. Besides such a drag chain on his undertakings, sudden death or unpleasant surprises may take the wind off his sails and nip his enterprises in the bud. A steadfastness ready to face any tests is therefore the catchword here.

Engineering may be a congenial profession; a mechanic's job seems to be the right trade.

Example: In the pattern of the armistice May 7, 1945, Uranus, as ruler of the Ascendant, is in this degree.

13° Gemini

Symbol: A corpse exposed to birds and beasts of prey

And left their bodies prey to birds and hounds horrible sight.—Homer, *Iliad* 1, 3-4

And of a wolf which seemed to harbour all cravings and yearnings in her scraggy shape.—Dante, *Inf.* 1, 49-50

The native cannot be denied inner power, but lacks character. He is more active than constant and even more restless than active. A man of bristling project, though vague and blurred, if lofty; the native runs the risk of leading astray his winged gifts. Especially natives having the Sun above the horizon and their Ascendant in this seventy-third degree are a living proof of the saying: "Hell is paved with good intentions."

That he who was born an eagle may not become a hyena! The unsatisfied natural craving for earthly goods will become an inexhaustible yearning. Not having exploited his gifts properly, he may be led to wonder resentfully, "Why should the others, if I don't . . .?" This envy of other people's luck may become hatred, as if the welfare he could not conquer were an offense to his misery and a constant reproach to his unsettled, wasteful, roaming life, and as if he had a right to some sort of revenge.

Evil associations may lead the native far enough on the wrong path, but even in compact with worse beings than himself, he will still bear a sign of his fallen nobility; mental subtlety and the faithful keeping of secrets.

14° Gemini

Symbol: Two foxes devouring some chicken

Too few scruples and too many ruses. But to no avail, as in spite of tricks, the ill-begotten wealth may often have to be given back, as one cannot fool all the people all the time.

Should the horoscope in its other aspects not admit of dishonesty and incorrect methods, and should it point to an intense intellectual life, this native's subtlety may sublime into the meanderings of abstract reasoning. This would give rise to a mastermind in dialectical *distinguos,* the matchless skill of great logicians, and, in some cases, of the giants of thought.

In any case, an unharmonious and lustful nature.

15° Gemini

Symbol: A seven-headed human being

. . . as the man in whose mind thought springs from thought farther and farther strays from his own aim as each new purpose damps the former one.—Dante, *Purg.* 5, 16-18

Should the native successfully stem the onrush of his mental turmoil and impose himself a method, an inner order and an intellectual discipline, the lively originality and the boundless manifoldness of his versatile mind may recommend him to everyone's admiration and open a bright career for him.

I said *if.* Otherwise, his restless desultoriness will lead him to do too much at one time, getting him all tied up in the knots of his scattered activity. What could have been original becomes eccentric; whatever is gained in extension is lost in depth.

16° Gemini

Good initiative and charitable work, however, will be profitable only for others and unfruitful for the native, who will be a modest, peaceful, though emotional, being devoid of the sound judgment and the luck necessary to reap the fruit of his long labors.

17° Gemini

Symbol: A handless man

Birthright, personal prestige or occult powers may grant the native supremacy over others, who will then be the material tools to carry out what the native has conceived. Should practical execution fail him, he would not be able to perform with his own hands and translate into concrete reality what appeared dazzlingly clear to his mental eye. Either he will be totally devoid of manual skill and practical sense, or will be maimed or otherwise invalided.

Should he work with supernatural means, one has then to bear in mind that magic consists only in working without hands and walking without feet. Let those who have ears understand. But magic practice will not suit anyone who is not physically whole.

Example: Charlotte, Empress of Mexico (Sun's degree).

18° Gemini

Symbol: Two foxes in relay according to their custom.
(One rouses the game while the other lurks in
ambush ready to stalk it.)

Inner duality. A close cooperation, a very subtle mind and, in lower beings, shady cunning and complicity. Mental suppleness and penetration, swift and unconstrained gestures, a great experience in business and politics. On the strength of his own undeniable practical ability, the native may conceive too ambitious plans, demanding exceptional timeliness and utter precision of movement. These undertakings can be crowned with full success, but then the results run the risk of not being equally divided between the subject and his partner.

Examples: Lloyd George (degree of Uranus, rider of the Ascendant). Tradition places here the town of London's Ascendant (17°54').

19° Gemini

Symbol: A pilgrim holding his staff

A wretched and roaming gypsy's life. The native's mind may well be endowed with some artistic gifts, but he will lack character and will shun constant work. Forsaken by all, he will painfully

53

drag his tramp-like existence through the world. A deep religious feeling may give a sense to such a life.

20° Gemini

Symbol: L'apprentis sorcier

Some of the bright gifts of this native are not in keeping with the whole of his being. If the rest of his horoscope restricts his activities to the practical field, his hard work, well-trained mind, and influential friendships will permit him to achieve some aims. He may improve his position, gain wealth for himself and his family, etc. On the contrary, should other astrologic data confirm, or simply not hinder, the occult, mystical, or spiritual powers present in him, the native may attain higher results, but on the indispensable condition that he take in a reef, not trust his visions too much, and not overreach himself. Above all, he ought to remember that anyone who rouses powers beyond his own control runs the risk of being crushed by them.

This applies, of course, to political power as well, though the danger is far greater in the super-sensible field.

Examples: Astrologer Regulus (degree of the Moon and Neptune joined here). The Sun was in this degree when Benito Mussolini declared war on Great Britain and France on June 10, 1940.

21° Gemini

The native can hardly expect a free and independent position as, in spite of his quarrelsome, eccentric or otherwise unsociable character, he will have to put up with playing second fiddle to someone.

He will not shun work, but will be very fond of sport and full of competitive spirit, which will let him miss many a good occasion, and eventually be his undoing if the horoscope is bad.

22° Gemini

Symbol: Chirping birds peck at their seed

A gentle, winning disposition, a delicate but communicative nature, a rather too talkative but pleasant character; a person led by the honest desire to be in harmony with everyone and to bring peace everywhere, fond of nature and in some cases highly gifted for fine arts.

This native might incline to the corresponding failings and be overconfident; or his gentle nature might not stand the hard struggle for life and might resent its cruel blows; or he might entertain lofty desires which can hardly be satisfied on earth. The demonstrative strain in his character can be warped into a random talkativeness apt to waste away his creative faculties; and his conciliating tendency might sink to weakness of character.

Reference is to be made as usual to the horoscope as a whole. Should the rest of the chart offset the excessive idealism with a solid sense of reality (prevalence of the earth element; role played by the sign Scorpio; opposition of luminaries; trigonal position of the Moon, Mars, Mercury to each other, etc.) and be good on the whole, the subject would be skilled and successful in his work, happy in marriage; harmony and well-being would sway in his home and about him.

A woman born under this degree will land the man she wishes, though leaving him the pleasant delusion of having made his own choice, if she is wise enough not to let him go too far before wedlock. Should she have other aims, she could have all the men she wants, and would manage to stay on friendly relations with them afterwards as well. The horoscope as a whole will show whether she will be prodigal other own or of herself.

Example: The Republic of Italy (Sun's degree).

23° Gemini

*Symbol: A withered, ragged old man, bent by age
and by suffering, standing alone, leaning on a stick
in an attitude of utter dejection.*

If the horoscope at large does not offer any particular hints of good luck, the battles of life will prematurely sap the native's energies. He will feel powerless to put his otherwise original ideas into practice, will not only refrain from reaction, but from action as well, and will give up the struggle and waste away. His breakdown ought to be followed by the estrangement of his children and everyone else; his old age will be miserable and lonely.

Example: The government come to power in Syria with the *coup d'etat* of August 14, 1949 (degree of Point of Equidistance).

24° Gemini

Symbol: A merry fellowship

A demonstrative and jovial fellow whom all will like. The native would seem unable to live alone, as the frankness with which he declares his friendship, the selfless pleasure he feels in the company of his comrades, and the proof of true friendship he can give when needed, will win him the largest possible number of hearts. Few people will enjoy so many and so sincere affections.

The native's mind might turn to deep scientific research. He is in love with fine arts and music but his inborn innermost gift is the art of persuasion.

25° Gemini

Symbol: A man holding an open book

An original and uncommonly bright intellect, a great passion for study, especially of ancient times; a profound education, a steady delving into scientific research. The native's chances of success in clamorous feats, in great undertakings or outward conquests are equal to nil. Instead, he stands more than a fair chance of emerging into eminence in scientific pursuits and of finding his delight in them. Parents willing to direct such children to worldly careers **are** wrong as, barring pointers of great luck in fields other than intellectual research, they never will make any headway.

Examples: I think Dante Alighieri's Ascendant is in this degree (see my note on 13° Cancer). Here is the degree of the Point of Equidistance of the *coup d'etat* which overthrew the Fascist regime on July 25, 1943.

26° Gemini

This degree's influence is in open contrast with the one of the sign to which it belongs, as it muffles down its foremost feature-reason, and sharpens, on the other hand, its second main trait—strife. The native seems to be born to argue and quarrel, but not on the solid ground of logic as he does not want either to offer reasons or to listen to reason and simply sticks to conventional ideas and popular fads current at his time in order to support his arguments.

Yet he likes arts, though in a conformist way, and might even cultivate them, but without the least trace of personal style. An ambitious, jealous being, alive only to his own merit and blind to the merit of others; stubborn, unreasonable, quarrelsome and revengeful, he is not liked by many and can go so far in his blunt recklessness as to court death at the hand of others. The rest of the pattern might emphasize this threat or offset it, as the case may be.

27° Gemini

Symbol: A gypsy woman, shedding copious tears

All good features of an artist (human sympathy, sensitivity, sense of universal suffering) as well as the evil ones (wanton untidiness, unfitness for the struggle of life) might have fallen to this native's lot. His horoscope as a whole can answer only the question whether this gift will find expression and materialize, or stay potential, whether the native is to reach the peak of genius or to grovel in the lowlands of modest craftsmanship. In any case, his is a precious and refined, rather than a mighty and rugged, talent; the blight of mannerism is dangerously near.

A life interwoven with roamings, disappointments and sufferings.

28° Gemini

Symbol: Two bulls of different size on a thriving field

Mens sana in corpore sano: a topping health, an active nature, an open mind fit to pass sound judgment on people and things. There is love for work in its pithiest and most substantial form—farming. The native worships Mother Nature and must live in her bosom; though not harboring any prejudices against the modern machines and newfangled methods, he will still prefer the good old ways as his horse sense whispers to him that whatever is nearer nature has something more vital in itself. Therefore, he hates whatever goes against nature, but also has a deep contempt for what lies beyond nature's ken.

A conservative by instinct and a worker by temperament, financially and sexually fruitful, there is nothing sophisticated about him, though he is capable of delving deep into research of what he loves—especially antiquity. An honest and true friend, he is universally esteemed and loved by many. An emotional and, in certain senses, an impressionable or rather a passional being, he is no such highly spiritual creature as his great concrete intelligence may lead a superficial observer to think (one should bear in mind that there are two bulls in the symbol, and of different sizes!). It is but his horse sense, not any lofty spiritual force, that leads him to hate materialist mechanism and economic determinism. Which does not prevent spiritual forces from operating in him, though they might do so more through his moral sense and his feelings than in a direct way. The native may expect, though not with certainty, a happy and prosperous destiny.

Example: The Zionist State Erez Israel (degree of the Point of Equidistance between Sun and Moon).

29° Gemini

A rather pessimistic degree inducing skepticism and mistrust, apart from which its influence is a typically divalent one.

Helped by other astral aspects, it will confer kindheartedness coupled with ability to command; an imaginative, manifold mind; the makings for occupying a high position and for nobly exerting the attending authority; skill in hunting and sportsmanship.

On the contrary, where other aspects are mainly negative, these features will shift into opposite polarities or will stray into corresponding vices. Kindness will become affected courtesy, prestige will be disfigured into autocracy, love of hunting into cruelty or even sadism; there will be misuse of power closely followed by ruin and misery. Likewise, imaginative power will sidle into fruitless daydreaming, too many plans will cram the mind, all shifting and inconclusive, as no steady power behind them will help carry them out.

Example: Sir Douglas Haig, British commander-in- chief from 1915 to 1918 (Sun's degree).

30° Gemini

Symbol: The cow, the goat, and the ewe in society with the lion

As in the previous degree, this one also can make the native into a fond and efficient hunter, but the point lies elsewhere and can be summarized in the expression, a lion's share.

It will have to be left to the horoscope as a whole to decide if the native himself or partners will have that share; and whether he is endowed with a deceiving, cunning nature apt to rob others of

59

their luck or is forced by circumstances to pay for one of the partner's misdeeds; but in either of these two hypotheses, the former item does not on principle exclude the latter. The native undoubtedly has formidable persuasive or seductive powers, a strong character, a hard worker's temper, and can weave and unravel plots. However, destiny will disappoint him in the end.

Examples: Dumas père (degree of the Point of Equidistance); Giuseppe Mazzini (degree of the Sun, which is, by nearly a half, in Cancer's first); Calvin Coolidge, U.S. president (Moon's degree).

N.B. The senior Alexander Dumas had reached perfection in his system for exploiting and appropriating other people's work. His "negroes" wrote that he led, corrected, gave the finishing touches and collected the royalties. Yet he died poor.

Mazzini is even a clearer case in point. Sublime as his ideal may have been, he sent others to face the gallows and took a personal part only in the Savoy expedition. Yet someone else has earned the title of Father of the Country and enjoyed the results of Mazzini's efforts, whereas this latter died an exile in his own country.

CANCER

01°Cancer

Lasting and close ties of affection, probably legal union, tender and sensuous married love; completely given over to her marriage partner and her own relatives. Inborn goodness and fidelity, natural merriness and fortune's deserved smile makes her popular and universally liked. These bonds of affection will, however, tie her and limit her freedom of movement, as well as her chances of fully exploiting her good luck.

Many are the native's gifts: a musical aptitude with a pronounced sense of rhythm; a faculty for exact sciences in general, especially mechanics; a rigorous logical mind, keen on seizing the cause-effect relationship; business sense, particularly for sea trade (provided that the family does not contrast the native's passion for travel). The other aspects will have to show which of these tendencies ought to be followed.

Example: Here was nearly half of the Sun's orb at Giuseppe Mazzini's birth (its center being in Gemini last degree).

02° Cancer

Symbol: A knick-knack in a glass case

Whether the native is hard-working or, as he is likelier to be, lazy and sluggish, he will usually not prove up to the task of earning his keep. If he works at all, his work stays unfruitful, or goes to produce only superfluous, trifling and refined objects, the only things the native seems to be fond of. He ought to take a job connected with perfumes, luxury and fashion, the dressing or tailoring trade and the like.

Favorably aspected elsewhere, he may become an artist in the highest sense of the word, in the domain of figurative arts; in which case his anarchic sloth, his individualism and his jealousy toward his colleagues would fit into the pattern of those moral failings even Philistines are willing to pardon in artistic bohemians. Whether an artist or not, the native is only too prone to depend on others for his maintenance. But even as a toady, there is something noble about him. His inborn virtues will be sweetness, nicety, smartness, above all, a sincere love of beauty.

One physical feature is his often abnormal fear of air drafts.

03° Cancer

Symbol: A scene from the eighteenth century; two seated ladies, and two squires standing in front of them

The native will be inwardly split into two contrasting halves—a thinker's mind and a lecher's tendencies; an old man's sedate wisdom and a boy's reckless wishes; feverish activity alternated with dull idleness; refined servility strangely coupled with a refined, aristocratic haughtiness. The result may as well be fame as infamy or success closely followed by failure due to passional follies.

In a man's horoscope, will power will be lamed, as this emotional influence inclines more toward fatalism than toward action. In a woman's chart it is just the other way about. Any native woman will have everyone at her beck and call; a termagant or a Xanthippe, as the case may be. Be it a woman or a man, mannerism will affect the native's attitude, which will be neither simple nor sincere.

Seer Charubel maintains there ought to be a special ability for geology or meteorology, which I report here on his own responsibility.

Examples: Elizabeth Tudor, Queen of Britain (degree of the Point of Equidistance); Lord Kitchener (Sun's degree); Edward VIII, King of Britain (Sun's degree).

04° Cancer

Symbol: Walpurgi's night

Here the challenge to the existing spiritual order will reach its uttermost degree. An orgiastic temper, a defiant impiety, a craving for sexual or alcoholic intoxication, misuse of drugs or dope, the practice of Satanism. In the eyes of the world there is no understanding the native, who will seem eccentric, extravagant, if not altogether a lunatic. But his intellect is quite healthy, and he does not mind at all openly countering other people's prejudices, which he is content to ignore. His heart is healthy as well, but lust is apt to bite deeply into it, ravaging his feelings and threatening mental sanity with its intoxication. The social and financial position, health and the whole being are in danger owing to this.

All of which ought to be looked at in the light of other astrological factors. Where other aspects point to occult practice, this native would rather take to black magic, sexual rituals, witchcraft, and might come in touch with more or less shady sects. The prospect of a superior initiation (although through the way of corrosive waters) is not to be ruled out. It is up to the astrologer to distinguish.

Should the horoscope show no super-sensible features, the native would simply, according to his degree of evolution, take to one or another form of violence against God, from vulgar blasphemy or oaths to blasphemous philosophic systems; attend the sophisticated orgies of the cream of society, or plunge headlong into ribald revelries; gain admission to Baudelaire's artificial paradise or stoop to the fuddles of a miserable drunkard. This degree's peculiar feature will give the bouts and feasts a ritual character making them nearly solemn, and will philosophically induce a mood of perverted mysticism, which can be observed easily in the systems inspired by it.

At the lowest level of intelligence, this degree will produce a type of blase townsman, looking at things with a Mephistophelian smile.

05° Cancer

In this degree there is a Libra-like strain coming to light as love of justice and truth. The native will be friendly and will feel the need to lean on someone else. A loving—or even passionate and sensual—temper might give the male native many a headache, and might lead a woman into trouble. No adequate prudence balances the intensity of feelings. The native is better suited to win new friends than to keep the old ones and runs the risk of being seduced or easily deluded about the firmness of the ground on which to build his existence. In any event, there is an inordinate imagination and a misplaced confidence.

Confronted with the unfairness and double-dealing of the world, the native's sense of justice will champ at the bit and rise in arms; he will call for justice, demand to have things straightened and facts revealed at any cost. This rebellion will be naive, reckless, untimely and might even make things worse for the already deceived native, who is unfortunately not acquainted well enough with human baseness.

Examples: Louis XIII, King of France, named The Just (Ascendant's degree); Louis Lazarus Hoche, general of the French Revolution (Sun's degree).

06° Cancer

Symbol: Alcidiades, walking through Athens with his famous dog, whose "most beautiful tail" he has cut

The native is a spendthrift, devoid of practical sense. He is not devoid of heart and has much tact, but is persuaded that everything is due to him, and might, therefore, appear unjust. He is nice but vain, might sometimes sound high-flown or appear gaudy, but will give himself airs; nothing matches his fatuousness and extravagance. His recklessness might go so far as to bring about his own ruin.

However, barring especially unfavorable aspects, Fortune's boons are lavished upon this irresponsible being; he will gamble successfully, will have luck in absurd speculations against the most reasonable expectations, will reach what he has set his heart upon and go on throwing money out of the window with the utmost composure, certain that he will somehow manage to earn more.

The rest of the horoscope is expected to tell us what all this will come to.

Examples: Marie Antoinette of Habsburg, Queen of France, 1774-93 (Ascendant's degree); the Versailles treaty (June 28, 1919; Sun's degree).

N.B. About Marie Antoinette, see also the degrees of Sun (11° Scorpio, and the Point of Equidistance 01° Scorpio), and above all, the two degrees astride of which is her Moon, ruler of the Ascendant (21° and 22° Libra. This for the degrees. But the whole pattern is as unlucky as it can be: the Moon in quadrature with depressed Mars; the Sun and exiled Venus in quadrature with Neptune and in semi-quadrature with Pluto; Mercury, Jupiter and Saturn isolated, etc.)

07° Cancer

Symbol: God Thor brandishing the thunderbolt hammer

You may well shout Death at me, but not shout me down, as Nature has placed me high.—1906 Nobel Prize winner Carducci's answer to university students heckling him

A genuine he-man, rugged, indomitable, apt to face and conquer any adversity.

All the manliest features, a marked personality, a nature obviously above the average, strong and healthy instincts; no shilly-shallying, no retracing one's steps; an extreme deliberateness, a lenience bearing no trace of weakness; a self-consciousness to which both showing off and false modesty are unknown.

He has all the corresponding shortcomings. According to the Roman expression, the native "sees nobody in front of himself; viz. has neither regards nor respects. He will show fight and violently react to anyone's attempts to block his way or to undermine his ground. He takes for granted that he has been singled out to lead and to order all others about.

Should the horoscope bear any other features pointing that way, that lack of regard might stray into ferocious brutality, that lordly spirit into arbitrary overbearingness, that warlike strain into sheer quarrelsomeness, that superiority into selfishness, isolation and indifference to other people's sufferings.

The virile qualities will be courted and smiled upon by a true *fortuna virilis*. Of obscure or even very humble birth, the native will reach the top in his chosen career; unless unfavorably aspected elsewhere, he will have all his opponents topple and crash out of sight, and even before reaching the summit the conqueror will see no rivals around him.

Examples: Giosuè Carducci (Ascendant's degree); Calvin Coolidge, thirtieth president of the United States (degree of the Point of Equidistance); John Franch, British commander-in-chief, 1914-15 (degree of the Point of Equidistance); Pierre Laval, premier of the Vichy government (Sun's degree); Franklin Delano Roosevelt, our thirty-second president (Moon's degree).

08° Cancer

A lazy and sensuous being, much too prone to self-indulgence and wantonness. But he has horse sense and a mind cut for life's rough-and-tumble existence and is not totally destitute of that cunning that often replaces intelligence in fools. A general tendency to aberration and to illicit ties (in a woman this will mean easy seduction) will expose the native to the danger of adulteries or otherwise guilty intercourse threatening his married happiness and his renown. As he knows no measure, not even in speaking or in writing, he will be led to more or less serious indiscretions which, according to other pointers in the horoscope, may range from petty, mischievous gossip to veritable libel, from the dutiful report of a crime to delation, even to breach of friendly trust. Therefore, he might be sued for slander, not for abuse (unless other components give him courage enough to voice his opinions openly) as he is too cowardly to face people directly, and delights in publishing spicy gossip about them. He usually likes to entrench himself behind the responsibility of others and to hide the hand that flings the stone. A gazetteer more than a journalist, he might have success with the *chronique scandaleux* and, if the horoscope helps, he may even lead a paper with success; otherwise he will stoop to publishing infamous defamation and anonymous letters.

Examples: James I, King of England (Sun's degree); Benito Mussolini (degree of the Point of Equidistance)

09° Cancer

Symbol: Spinning and weaving tools; spindle and loom

A hard working, patient, thrifty being, will be only too modest and will lack that trifle of individual aggressiveness necessary for self-assertion. He will not be kept back by cowardice, but rather by a shy reserve, by an inborn, humble goodness making him put up with an obscure life in which he feels happy. It may take him long to make up his mind as to his own road, but once at it he will draw on all his resources in order to carry his work out to perfection, even in inconspicuous things, and will meet with real success in his own field. None knows better than he does how to apply Boileau's advice: *Vingt fois sur le mètier remettez vôtre ouvrage: polissez-le sans cesse et la repolissez.*

As with all shy people of this kind, he is apt to develop a great eloquence once he has conquered his inhibitions and will then move and stir his listeners all the more, finally overcoming the pent up feeling which made him tongue-tied. As he has an eminent juridical and social sense, he may make a good lawyer and a good political speaker, but will not become a king of the bar or a party leader, as he has not that minimum of charlatanism and intellectual exhibitionism needed. A less noble horoscope might lead the native into a police career, but his natural goodness will make him prefer the offices of the C.I.A. or a detective's profession, to the direct guardianship of public order.

10° Cancer

A mighty and productive will power, firmness and decision, activity and steadiness. The native is honest, generous and hard working; displays a great vitality, both physically and mentally. He seems to be endowed with magnetic force.

Luck will be deserved; his renown will be good. The native, or his undertakings, will give many people work and bread; his own work will thrive and he will reap the fruit thereof in his late years; all this provided that the rest of the pattern does not exclude success. The whole of the horoscope will show which is the pursued aim and on what plane the native's activity will develop.

Examples: Pope Jules II (Sun's degree); George Sand (Sun's degree); Charles Maurras (degree of Uranus, ruler of the Ascendant)

11° Cancer

Symbol: Some very young fishermen, still nearly boys,
try to disentangle their boat stranded on a shoal
and containing fishing tackle and string
nstruments for their leisure

A perennially youthful and inexperienced nature, its main

features being artistic temperament, musical talents, bombproof optimism, enthusiastic impulsiveness, carefree merriness and reckless light-mindedness. The character needs guidance, as it is unfit for independent work.

There will be repeated shipwreck. The native's affairs will slacken often, and he will be left stranded. If very unfavorably aspected elsewhere, a final failure might be expected. In most cases, however, the native will pull himself out of the scrape and begin all over again as if nothing had happened.

There is one thing the native ought never to do, even if he dies to: to sail.

12° Cancer

An incurable sadness, a murky character, a taste for mournful and gruesome things. A destructive instinct; a mind bent on criticizing things and itself; always on demolishing, never on building up. There are the worst tendencies-a deep and pent up passion bound to break loose all of a sudden with tragic violence.

The native is far from being sociable; on the contrary, he is cruel and arbitrary. He might be the author or the victim of a crime, as the pattern will show, toward life's end.

A certain skill in business is not unlikely; joy of work and constructive serenity are present.

13° Cancer

I, who can turn and change in a thousand ways.—Dante, *Paradiso,* 5, 99

. . . There is no learning if one does understand, remembers not.—Dante, *ibid.,* 5, 42

Science and wisdom. This degree is a lucky blend of taurine, mercurial and lunar features, endowing the mind with the brightest gifts; versatility and sharpness; deep understanding and a retentive memory; passion for learning and modesty in front of science; assimilation and originality; an inborn diplomatic aptitude. There might be peculiar faculties in the most different branches of learning, ranging from medicine to linguistics, from natural to occult sciences. A remarkable craftsmanship. All of which does not exclude a typically taurine nature; before getting one's work in hand, there is an inner drag to overcome, but once started, the rut thus dug will make the going steady and smooth and will prevent interruption of the effort undertaken.

An unsteady destiny, a mood liable to frequent change, owing to the native's excessive sensitivity. In less good horoscopes, the frequent shifting from enthusiasm to depression might reach cyclothymia or dysthymia. The native's youthful features, although promoting study, might prove harmful to the mind and might let it stray back into childishness.

The family might try to hinder and thwart the native's ideas or initiative. He seems likely to be destined to travel and change his residence often. His relatives, however, do not seem likely to hinder this.

Examples: The U.S. (Sun's degree); Calvin Coolidge (Sun's degree); Madame Curie (degree of Uranus, ruler of the Ascendant). I am inclined to place here Dante Alighieri's Sun, although it cannot be ruled out that the orb's rim overlaps into the first minutes of the following degree. Albert Einstein (degree of the Ascendant).

N.B. In the twenty-second canto (112-117) of his *Paradiso,* Dante states that he was born when the Sun was in Gemini. This constellation embraces some twenty-five zodiacal degrees, but strictly speaking, the eternal twins are Castor and Pollux, both stars of the first magnitude, the former of which was in 10° Cancer and the latter in 13° Cancer in Dante's time, the entire constellation ranging from the end of Gemini to about the middle of Cancer.

70

14° Cancer

An inborn nobility, such as to raise a peasant's son to a higher status on account of his native superiority; a natural sway over others, high feelings, kind manners. The native's judgment will be right and will be listened to. He will be fond of art and, in art, of the sublime. Though usually smooth mannered, he might become boisterous at times owing to an excessive emotivity.

His mind's adaptable manifoldness is, so to speak, boundless, and will balk at no practical problem. His favorite sciences are natural history (especially botany) and mathematics (above all, astronomy); among arts, poetry and painting and among crafts, goldsmithy. Whether practicing them or not, the native will become a protector of arts as soon as he can.

A fresh, healthy complexion, possibly withers early. The marriage partner comes of a noble family, famous through its old lineage or through artistic achievements or otherwise. Usually there is plenty of luck, but other components must be recognized.

15° Cancer

Symbol: A coil of rats' tails in an attic

And Jesus asked him, saying, What is thy name? And he said. Legion; because many devils were entered into him.—Luke 8:30

The native will unaccountably be laden with titles, honors and benefices in spite of his utter worthlessness, as he will be able to hide his slow wits and lack of personal ideas from the world's gaze under a display of great self-assurance and successful bluff. An uninspiring and unimaginative crammer who never will attain real culture, a jingo rather than a patriot, sophisticatedly shallow and destitute of real personality, an empty ranterer or even a vicious hypocrite, he never will be more than a stooge, ready nevertheless to deliver his void phrases with consequential pompousness and to cloak with hideous priggishness his blunt indifference for anything that does not touch him directly.

A dull and sluggish being, possibly potbellied and anyway unable to move, he will have to make up for his lack of intelligence by having recourse to tricks. His only redeeming virtue will be a watchful and tireless attention paving his way to self-assertion, and a deep attachment to his home.

Examples: Maximilian of Habsburg, Emperor of Mexico, 1864-67 (Sun's degree); Marie de Medici, Queen of France (Moon's degree).

16° Cancer

Symbol: An eagle holding a snake in its claws

This degree will grant courage, toughness, ready wit, inner and outer strength, a scheming and adroit mind, an intelligence that does not exclude cunning; in a word, all the makings of a great captain and the requirements for engaging in a successful battle. These traits will be enhanced by courteous manners, great tact and a good deal of tactical ability.

The native's foes will be his matches as far as gallantry and doggedness in fight goes, but will be unworthy of him for their unfairness and wickedness. A clue as to whether he will leave the battlefield as a conqueror or a loser may be drawn from his horoscope at large. But even in the latter case, his enemies will not be able to make him bite the dust.

Example: Hirohito, Emperor of Japan (degree of the Point of Equidistance between the Sun and the Moon)

17° Cancer

An apparently contradictory influence, as it seems to beget on one hand people in whose veins water runs instead of blood, and on the other, the sturdy leaders of the human herd.

The key to this riddle is to be sought in this degree's feature of extreme jumpiness; whatever amount of energy has fallen to the native's share, it will be of an entirely nervous character, and will lead him on by leaps and bounds. Therefore, a close study is to be made of the planets ruling the nerves (Mercury, Uranus and Lilith) in connection with the ones ruling will power (Sun, Mars and Pluto).

Whether the character is weak or strong, there is no room for prejudice or superstition. The intelligence is deep, lively, original, though discontinuous; there is great executive ability and a high education. If favorably aspected, the native might become an explorer, a pioneer, a political or religious reformer, never an impassive or a phlegmatic being. Provided that Jupiter does not stop him, he will go very far.

18° Cancer

The subject is weak with himself, has unhealthy tastes and an unbalanced will; he is cowardly and overbearing, shy and foolhardy, intrusive and lazy. His whole life is aimed at pleasure; he loves gambling most. When his money and vigor run low, or when he is sated and disappointed with life and has exhausted all other ways to enjoy himself, he will seal his own ruin by taking to booze and dope. Should other factors concur, his likely pitfalls will be sharping, misuse of trust, embezzlement, theft, rape, corruption of minors, and homosexuality. Should the stars portend mental deficiency as well, the native could even stoop to murder. (Criminology teaches that stupid thieves kill and clever ones steal without. attempting to take their victims' lives.)

19° Cancer

Symbol: A renaissance gentleman, sword and dagger at his side, plays the flute before a book stand on which an ancient illuminated score rests. Other courtiers stand respectfully around.

Though wearing a sword, I am of courteous manners.—Heraldic device to be read on the sword-bearing

73

coat of arms of painter Courtois Bourguignon, still standing on the house where he lived in Rome.

Gallantry in war, civil courage, a great passion and gift for art, a taste for polemics. The native will be capable of profound thought, will love books and research and will hold, for all his refinement, a marked sway over others. His is a terribly difficult character. He will be apt to fly off the handle for a trifle; he will be very kind when not roused, but will frighten everyone when angered. Should the horoscope bear evil influences, his artistic gifts would degenerate into histrionics, his gallantry into quarrelsomeness, his spirit of research into fruitless bookishness.

Great as the genius bestowed by this degree may be, it does neither give nor deny a creative turn of mind by itself; it only secures success in rendering and performing other people's works (as a dramatic actor, an opera singer, an orchestra player or conductor). That he may work creatively himself, he needs other stars to determine in what particular art, or other trade, his talent or genius may take concrete shape.

The parents might be of illustrious descent, even if they do not display their title officially.

Examples: Michelangelo Buonarroti (degree of Saturn, ruler of the Ascendant); Giuseppe Verdi (degree of the Point of Equidistance); Paul von Hindenburg, second president of Germany (degree of Jupiter, ruler of the Ascendant).

N.B. Paul von Beneckendorff und von Hindenburg was German field marshal from 1916 to 1918, and Reich president from 1925 to 1934, when he died. He had been born in 1847. Before World War I, during the great maneuvers, he had been forced to let himself be beaten by the kaiser. In the idiotic way of all tyrants, William II mocked the defeated general during the final banquet. Hindenburg answered as the kaiser had deserved, and had to go into retirement. At the beginning of World War I, the Germans were shamefully put to flight at Gumbinnen, and Prussia was invaded; the police found disbanded soldiers at 200 miles distance from the front. The old general, aged 67, had to be recalled into active service and was allotted the eastern sector. In the two battles of Tannenberg and the Masurian Lakes he turned the tables in his own favor. From then on, like Hannibal, he won all battles except the last one which, like Zama, decided the outcome of the war.

20° Cancer

Symbol: A watchdog slumbering at the entrance
of an old palace

Masters is what dogs have.—Italian proverb

The native never will be in want of either a piece of bread or of a roof. Though poor, he has, all considered, an easy life of it. His days are spent in blissful idleness. An easy life, not a dignified one. He cannot even think of being independent; as soon as the old master has gone, he will look for a new one. When kicked, he will whine like a coward and will think nothing of kissing the hands that enslave him.

I think he cannot lead an independent life because nothing weighs so heavily on his shoulders as a personal responsibility or thinking with his own head. Should the master allow him a minimum of authority over others, he will misuse it or at least make a display of it in front of those less well-dressed.

A lustful and lazy being, of ready wit and watchful character, he wants to be left in peace-that is, in idleness—and does not bear anyone other than his master daring to prod him in the ribs to rouse him from his slumber ("Do not rouse a sleeping dog"—Italian proverb.)

For his master he has a faithful attachment which is both base and heroic, despicable and moving. A thorough craven, he will boast of his master's valiant deeds; in his own utter poverty, he will brag of his master's wealth.

The native is hale and hearty, though no great friend of water and soap. Though he is financially poor, as we said, this poverty is at times the result of an heritage too costly for his income, which it would be wis? to waive, though none would dare advise him to do so. A bastard (or a degenerate) scion of a very old lineage, he would die rather than forget it.

What has been said till now about the native's despicable nature ought not to deceive us as to the real, indisputable usefulness of his task. As long as mankind stays what it is, policemen, customs officers, sextons, career soldiers, jail wardens, harlots, are all necessary evils. The frontier needs watchdogs, justice needs bloodhounds, and the male needs the female.

21° Cancer

A sociable disposition, perhaps not free from inquisitiveness. The native's mental makeup is supple and fit for scientific research, if it were not for its jumpiness, its unsteadiness, and its scarce faith in success. There is a marked ambition, but success depends on other factors; should these offset the subject's fickleness, he could exert some authority over others. But even in the exercise of this authority, his mind will trifle its power away and luck will not become more constant, nay perhaps it will prove treacherous.

What is certain is the native's love of travel, a veritable craze for journeys, which, however, may prove far from lucky.

Examples: Elizabeth Tudor, Queen of England (degree of Saturn, ruler of the Ascendant); Palmiro Togliatti, Italian Communist leader (Moon's degree).

N.B. Compare this with Queen Elizabeth's other essential degrees: 12° Aries Moon, 03° Cancer Point of Equidistance, 25° Virgo Sun). Read that note again.

22° Cancer

Symbol: A hothouse for exotic flowers

A haughty, fussy, dazzlingly showy, vain and lustful being, this native will incline toward a fantastic mood, driving her wayward refinement to the verge of morbid freakishness. She is inclined to strain at a gnat and to swallow a camel, this crotchetiness being perhaps due to an intensely artificial upbringing. Where other factors bear it out, the native's life might end painfully or tragically, and a pall of gloom might set upon those forced to live in the enervating, stifling air this being spreads around herself.

There is a great fondness of one's home. An interesting detail is love of perfume. The native might unconsciously absorb other people's vitality (what Indians call *prana*).

Examples: Catherine de Medicis, queen of France (degree of the Point of Equidistance); Cardinal Mazarin (Sun's degree).

23° Cancer

An inborn drive to rise higher and higher, to step aside from the beaten track and to follow new, untried paths. Other pointers have to show whether this impulsiveness will stray into fitful unbridledness, rudeness or brutality, or open its way upward into selfless dedication to an idea. The need to soar may be taken in a literal (mountaineering, aviation), financial or spiritual sense.

In any case, the danger of tumbling on the way is attendant upon this degree, as well as a manly daring and the chance of overcoming all obstacles at the end of the road, thus victoriously winding up the climb to the peak of glory or, in an humbler way, the scaling of a still untrodden mountain top.

The whole of the pattern will give a clue to the particular case. Anyway, the native is no common being, as he seems to dispose of always fresh energies and exceptional gifts; but he is unsteady and, at times, too rash. Great is his love of nature, irresistible his need to wander and open up unexplored territories.

In a humble horoscope, he will be an alpine guide; when the necessary scientific features are present, he might become a great explorer. According to seer Charubel, this degree rules over work connected with catering for the public and produces innkeepers, managers of restaurants, or butchers; which I am quoting here under his responsibility. I personally think that an uncommon gift of gab has fallen to the native's share, enabling him to shine as a teacher.

24° Cancer

Symbol: On a mountain peak, a fortress-like cloister
whose abbot is engrossed with the neighboring region

The native's soaring ambition is fanned by great qualities and as great failings; it takes but little help by other astrologic factors to have that ambition satisfied even beyond expectations. This degree grants an inborn prestige, admirable courage and untiring industriousness, but a snake-like hypocrisy as well, a tendency to cool-blooded, ruthless scheming, a mean way of cowering and cringing until the desired aim and the attending distinctions are in sight.

Such vices are hard to sublimate into virtues. The native's religious spirit would offer a chance, although exactly the contrary-namely, perversion of that outer intolerant and hypocritical formalism-might be expected. But the importance of the other factors and their marshaling, can never be overly stressed.

There will be no lack of enemies, whom the native will not fear. He may instead go out of his own way to bargain with them, if this can lift him but one step higher. As soon as he has the whole flight of steps behind himself, he will have them all under his heels and will rule over them all as a tyrant.

Example: Rome (Ascendant's degree).

N.B. See also 05° Aries, where Rome's Sun is to be found, and the note referring to it.

25° Cancer

Symbol: A wild horse

The strongest man is the one who stands most alone.—Ibsen, *An Enemy of the People*

A high-spirited being, full of noble purposes and setting his aims high, cherishing freedom above all earthly things and driving this love so far as to stray away from his kind into silence and seclusion. If other stars help, this will not prevent his doing great works likely to exert a deep influence on his neighbors and to leave a mark in history. The secret of his success is his unshakable self-confidence supported by a fiery will.

Under less favorable influences his daring may become a reckless love of adventure, his zest for work wild and fickle fanaticism, his lofty aspirations selfish ambitions.

Travel will play some role in his life. Concurrent emergence of suitable factors might make him into a pioneer.

Example: Ignatius Semmelweiss, physician and forerunner of asepsis (Sun's degree)

26° Cancer

A fickle, inconsequent or shilly-shallying character, a shifty destiny, foreboding pitfalls. This native's conflicting features will be a soaring mind and an eager lustfulness; religiousness and recklessness; a bright mentality adorned with good taste and dialectic drive, at a loss in front of the practical problems of everyday life. The native is blessed by a sincere good-heartedness, a poetical turn of mind and a generosity bordering on lavishness.

The tumbles that destiny has in store for the native might affect his financial life (bankruptcy) as well as his health (bodily falls). Therefore, violent sports, air travel and alpinism ought to be discouraged.

27° Cancer

An exceptionally good, mild and conciliating being, the native's keynote is a thorough and essential passivity. He might even carry out great works, which, however, he will not have undertaken himself; he might be a model of perseverance and hard work, but will sit pretty when no one else prods him in the ribs. In a word, he has been born to obey, and only in a subordinate position can his diligence result in useful work. The only initiative such a meek and unambitious fellow can take is to patch up quarrels.

He has a slow, short-sighted, blunt intelligence.

Example: Anne of Austria, France's queen (degree of the Moon, being also ruler of the Ascendant).

28° Cancer

The native is deeply in love with nature and its beauty, its contemplation being for him a source of fresh strength. He abhors whatever is unnatural and can be naturally kind and attract lasting affections. He lives in harmony with the cosmos and the beings inhabiting it. Yet he can display a remarkable political skill and a more remarkable administrative ability.

Barring pointers to the contrary, the native is sure to get money galore as soon as he is of age, whatever the conditions of his family at his birth. Unfortunately, the gift for earning money might be warped into greed, and his foresight into stinginess.

On the other hand, even that admiration of beauty might edge off into loafing, political tact give way to scheming, servilism or even worse; even the relations with neighbors might turn into rivalry. Only a look at the whole can enlighten us as to the right meaning one can ascribe in each concrete case to this dual influence.

Example: The so-called Third Reich, namely Nationalist So-cialist Germany (Ascendant's degree).

N.B. Compare the other essential degrees of the quoted Example: 01° Aries Sun, 04° Aquarius Moon, 03° Pisces Point of Equidistance. Remark as well the Third Reich's victorious struggle against neo-malthusianism, a unique case in the history of people whose birth rate is sinking.

29° Cancer

Where there are pointers of honesty and decency, this degree bestows a superior intelligence and a sense for business. Unfavorably aspected, it will produce a low cunning leading to unscrupulous doings, cheating, and even theft.

Strange as it may seem, the native tends by nature to be shy, yielding, self-conscious, and close. Such a pliancy will remarkably relieve the educator's task, provided he can see through his pupil, but will increase the danger of evil influence as well.

Should other astrologic factors concur, an unhappy end might be foreseen: jail, death sentence, violent death and the like. The ambushes of men and fate are, in any event, to be feared.

30° Cancer

As are all over-compensated half-wits, the native is firmly persuaded that other people's opinions count for nothing. As far as he is personally concerned, no one can deny him a certain ready wit, a certain insight and a degree of psychological penetration, or the sense of justice. But unless very favorably aspected elsewhere, he cannot be expected to be modest and to harbor any feelings of human brotherhood.

His force does not lie in his thought, but in his will power, which, if backed by other good aspects elsewhere, can really be above average. He will disdainfully reject help and shun depend-ence, plunge boldly into action and engage singlehanded in fierce struggles-and will still succeed best in that very field any logical mind would deem the least congenial to him, namely, government career. He might take to the sea and have to stand the hardest ordeals and face the worst dangers in his career, which, in the light of abstract reasoning, would seem to fit him to a tee.

LEO

01° Leo

*Symbol: Alone and weaponless, Samson tears up with
his bare hands the lion come to attack him*

*Out of the eater came forth meat and out of the strong
came forth weakness.*— Judges 14:14

But for modesty, the native is endowed with all the qualities
required to master himself and others. A man of high standing, he
will reap victory over his enemies.

Should he curb his inborn daring and strength with mildness
and restraint, he might become a benefactor of his own subjects.
Otherwise his exceptional power and unchallenged faith in himself
will drift into high-handedness, inner dignity will stray into exterior pompousness; the flatterings of men and the enticements of
women around him to which he is apt to lend much too willing an
ear, will prove his undoing.

The native's karma might be bound or interwoven with that of
his nation, a thing of which he might have to bear the consequences
as well for evil (obscurity and oblivion, at least for awhile) as for
good (lasting renown). The horoscope as a whole will have to lead
the interpretation on this point.

Examples: Dumas Père (degree of the Sun); Lord Kitchener
(degree of Venus, ruler of the sign intercepted in the house of personality); Herbert Hoover, thirty-first president of the United
States (degree of Mercury, ruler of the Ascendant).

02° Leo

Symbol: A rudderless ship, prey to the waves

Danger of shipwreck ahead. Devoid of moral strength, lacking decision and self-appreciation. This one hundred and twenty-second degree of the zodiac is the reverse of the previous one, though, being in common with it, exposed to trouble and having karmic connections with the surrounding community.

The native is besides a nervous and oversensitive subject. He might often be an artist, and might be blind sometimes to his own uncommon gifts. Unable to steer the course of his own life, he will go adrift materially and spiritually, will be tossed and bounced right and left.

The omen of the shipwreck might literally come true; there might be shipwreck in the real sense of the word.

Examples: Carlota, Empress of Mexico, 1864-67 (degree of the Point of Equidistance between Sun and Moon); Erez Israel (degree of the Moon). Compare this with 27° Leo (degree of the Ascendant), with 24° Taurus and 28° Gemini (Point of Equidistance between Sun and Moon). In this same degree is to be found Pluto as ruler of the Ascendant in the pattern of Mussolini's war declaration on France and the British Empire (June 10, 1940, about 5 p.m.), as well as the Sun of the *coup d'etat* which overthrew the Fascist regime (July 25, 1943). Also compare 17° Taurus (Moon), 25° Gemini (Point of Equidistance), and 27° Libra (Ascendant).

03° Leo

Symbol: A newly born lion cub, its eyes still shut

This symbol, while on one side pointing to the unripeness of the native's lion nature, emphasizes on the other side what chances he has to progress.

The horoscope as a whole will show whether the native will be able to open his eyes within the bounds of this one embodiment, and whether he will succeed in gradually developing the powers he hides slumbering in himself. If so, stumbling and tottering, forcing his way through pitfalls and thorny briers, he will work himself up to the highest peaks of human achievement. Then the very utterness of his ignorance and his native childishness might enable him to do some great and original work, untrammeled as he is by the yoke of scholastic tradition. His very lack of moral tenets might lead him up to a noble and freer stage of morality, where convention and prejudice play no part. In front of the mystery of the universe he might preserve that divine sense of wonder from which the, sophisticated fool struggles to free himself.

All this might happen. The subject is, of course, unlikely to follow the entire path of such an evolution till its end within the short span of one earthly life. In most cases he will be able to open his eyes only in a following embodiment. In the present one the native is likely to grope in the dark. Even worse, pushed back on his defensive by the first rude jolts from the outside world, and unable to account for them, he might freeze into immobility, shun any further struggle and take a mistrustful attitude toward life. Thus, while trying to avoid development through experience, he never will avoid suffering. Driven by his childish nature, he will flare up quickly into a mood of unjustified elation, and will subside into discouragement and despair even more quickly.

An extremely lively but unruly imagination, eager but fruitless passionate-ness, inconsequent behavior, as one aimlessly fumbling in the dark. The subject is not to be relied upon.

04° Leo

Symbol: On the polar pack a white bear lies in ambush by a cleft, waiting for a seal to emerge for air

. . . my breast, where hate and love are never stilled—Carducci, *Rime Nuove* 2, 24

All virtues born of prudence and reserve; and all attendant

vices as well: suspiciousness, cunning, and malice.

The native might display great activity and practical sense and might push his endurance in work to a superhuman level, but always with some selfish goal in sight. His gaze is sharp and unfailing, but he will not make up his mind before ripe reflection.

He will be constant in love, unflinching in hatred; he will make a staunch, devoted friend and a formidable foe, who will hardly fail to take revenge sooner or later for any offense, mighty as the offender may be. His wrath will not seek an immediate outlet; he will bide his time like a well-laid trap ready to snap. Only after detecting the vulnerable side of the one who harms him or hurts his feelings, he will strike with ruthless deliberation.

His success seems to be bound to travels, especially overseas. He is likely to draw the greatest profit from his native cunning and practical sense for trade and diplomacy. The rest of the pattern will supply more precise details.

Example: Giosuée Carducci (Sun's degree).

N.B. Compare 12° and 20° of this same sign, where the poet's equidistance and the Moon are; and especially 07° Cancer for his Ascendant.

05° Leo

Symbol: A snake

It is a degree of ungenerosity. The native has something eluding grasp and will slip away from your hands on the very moment you think you have caught him.

He will delve deep into the most hermetical sciences, whether material or spiritual; tackle intricate and baffling problems and master their result with matchless skill, but the work thus done he will turn to his exclusive profit. A thankless egotist, with a strain of mockery and scepticism, cunning in spite of his undeniable intelligence; full of lust but not its slave; jealous of his discoveries and venomous toward his rivals, the native will be able to reach success, but will fail to achieve the popularity he craves and can reasonably expect. It is not even to be ruled out that he will have to suffer—and much at that—and leave his native country under grave circumstances. He should avoid positions of responsibility, refrain from running any concern on his own, and put up with a lower status than he bargains for, living up to it in the quietest possible way.

Example: George Bernard Shaw (degree of the Sun)

06° Leo

Symbol: A man of stately appearance, riding a horse, brandishes a sword. A snake lifts its head between the animal's hocks.

. . . a *serpent by the way, an adder in the path, that biteth the horse heels, so that his rider shall fall backward.*—Genesis 44:27

Bodily strength and inner power, which might degenerate into material and moral violence; daring bordering on recklessness; fondness of sport contests, weapons, polemics and duels, with a quarrelsome bent toward aggression in word and fact.

The native might have a mission to fulfill, might become a great military or political ruler and stand out like a giant. Something, however, will undermine his greatness at its very foundations; his inordinate pride or his self-ostentation.

Examples: Prince von Bismarck (degree of his Ascendant); Benito Mussolini (degree of the Sun and Mercury in conjunction, though the Sun's orb overlaps by more than its half into the following degree, its center at about 06°00'52"; George V (degree of Mars, ruler of the Ascendant sign, or of the sign intercepted in the house of personality).

07° Leo

Symbol: A man riding a lion

The native is a tamer born and none is possessed of a greater instinctive gift for ruling human beasts-or wild animals, should the stars point to it.

On the noblest souls this degree may bestow a nearly heavenly wisdom such as to transcend human reason and connect the individual with the Whole. The subject might then attain the gift of prophecy, or better, be enlightened with a nearly divine sense of the universal mystery and of the Infinite.

In less exalted beings we may find a more or less earthly wisdom, a direct, non-rational insight into reality or, in a still humbler way, into practical problems. Whatever the field the stars allot to the native for his activity, he will hold a natural sway over others and direct them at will or, according to his whims, as if he could dispose of supernatural means. Should luck be on his side it would not be risky to forecast that he will become the pivot of the circle—whatever its size—where he lives and works, that he will step into the limelight in spite of his doggedest opponents and will outshine even much worthier rivals.

According to Charubel there is sympathy between this degree and 07° Libra. I contend that this sympathy ought to extend to the whole of Libra.

Examples: Giuseppe Garibaldi (Ascendant's degree); Benito Mussolini (Sun's degree); Sir Bernard Law Montgomery (degree of Saturn, ruler of the Ascendant); Napoleon has in this degree Mercury, as ruler of the war and death house

08° Leo

Symbol: The burning bush

As above so underneath.—Hermes' principle from the "Emerald Table"

Per manum benedicentem maledictus adumbra-tur—Esoteric sentence of mediaeval origin: viz. E. Levi, "Dogma and Ritual of High Magic"

In a highly spiritual horoscope this degree's influence will endow the native with the power of heavenly fire surging forth with ardor unquenchable, unsullied, and all-consuming. Its light will be hidden from the sight of the unworthy and might even stay invisible to most eyes or escape notice altogether. In the bush blazing with unearthly flame, much-too-human beings will fail to see the light of the Absolute and will be alive only to the fact that the thorns in the bush sting anyone attempting to violate its mystery.

Such are the conflicting features of the zodiac's one hundred twenty-eighth degree; fieriness along with reserve; aims sublime yet secret; a nature flashing with hope and led by the most generous impulses of self-denial, yet constantly on its defensive, as the thorns and the flames in the bush clearly imply.

On the contrary, should the horoscope as a whole point to a lustful nature, the Lion's eighth degree would shift to its opposite polarity and, instead of a divine imprint, give it a luciferic bent. The burning bush will thus change into the lunar devilish image of Cain and the thorns. Then an unquenchable passion, impure yet devoid of hidden motives and mental reservations, will slowly and steadily eat up the whole being, body and soul. The fire might not die out before having wasted the mind to its innermost reserves and burnt out the organism to its last shred.

Even a third case is possible: when the stars point to neither outspokenly spiritual nor lustful features, and the whole pattern appears uninspiring and mean, the subject proves a modest being of limited scope. The degree's fire then will enter the existence from outside. The native's activity might be bound to the fiery element, giving him a chance to rise to success and even to emerge into fame (should the whole contain hints of luck). Such might be the case of a smith working his way up to becoming an artistically gifted craftsman, or an industrialist running a successful foundry;

also of a fireguard meeting an heroic death and rising to short-lived fame.

Whether heavenward or earthbound, such a mind will be ruled by instinct rather than by reason. His spirit of justice and honesty, his sense of unalloyed integrity and fairness, often would entitle the native to a higher social status than he occupies.

Example: Herbert Hoover, thirty-first president of the United States (degree of the Moon and Mars in conjunction).

09° Leo

Symbol: A great show of fireworks. Rockets, bombs and tourbillions unfold their dazzling pattern in the sky.

The native's talk also will sound like a show of fireworks. The positive side of this influx is its utter distinction and refinement. The native is keenly aware of his own worth, has self-respect and commands respect from others; has sincerity, grandeur and elegance at the same time.

Overdone and disfigured, all these virtues might present themselves in the shape of defects or even vices. We shall then meet a vain haughtiness, as contemptible as full of contempt, an antisocial and destructive character, apt to burst out into fits of rage. There will be a vain self-ostentation, a misplaced fastidiousness, a splash of dazzling extravagance, a splurge of rank pageantry devoid of any inner foundation. In other words, a lot of money will go up in smoke; the permanent will be sacrificed to the transitory, the useful to the pleasant, and substance to appearance.

In particularly unfavorable horoscopes the virtue of sincerity will disappear and the nastiest surprise might be expected. The native seems, however, to have luck on his side. He might travel to places very far away.

90

10° Leo

Symbol: Death, holding the scythe

Ananke! In a previous life the native has taken someone's life in cold blood, but not for selfish purposes. Therefore he is either an instrument of fate or its victim. Whether good or bad, such a man is destined to destroy, not to create.

In extremely lucky horoscopes the native is an indomitable being. No one can oppose his cunning and his cool determination. He can bide his time, but will not argue or listen to objections when he has made up his mind to act. Nothing equals his timeliness, nothing can shake his deliberation. You might ward him off for awhile but never finally thwart his plans, as he simply will lie in wait for a better opportunity to strike again, this time more unpredictably and more decidedly than before.

He knows neither privileges nor distinctions; all are equal in his eyes; and he cannot bear the big shots. If he is good (which is not excluded even side by side with the ruthless will power we credit him with) he will extend his kindness and hospitality even to the undeserving. If he is bad, nothing will limit his capacity for evil; no one will deserve pity in his eyes, no power on earth will be able to ward off his murderous hand.

So far the extreme cases. The average man born under this influence will inherit only its destructive bent and will not be able to build anything on earth. Death's wing will be ever at his side, ready to carry off his dear ones, his irreplaceable cooperators, or himself. His best-engineered plans will stay fruitless, his earthly work remain unachieved. Others might reap what he sows down here. He can sow only for eternity.

Example: Pandit J. Nehru's Moon is here, in conjunction with his Ascendant (see 13° Leo).

11° Leo

Symbol: A very young woman lifting her dress

An impulsive, restless temperament bent on all pleasures and devoid of inhibitions. The character is weak and open both to enticements and to bad advice from other people. At life's turning points there is a dangerous tendency to lose control.

As the native is good-natured, sociable and endowed with precocious gifts and attractive brightness, one is likely to be lenient toward his excesses, which are apt to be labeled as the wayward youth extravagance peculiar to budding genius. A bright promise which is hardly ever kept; in spite of current opinion no one will achieve artistic creation who does not submit himself to a hard, unrelenting rule, in possible contradiction to the, accepted middle-class morality, but still to be observed with an inflexibility unknown to the nameless mediocrity.

Examples: Philippe of Orleans, France's regent during Louis XV's minority (Sun's degree); the Duke of Main, Louis XIV's legalized bastard (Moon's degree).

12° Leo

*Symbol: A fair lady dressed with Christian modesty
and uncommon elegance*

Life under this lucky star will be sheltered against storms and earthquakes and will glide along thriftily and smoothly. Wealth accruing to the native from inheritance or dowry, barring indications to the contrary, will give him a measure of independence, saving him at the same time the trouble of striving after money, as either the native personally or the native's marriage partner, or both, will be born rich unless, as I have said before, the stars point to the contrary.

Even if not possessed of any relevant wealth, the marriage partner certainly will bring the most welcome gifts, above all, the gift of making the other partner happy, but may well be possessed of both.

A sound, straight, inwardly felt moral code; a sensible and fair behavior; an instinctive reserve; an easy and gentle firmness of character; a natural balance of feelings-these are the virtues completing the picture.

Outward success ought not to fail; even fame might be attained if the pattern as a whole is favorable, though the native's name is not likely to survive him. Should other aspects point to renown, this ought to dim after the subject's death. Whatever the native's merits, even if very high, his renown will be greater than reasonably expected among his contemporaries, and less than his due among his posterity.

Example: Giosué Carducci (degree of the Point of Equidistance between the Sun and the Moon).

13° Leo

Symbol: A black bull

All good and bad features of an extreme steadfastness and positivism; on one hand, firmness, constancy, sturdiness, endurance in exertion and a sense of phenomenal reality; on the other hand, stubbornness, restiveness, pigheadedness, hypercritical scepticism and unappeasable lustfulness. As a result, the sources of income and means of subsistence are lastingly assured—nay, too lastingly—which might hinder and thwart progress, even mobility in general.

There is no enthusiasm, no spiritual urge, no faith in men or in the future, not to speak of faith in God. The character is, therefore, skittish, sullen, sometimes cynical, often unpleasant on account, or in spite of, the fact that the native professes very firm principles and sticks to them.

Whatever his luck, the subject never feels happy and is therefore in a state of constant dissatisfaction.

Example: Guy de Maupassant (degree of the Sun); Pandit J. Nehru (degree of the Ascendant).

N.B. According to Axel Munthe, Maupassant was nicknamed "the sad bull" by his friends.

14° Leo

Symbol: A waterfall, on its bank a deserted mill.
A rainbow rises from the spray.

This influence tends to promote an intensely spiritual and artistic life and to damp the native's practical and businesslike faculties. There is no lack of intelligence, but a marked absence of executive skill, so that the native's abstract ingenuity does not prevent his feeling helpless and shilly-shallying when confronted with the small problems of everyday life. As a result, in the outward sphere uncontrolled impulses and noble urges prevail upon organized activity. The subject does not either feel it in himself or bring his influence to bear on others in any given direction.

When they cannot praise a girl for either her looks or her wits, they say of her in France, as a piece of mischievous cold comfort, that she is "so fond of her mother anyway." But this can be said in all earnestness of the native, who is really attached to his parents. If these have bequeathed him any estate, it will dwindle away sooner or later, as the heir is nearly always an inefficient, often idle, idealist, lost to material reality in his worship of the sublime and his love of the beautiful.

15° Leo

Symbol: Odin, in a wanderer's disguise, brandishing the magic
spear, hits the ground and rouses the thunder.

Inborn power and superiority over others; whether bodily or moral or else, other pointers in the horoscope must decide. The native is conscious of his own worth, whatever it might be. In well-developed beings this degree will nurture lofty aspirations and inner pride; in the coarser ones it will lead to vain ambitions and display. Something special will single out the subject anyhow, be it for good or evil, through bright mental gifts or spiritual prominence, through money or even brute force; in what manner and how far will depend, as mentioned above, on the other threads in the astrological pattern. But whoever is born under this sign is very likely to become a ruler in some sense and to have the makings for it as well; he is likely to couple his inborn power with kindness and human warmth, and to win many friends. This can even go so far as to entangle all mental activities in social life, in which case the native is in for a more or less wide popularity as the soul of dancing parties and the organizer of merrymaking.

Barring indications to the contrary, travels in connection with friendships or social engagements can be foreseen, as for instance on friends' or relatives' invitation, journeys undertaken in order to assist friends, etc.

Examples: Louis, Duke of Burgundy, the great Dauphin's first-born son (Sun's degree). In this degree we find Saturn, as ruler of the Ascendant, in the horoscope of Soviet dictatorship (November 8, 1917).

16° Leo

Symbol: A baby giant riding an unharnessed ass

An impulsive, enthusiastic and demonstrative nature, impatient of discipline and advice, stubborn and foolhardy, hard to repress and to check.

An open-hearted, generous and affectionate friend, he will make an uncomfortable and often dangerous enemy.

To all this he adds the utmost frugality, thanks to which he might bear the distress his unripeness is more than likely to bring upon him.

Potentially a man of many sports, endowed with a lopsided but bright and sometimes outstanding intelligence; he is conspicuous for the utmost development of some of his gifts and the utter infancy of other sides of his being, which exposes him to the risk of wasting his mental power on childish trifles.

There will be a tendency to a large body size; great head, broad hands, tall stature, etc.

17° Leo

Symbol: A dromedary

An extremely outstanding personality. The native will cut out a place for himself in all he does, supported by a fierce, altogether indomitable nature, an inexhaustible energy, an exceptional resistance to exertion, a toughness, a sturdiness and a steadfastness ready to stand any test. On the reverse side of the coin appear petty formality, headstrongness, bad manners, a wild roughness and sometimes even ferocity.

Mindful of benefits as well as of injuries, he simply cannot dispense with the glee of revenge. Strangely enough, though fond of display and notoriety, he is apt to turn a deaf ear to the often vicious taunts and snubs leveled at his surly character, as only what may harm him is an offense in his eyes, and such complaints against him as may end by enhancing his renown as an awe-inspiring being are far from displeasing to him.

Lucky and endowed with an inventive turn of mind, he will reap abroad the success to which his long toils and his often gigantic works entitle him. Material danger might, however, lie in wait for him, either on his journeys or on his undertakings and might stand in his way to wealth and renown.

Examples: Georges Clemenceau, "the Tiger," premier of France (degree of Venus, ruler of his Ascendant). In this degree is to be found Pluto as ruler of the Ascendant in the horoscope of the government set up in Syria through the *coup d'etat* of August 14, 1949.

N.B. To Clemenceau as president of the council during and after (1917-1920) World War I, goes the glory of the *revanche* and the infamy of the treaty of Versailles.

18° Leo

An uncommon mind, thorough and brilliant at the same time, qualified both to create by itself and to successfully assimilate other people's hunches and doctrines. The native's personality is a powerful one and will leave its mark; obscure as his birth may be, he will rise to distinction through his own ingenuity. By dint of hard work and such a toil as may let him appear a drudge and a grinder, he will get in his life the share he deserves and, as he is not duly endowed with intellectual gifts, but kind, generous and plucky, he will win many hearts.

Examples: Philippe of Orleans, France's regent; Oamillo, Count of Cavour (degree of the Sun).

19° Leo

Should the horoscope as a whole show outstanding features in point of originality or initiative, the mysterious component of this degree then would make itself felt as a force not of this world, which through often superhuman ordeals can lead the native beyond all earthly limitations (e.g., prevalence of the Fire element, more planets in the house of spirit, role of Neptune, etc.—spirituality—besides, for what concerns originality and initiative, a strong component in Aries, well posited Sun or Mars, majority of planets in the east, rulers of the Ascendant dignified, plenty of planets in the house of personality, etc.) But as it is not within everyone's power to go through fire without being burned, less exceptional beings may register only the discordant harmonics of this influence. This is why we shall find little personal initiative, productiveness, or practical aptitude in the man in the street born under this sign, and usually nothing but a certain aesthetic taste. Apart from this, the native is utterly devoid of initiative and seems born to serve, or at least to obey. But, surprisingly enough, a senseless and stubborn arrogance sets him against those worthier, mightier and better than himself. What in higher beings is contempt for the world, or conquest of what the Church defines as human respect becomes, in lower individuals, grudge against mankind and unjustified rebellion against public opinion. Which will only call for sharp reproof from his neighbors, and for harsh but deserved lessons. The native is heading for more than one fall. But never fear! He will always fall on his own legs as, even thus distorted, this degree's providential component will still make itself felt.

Examples: Herbert Hoover, thirty-first president of the United States (degree of the Sun). In this degree are the Third French Republic's Venus and the Italian Unity's Jupiter, both indicating the working classes, viz., as rulers of the sector of labor in the respective patterns.

20° Leo

A strong character, resentful of outward restraint and impatient of any fetters; a bright and manifold intelligence, an intuitive and imaginative mind. Famous and influential people will like and support the native, who will enjoy also the friendship and cooperation of the best minds.

In a word, all the makings of success; which, however, will keep him long waiting. For quite a time every effort will stay fruitless, every undertaking will seem doomed to failure, no sizable result will be apparent. He will have to start all over again.

Unwavering steadfastness is the catchword here; try and try again. Luck is likely to^await the native far away from home. A diplomatic career, a commercial or industrial agency abroad, or other such activities might suit him. Destiny seems anyhow to be bound to paper, as to documents or other writings, drawings or engravings.

Examples: Giosué Carducci (degree of the Moon, ruler of the

Ascendant); Rudolf Steiner (degree of Jupiter, ruler of his Ascendant); Cardinal Newman (degree of Saturn, ruler of his Ascendant)

N.B. Compare this degree in the poet's horoscope with 07° Cancer (degree of the Ascendant); with 04° Leo, where his birth Sun is; and with 12° Leo (degree of his Point of Equidistance between Sun and Moon). Jupiter's degree (04° Cancer) ought not to be lost sight of, as it offers a clue to his Hymn to Satan.

21° Leo

Symbol: Isis' Key

The native is a ruler born, but his sway over others has nothing challenging, high-handed or overbearing; it is but the expression of a surging inner strength, based on a perfect harmony between power and action, on a deep knowledge of human nature and life's laws. There is a highly developed power of mental concentration and insight into others' characters, from which the native draws a clairvoyance and a foresight that might seem supernatural. An uncommon intelligence and an outstanding memory complete the excellence of such a mind. In the field of human relations, a very kindly and hospitable touch, an utter sincerity coupled with the strictest discretion, a distinguished handling of people, full of worldly wisdom and yet above any diplomatic double-dealing, will earn the native widespread popularity and will win him loyal friends.

Unless ominously aspected elsewhere, the native ought to obtain success. It is not to be ruled out that he is on his way to initiation; he may even be a master already.

22° Leo

Symbol: Eccl. Homo!

As we had to remark above (e.g., about 19° Leo, 24° Taurus, etc.) this degree also possesses such a transcendent influence that no soul less than heavenly can bear it with impunity. Such enthusiasm and blindness to the world's mean ways, such candid artlessness as are induced by this sign can only be—without any possible compromise—the mark of a saint or that of a nincompoop. The native is his own worldly fortune's worst enemy and he will let those who ought to respect him most fleece him and cover him with abuse.

Should he stand—nay, desire—all of this out of his love for Jesus Christ, should he give himself over wholly to the service of suffering mankind and bear any disgrace in order to allay the most horrible social evils, should his astrological pattern, side by side with his primitive naivety, ascribe him an heroic character and a superhuman thoroughness, he then would rise to such a height as St. John of the Cross or Jacopone da Todi, as the case may be. Then the crowds would end by paying, however late, their tribute of honor and worship to the one in whose face they had spat.

On the other hand, should the horoscope be an indifferent one or simply not an exceptional one, the native would grow into a weak and powerless being, giddy and hotheaded, a prey to anyone willing to take advantage of him.

In any case, this degree implies danger from swiftly progressing illnesses and from fire. The holy man might die while tending the plague-stricken; the fool might die of his own imprudence.

Example: The government installed in Syria on August 14, 1949 (Sun's degree).

N.B. Compare 24° Aries (Moon), 23° Gemini (Point of Equidistance); 17° Leo (Pluto as ruler of the Ascendant), and 15° Scorpio (Ascendant).

23° Leo

Symbol: Janus, the two-faced god

(As everyone knows, Janus' temple, shut in peacetime, was opened in time of war, that the god might go thence and lead the army to victory.)

This is the great war leader's degree, although it does make not only the warriors but the authors of doctrines as well; the trailblazers of new thoughts and sciences, the legendary founders of traditions. The native never will deny or despise the past but, on the contrary, will draw enlightenment for the future from its study.

The secret of the native's ascendancy, enabling him to get many followers and to steer them along as he likes, is to be sought in his mind's superiority, which is based not so much on its power as on its unique type. This original and many-sided intellect, often capable of more than one work at a time, is coupled with a stunning psychical insight, a deep knowledge of human characters, an inborn aptitude for treating each person differently and for conquering everyone's heart. He is, moreover, possessed of alertness and penetration, a powerful and well-trained memory, and a subtle diplomatic sense.

Although this is a war leader's degree, the native will appreciate greatly the benefits of peace and culture. Possibly many of those Renaissance *condottieri* were born under this sign, who opened their way to leadership with the force of arms to become from then on the protectors of the painters, poets and artists of their age and who held in their courts scientific and literary academies.

Examples: Napoleon (Sun's degree); Lord Kitchener (degree of Mars, ruler of his Ascendant)

24° Leo

Symbol: A scene from Sienkiewicz Quo Vadis; gigantic Ursus, the slave, chops wood in his royal mistress's yard.

Apart from whatever other astrological factors there may be, this degree tends to produce the typical figure of the good giant, so dear to late romanticism. A modest, utterly unambitious, wild and childishly artless, friendly, clumsily devoted being, he loves the rough toils allotted to him since his birth and displays the greatest painstakingness even in the longest and hardest labors. He is very fond of the country and especially of the woods, as he feels at home only in primitive surroundings.

His honest and faithful nature might make him dear to beings more developed than himself. His roughness does not exclude either a rudimentary kind of musing about religious matters or a deep effort to grasp and follow a higher or less primitive moral code than the jungle law; if the pattern as a whole points to a very clever, cultivated being, this feature may be interpreted as portending conversion to another religious faith.

According to the seer Charubel, the native must move only southwest of his or her place of birth and trade in only white things or white animals. To him goes the responsibility for such details.

25° Leo

Symbol: A man swimming in the waters of the sea

Should the other threads in the pattern correct the negative sides of this degree, the native's work would yield splendid results. This is, however, unlikely to happen, as his otherwise gifted, enterprising nature is hampered by his lack of stability and his aversion to steady effort. His taste is refined but lustful, his disposition sensitive but an easy prey to passions and craving for pleasures. The native is in for hard struggles and not with the brightest of perspectives, as both his possessions and his trade skirt disaster through intemperance.

The native is awfully fond of the sea and might sometimes be fond of the sport of fishing. Unlucky aspects might induce death either through drowning or stilling.

Example: Elizabeth, queen of England (Sun's degree)

26° Leo

Symbol: A tiller breaking the soil with a hoe

102

If other astrologic aspects bear it out, the native will be a deep investigator of nature and will love it from the depth of his soul. A clever and unrelenting worker, he will be modest and stubborn enough to shoulder willingly the hard, ungrateful tasks which the majority shuns, but which tasks are necessary to science and society.

Luck is likely to reward the native's firmness and practical skill with well-deserved success, welfare and even renown.

As the seer Charubel has it, the native's lucky direction ought to be north of his birthplace, which piece of advice I am repeating here on his trust.

27° Leo

Symbol: Thrusting at it with his pruning bill, hitting it with a stick and pelting it with stones, a boy plucks the berries of a wild bush jutting off a crag.

This degree, like the former one, makes the native hard working and efficient; but in all the rest the two degrees differ greatly as this one plunges the native headlong into rash action aiming at immediate results, whereas the former one induces a level-headed, constant, peaceful and self-effacing effort.

Moreover, we are confronted here with a first-rate polemic mind, which may at times drift into quarrelsome recklessness and change the subject into a downright wrangle. It is also to be remarked that the native's industriousness is directed mainly toward works which, useful or even indispensable as they may be, result in a measure of destruction. Therefore, he is likely to reap more notoriety than affection, and will in extreme cases run the risk of bodily attack and violent death.

Nor is the blow sure to be driven by an enemy. The rebounding stone may hit the thrower; after .the seer Charubel, he has to beware of things falling by accident. The seer goes so far as to discourage work or residence at the foot of high buildings. To quote him again, and on his own responsibility, "the native ought to go south of his birthplace."

Example: The Zionist state of Erez Israel has its Ascendant in this degree.

28° Leo

Symbol: Two friends shaking hands

Natives exhibiting the marks of industriousness elsewhere in their pattern may only profit from this influence. It will make them into honest, fair, humane people whom everyone will find attractive and easy to deal with. They will promote or contribute to the setting up of cooperatives, cultural societies, social foundations, etc.

Should the horoscope lack any indication of useful work besides enjoyable pastimes, the native's gifts for efficiency and thoroughness would find no expression and would waste away in idle chatter and futile social events.

Those who look at human and personal ambition as a desirable gift would be disappointed by its conspicuous absence here, as the subject's only ambition lies in furthering human cooperation, in promoting or supporting collective work and spreading harmony around himself. Therefore, in the absence of any marks of financial luck, this idealist might bring about his own ruin.

The seer Charubel discourages travel; according to him the native's luck might be bound to what the Earth's bosom yields, be it mineral ore or archaeological remains. As above, I leave to him the responsibility for these statements.

Examples: Anne of Austria, France's queen 1702-14 (degree of equidistance between Sun and Moon); Arrigo Boita (Ascendant's degree); Raymond Poincare, president of the French Republic 1913-20 (degree of the Sun).

29° Leo

Symbol: Two newlyweds exchanging the wedding ring

As to the influence of this degree on the native's mind, see the foregoing one.

As to the course of life, the following difference is to be remarked: there friendship and social intercourse took up the subject's activity entirely, here family life is the pivot. The native may have to marry more than once, but great pains might have to be endured through the partner's divorce or death; happiness in marriage, general luck and a quiet old age spent in pleasant recollection of good work done are to be expected.

About the native's mind, one peculiar feature stands out-a gift for mathematics, which often will stay unheeded, unexploited, unknown to its very owner who, although not lacking firmness and enterprise, might drift toward less congenial activities, which are apt to yield less satisfactory results. How much store may be set by this minor feature of the one hundred forty-ninth degree, other factors in the pattern will decide.

30° Leo

Symbol: An old slave with a noble cast of features and a shadow of thoughtful gloom on his face

I warn you, if you twist it further it will break. Now, didn't I tell you it would break?—Words attributed to Epictetus while having his leg twisted by his torturer

I think that slaves like Aesop, Epictetus, perhaps even like Livy Andronicus, Phaedrus, etc., were born under this sign. This is another of those degrees where only a highly developed nature can save the native from being crushed under the weight of an influence overstepping our human boundaries. This Leo's last degree can make a superman of anyone whose stars should elsewhere supply the necessary requirements.

105

Upon a heart soaring beyond the highest peaks of human nobility, a heroically mighty will power, a winged mind, this degree will bestow the right of judging things and people from a higher standpoint and of drawing, although in perfect humility, an infallible moral law from the deepest sources of his overself, the right of being a master although performing the lowest duties, of feeling free and lordly while being socially a slave.

To less-developed beings this brings a feeling of oppression and wretchedness, a powerless struggling against material poverty and outward misery. Endless moaning and groaning will grow into a habit. The subject will take to finding fault with everyone and everything, although he has not the makings of a real judge, whatever his intellectual gifts, his human understanding and his literary taste might be. The continuous comparison between his actual standing and the one he thinks he is entitled to cripples his initiative and robs him of his will to work. He is, therefore, a useless servant.

Yet, whether a superman or a human wretch, he always will fit in with the self-styled definition of Christ's representative on Earth: *servus servorum–the* servant's servant. "As above, so below"; the lowest epithet is the one of the highest human dignity. That those who have ears may understand.

Examples: Dionysius Papin (Sun's degree); Henry Sienkiewicz (degree of the Moon); Raymond Poincaré, president of the French Republic during World War I (degree of Saturn, ruler of the Ascendant, or of the sign intercepted in the house of personality); Henry de Nicola, temporary president of the first Italian Republic (degree of Uranus, ruler of the Ascendant, or of the sign intercepted in the house of personality.).

N.B. This degree's influence is at present outshone by the presence in it of the royal star Regulus, whose conjunction with any planet residing in the sign is more powerful than the degree itself.

VIRGO

01° Virgo

*Symbol: A hunting party. Smart riders and fair
sportswomen gallop merrily to the horns' blare
and the hounds' yelps.*

A sociable, merry and probably frivolous and superficial nature, fond of collective games in general (but not of individual or athletic sport), especially horseback riding and hunting. One endowed with scanty wits, but plenty of friends and acquaintances, and love affairs galore. The native's gift for getting in tune with different kinds of people makes him the pivot of merrymakings, excursions and obviously of hunting parties. His gentlemanlike discretion will let people overlook his either sentimental or merely erotic adventures, which all will suspect, but of which none will know the victims with certitude.

Should the subject couple a certain earnestness to his outward smartness, to his worldly achievements and gallantry, he is sure to be successful, as many an association formed in pleasure and sport will immensely further his professional advancement.

In less lucky charts this influence will easily drift astray into cruel selfishness and double-dealing, which are natural tendencies in a libertine, as in Maupassant's Belami.

Where the horoscope is particularly bad, the native will be a sadist, a seducer of minors, a gangster, perhaps a murderer; but even thus perverted, a sociable spirit still will be traceable to him.

The native will tend to bodily fullness and will need plenty of sleep.

Example: Louis XVI, king of France (Sun's degree).

N.B. Other influences account for Louis XVI's frigidity and his pathological stupidity bordering on unconscionableness. But his psychological makeup is revealed by his diary. Which is little more than an over-detailed account of the royal hunts. There are brief hints of his religious practice and the drugs prescribed by his physicians. Nothing else. On days when Louis XVI neither took purgatives nor went to church or hunting, his diary shows the word "nothing." In July 1791, twenty-three days of the diary are covered by this word (see Dr. Cabanes, *Le Cabinet Secret de L'Histoire, 2 serie).*

02° Virgo

This degree confers a great abstract intelligence, a manifold versatility, a methodical and precise mental procedure, a special gift for military and mathematical sciences, a keen mind constantly on the lockout, but if no other influences in the pattern supply practical skill, the native will be as clumsy in carrying out as he has been brilliant in conceiving.

A dry and cool nature, whose earnestness can border on unwieldiness, whose endurance can drift into stubbornness and maniacal conceit. One endowed with great steadfastness but none of those deep impulses which only a feeling-not merely a reckoning-nature can give a human being. The resulting attitude is mostly one of apathy, sometimes of fatalistic indolence and sluggish-ness. Spiritually, the native is an atheist or, worse, an agnostic. Financially he is in for a miserable and roaming life when other aspects do not correct this one.

A decided prevalence of the elements of water and fire in the birth pattern can correct the dryness and coldness of this being. Water only would add to his sloth and fickleness; fire alone would heighten his dryness.

03° Virgo

Symbol: A man fingering a ledger

The essential features of this degree remind one of Libra: a fondness for justice and indignation at any breach of it. The likeness stops here. The native is an active and productive being. A deep researcher and experimenter, a writer (possibly of scientific things) and perhaps a philosopher, he upholds his activity with a keen insight and an inborn cool courage. A hopeful character but not too lucky in other fields, he will be successful in his scientific pursuits and professional undertakings, enjoying the fruit thereof and closing his accounts in the black.

Examples: Nicholas Copernic (Ascendant's degree); Giuseppe Verdi (degree of Jupiter, ruler of the Ascendant. Goethe's MC also is in this degree.

04° Virgo

Symbol: A steamroller

Prepare ye the way of the Lord, make straight in the desert a highway for our God. Every valley shall be exalted and every mountain and hill shall be made low, and the crooked shall be made straight, and the rough places plain.—Is. 11:3-4, routed by Matt. 3:3, Mark 1:2, Luke 3:6, and John 1:23

No grass grows where my horse has trodden.—attributed to Attila

A craze for planning and technology; a naive faith in purely mechanical progress; contempt for individual distinctions; love of the extreme and of the absolute. Some features of fatality in the existence, something inexorable in character. A massive strength, an ability to lay out on broad lines work to be carried out by others and to give it the finishing touches after completion.

This same force, instead of preparing and perfecting usefully the work of others, can stay fruitless and can sponge upon its environment; or, even worse, instead of leveling and paving the way for the execution of the work planned, he can be employed to destroy and raze everything aimlessly to the ground. The rest of the horoscope will show the right angle.

Where a sound, peaceful, constructive nature is at work, the subject might be really fond of nature and might run his or someone else's estate strictly but efficiently, heading for a quiet and affluent old age.

On the contrary, where the stars point to fondness for the fruitless, artificial life usually led by the smartest set of society, a rush for pleasure will swallow up wealth laboriously built up by the ancestors. Plenty of well-meaning and helpful friends will be powerless to save the native from bankruptcy; once collapsed, neither his taste nor his artistic gifts will be of any avail. A third case is possible: an aggressive, destructive, brutal and despotically leveling nature—in a word, a downright Vandalic or Hunnish character.

Undeniable in all cases is a profound sense of truth, unaccountably coupled with fast living or ruthless destructiveness.

Examples: Cardinal Federigo Borromeo, immortalized by A. Manzoni in his novel (Sun's degree); in this degree is the Third Reich's Mars as ruler of the Sun (Sun-sign) and therefore lord of the MC, viz., indicative of the government and the army.

05° Virgo

Symbol: A gerfalcon, or hunting hawk, on its master's fist

The native will be by temperament ever ready to act at any time or any age; young or old, tired or fresh, he always will rally round as soon as the trumpet of honor or duty calls.

However, his whole life might flow away without any call from that quarter making itself heard or any occasion presenting itself. The native being the very embodiment of discipline, he will not be able to create an occasion. An excellent executor and a gentleman every inch of his being, his lack of initiative and ambition can be offset only by his rigidly observed daily routine and his faithfulness to friends. An uneventful life will leave him as poor as a church mouse, but as long as he breathes and whenever his help is called for, he will plunge into action again, spot the burning point of the fight with an unfailing eye and wrest victory for himself or his party.

Example: Sir Douglas Haig, British commander-in- chief in World War I (degree of Saturn, ruler of the Ascendant); Admiral Ernest King (degree of Uranus, ruler of the Ascendant).

06° Virgo

The native is attractive, smart, good looking; he has a gift for experiment and invention, an exuberant and merry vitality, a perpetually young spirit.

The danger attendant upon such bright gifts is inherent in them; life has been too lavish with its presents and too sweet for the native, who will therefore be tempted very strongly to pursue pleasure instead of glory and will too often tarry along his mortal path to pick the flowers it is strewn with instead of making for the final goal. Money, love affairs, royal invitations and popularity in fashionable drawing rooms will come his way effortlessly and in plenty. In the end he will find himself old and empty-handed and will lose heart, unable to bear bitterness after tasting the sweetness of life.

Provided the subject can resist temptation and be as serious and steady in his work as he is merry and carefree in his parties and revels, provided he can stem his tendency to luxury and waste, and can join courage with brightness and firmness with affability, he will be able to build something durable and to leave a name behind himself.

The whole of the horoscope must show what is likelier to happen.

Examples: Wolfgang von Goethe (Sun's degree); Maximilian of Habsburg, emperor of Mexico (Sun's degree); Maurice Maeterlinck (Sun's degree); Albert Lebrun, fourteenth president of the French Republic (Sun's degree).

07° Virgo

Generosity and foresight; modesty, sensitivity and reserve; kindness and delicacy in the heart rather than in manners; chastity in thoughts, purity of feelings; in a word, all feminine virtues—except the good housewife's handiness. As to the male virtues, there is above all a lack of self-possession in front of others. The native is obsessed by a nearly pathologic shyness that makes him awkward, clumsy, unable to speak or act in public. In front of the opposite sex, he or she will feel almost paralyzed. This will render marriage very difficult, for which on the other hand there is little inclination. In a man, this degree can well produce an exclusively psychological impotence; in a woman frigidity, in spite of deep and sincere affections. Even in the case of consummated marriage, married life will imply a good deal of trouble.

As to profession, this one hundred fifty-seventh zodiacal degree will confer an uncommon juridical gift. By conquering himself and overcoming his-inborn shyness, the native may start a successful lawyer's career. In which case his extraordinary presence of mind, combined with the sensitivity distinctive of the shy, will develop into a supple dialectic and a moving eloquence.

If not a lawyer, the native might become a judge or a notary. Anyhow, his excessive modesty will be a drag chain on his way to renown.

08° Virgo

It is not meet to take the children's bread and to cast it to dogs.—Matt. 15:26, Mark 7:27

Let thy alms sweat in thy hand, till thou findest a righ-

teous one to whom to give it.—Didache 1, 6, quoted by St. Augustine P.L. 37, 1326, 1367

This degree will teach the native to love and contemplate nature's beauties, to cherish trees, often to like mountain climbing. Farming and tending cattle (which may be taken to mean pasture of souls) also will attract him.

A simple, truthful, unprejudiced soul swayed by ideals, he will give without afterthoughts, if not rashly, and will reap only unthankfulness. The native does not realize he is overreaching himself and thus sinning against moderation, as his indiscriminate lavishness is a crime against Divine Providence. Should he bear in' mind that before regaling strangers his sacred duty is to think of those God entrusted to him and, instead of casting pearls before swine at the risk of being rent by them, realize that it only stands to reason to consolidate one's position first and then to do good to others. Should he understand that these also can be helped much better by one who stands on both feet than by one tottering and led by the nose, in that case he may end by doing something really useful to mankind and avoid becoming a beggar-a burden to the good, a target for the evil's scorn, an argument of scepticism for those whose faith is wavering.

09° Virgo

The native is fond of literary leisure, in which he displays more or less proficiency (according to other astrological pointers); but he is fond of unqualified leisure or idleness as well. A smart, gaudy, sometimes prodigal being, he sticks to the device never to do today what can be done tomorrow. He is not likely to take his business or his duty too seriously, but can fly off the handle easily over things about which he feels keenly.

On account of woman (or better, of one woman) he will get into trouble. Marriage is certainly not made for him, especially as the outward activity that fits him best is traveling. It might be said that love of travel and thirst for exploration are perhaps the mainsprings likely to push the native to action. The fruit of his literary leisure as well risk to stay unachieved. Apart from this, fortune is not too lenient with him.

His complexion is apt to be ruddy, even flushed.

10° Virgo

Live and let live.—Commonplace saying re human laziness

None of us calls his vices by name. The miser will be "thrifty"; the spendthrift "generous"; the coward will boast of his "caution," the daredevil his "courage." Such lies do not fool anyone. But where the border lies between weakness and leniency is such a problem as to give wise people a headache. Where is the limit between welcome strictness and inhuman hard-heartedness?

This degree is a typical example of weakness disguised as leniency. Real leniency never will lead to such an amount of trouble as the character of those born under this influence. Whether hard working or not, the native will be lucky, extremely lucky in money matters, but however frugal and sparing with himself, he will be naively generous or downright prodigal toward others and will not listen to reason about his neighbors' real motives or the women's treacherousness. And it is from women that he will get the worst blows. Many friends are sincerely fond of him. This is enough for him to believe that all are sincere and that anyone saying he is fond of him really loves his person and not his money or influence.

He will understand nature much better than man and will be apt to meditate about the loftiest mysteries of the universe, neglecting to sound the abysm of human passions. Strange, freakish phenomena of the abnormal or the supernatural will engross him but he will never be better than hopelessly amateurish at human psychology.

Other features will be a liking for smart dressing and for taking walks or, better, the need of hiking.

114

Example: The sun was here when the armistice between the U.S. and Japan was signed on September 2, 1945.

11° Virgo

Symbol: A white stud racing at full speed, his bit white with foam

This degree promises success, honors and riches. The native will know how to command and, even better, how to secure obedience, as one joining kindness with imperiousness. His mighty will power has a way of sizing up situations and adapting itself to them without yielding an inch. His character is strong rather than despotic, steady rather than stubborn, and he has a large heart. Work goes on smoothly and swiftly without showing signs of wear and tear, and never stays unachieved.

There is an uncommon, prompt, supple, ingenious and inventive mind bent on the practical side of things and endowed at the same time with artistic taste. Here is more than a useful, precious personality for society, whose only besetting sin is lustfulness. This ought to be kept in check, but it would be folly to try to repress it. This horse must be given a run. If you keep it bound, it will become skittish and unruly, and you will have to look out for its kicks.

Examples: Sir Douglas Haig, commander-in-chief of the British forces (degree of the Point of Equidistance). The Sun was in this degree when World War II was declared, on September 3, 1939.

12° Virgo

The native is a mystic and a sensualist, as fond of research into mysterious things as of the opposite sex, and exerts a marked influence upon its representatives. For all his mysticism, the native is a ruthless egotist, and for all his lust-fulness he is a weakling; he may seduce and rape but will meet trouble in the end. His erotic relations ought, however, to stay hidden as far as it depends on him, as few people have such discretion and reserve.

His true force lies in his penetrating mind. Should other factors curb his erotic excesses, he would force his way forward through sheer intelligence and would end by making his own name famous. A dark, perhaps swarthy, complexion. Red is his favorite color.

Example: Here is the Third French Republic's Sun.

13° Virgo

Symbol: A rose on a Greek cross (Rosicrucian Symbol)

Per crucem ad rosam. Per rosam ad crucem.— Rosicrucian slogan

Much as human wickedness might rage against the native, it will have no power against his balanced and unruffled spirit. "For if God be with us, who can be against us?" (Rom. 8:31).

His features of unobtrusive modesty and unassuming helpfulness might let him appear somewhat childish, devoid of energy and luck. But in reality his ascendancy on the others is great, even if not felt on the physical plane; his enemies' weapons will blunt themselves.

Bearing his poverty with a swing and a smile, taking the hardest ordeals in his stride, he breathes an atmosphere of utmost serenity and, even if not with full awareness, confides for everything in Divine Providence. He is possessed of the magic secret of nonresistance and can easily tune with his surroundings. His family might thwart him, wicked parents expose him, envious rivals run him down and the world ignore him. But the measure of his joy, and not only in a spiritual sense, will be as full as that of his opponents' unhappiness.

His birth might be noble, certainly his nature will be, but no burden of tradition will hamper him; he will be rich at least in imagination, but will do as well without any inheritance. He might

116

love fine arts, protect them and even cultivate them. He is likely to be fond of gardening and to worship flowers.

The occult will at any rate attract him, if not lead him to some degree of realization. Among occult sciences magic will be the most congenial to him. A real initiation may come his way, should other aspects not prevent this.

Example: Remarkably enough, Napoleon's Mars is in this degree.

14° Virgo

Symbol: A cow standing in the middle of a plain

. . . Sic vos non vobis fertis aratra boves.—from an epigram attributed to Virgil

Steady, unceasing and probably sedentary work, exposing the native to weariness and great hardships, to the danger of others exploiting his relentless and fruitful efforts, and to the danger of gains not corresponding to exertions.

The native totally lacks imagination and, for all his honesty and good-heartedness, cannot harbor any ideals. This is not due to any cynicism but to an inborn inability to visualize what has never been met or experienced, making the native loath to look or believe beyond the range of his bodily senses.

Lack of imagination makes him commonplace as well—not altogether dull, owing to his skill in handiwork—but surely a hearty blockhead devoid of ambitions and proud of his portly build and his excellent craftsmanship; and very, very talkative.

His sexual life is not normal; excess rather than aberrations are to be feared. The glut of vigor is hindered queerly by a dull stagnation, and by an absolute lack of the inquisitiveness and fantasy which are the main incentives to the third capital vice.

A kindly soul with the temper of a commoner, he has a primitive and elementary sense of justice. He is serviceable, generous, easy to take advantage of; but he draws the line at being pilloried and, if driven too far, will not budge an inch.

Should the horoscope carry other dangerous pointers, accidents-even deadly ones— mutilations and wounds are to be feared.

Examples: Louis XVI, king of France (Ascendant's degree). The Sun was at the end of this degree when the League of Nations was founded, on October 7, 1919.

15° Virgo

A feminine nature, whose most pronounced features are self-surrender and tenderness, and whose corresponding vice is effeminacy. For all this, more than one good soldier will be born under it. Military virtues are not excluded, as this degree vouchsafes that virtue of taking things off at a glance for which Napoleon praised Frederic the Great as for the greatest asset in a warrior.

This influence tends to make a helpful, modest officer, mild toward his subordinates, gallant with ladies, always beaming and kind to everyone; his only failing being timidity which, if not offset by other aspects, may even go so far as to ruin his career, though not so far as to make him cowardly.

On the whole and for any chosen career, luck will favor him and will accompany the often great undertakings the native might conceive and carry out.

Example: Here is the Italian Republic's Point of Equidistance.

16° Virgo

This is a degree of commerce in all senses of the word. The native is born to live in society, is a sociable being (what Aristotle called *zoon politikon)* who will thrive in association and die if left in isolation.

His natural gifts are a way with people, a social sense and adaptability, enabling him to act constantly and successfully as a connecting link for people who, but for him, never would enter association. He is, so to speak, the mortar and plaster of the business firms and social circles to which he belongs. He will draw large profits from his social connections and will be asked to all kinds of entertainments and parties. His favorite game is hunting.

However, he is a more serious and contemplative mind than one could guess; a philosopher might lurk behind that brilliant facade.

Bad aspects might disfigure those features and lead the native toward shady business and shameless dealings with the dregs of society.

17° Virgo

Symbol: A splendid castle by a river, whose streams have partly been turned from their course to flow into the moat. Within the outward wall enclosure thriving gardens and orchards can be seen; in the towers, supplies of oil and wheat to last through long sieges; in the cellars, thick rows of dusty bottles; at the bottom of the dungeons, captives loaded with chains. Laboring servants and watchful sentries are all over. The aged lord is carried through his domains on a sedan chair.

There is either a noble pride or an arrogant haughtiness based on lineage, social rank or on one's own self. The native is fond of home and its comforts; he nurtures a deep-rooted ambition and works up to it, harbors a wariness bordering on mistrust. An exacting, hard-headed, close, dour, strict nature, prematurely aged by its cantankerous faddiness, by a steadfastness not devoid of whims. The native's self-centeredness can stray easily into selfishness, and can drift into eccentric estrangement from his fellow beings. There is a lord-like love of pomp and luxury, coupled to a wary and watchful utilitarianism, with a touch of hedonism.

119

An idle fellow who fondles his ideas and knows very well how to have others work hard to carry them out. If he could have his own way, he would employ crews of slaves ready at his beck and call. He is not unwilling to work himself, but only when it cannot be dispensed with. Work for work's sake is nonsense to him. Any activity by himself or others must, according to him, be foreordained to future welfare. Once his own comfort is assured, there will be room for the comfort of others, if both can co-exist; but once that aim is reached, there is no reason to take further trouble. There is, in one word, the estate holder's mentality. Ambition is furthered steadily but not in such a way as to disturb one's comforts, ranking high among which are the delights of a good table.

A great stroke of luck might hasten the day the native's fortune is established in a way after his own heart. From then on, barring pointers to the contrary, he lives on his income, journeying for his pleasure or for health (which leaves much to be desired, and he hates moving on his own legs), or tarrying in; learned leisure, musing idly, leading the household punctiliously and closely watching the kitchen. A peaceful old age, if the stars do not point otherwise, will close his career.

The rest of the chart is not to be lost sight of. There might be unforeseen trouble lurking somewhere or unexpected blows of a hurricane sweeping everything away and dashing to pieces the carefully planned prosperity, leaving the native dispossessed and dazed.

After all, he is a sceptic, and harbors no ideals beyond and above his empiric self. Should the storm overthrow his well prearranged plans, his self-indulgence will prevent him from beginning all over again, and he may collapse together with his castle of cards never to rise again, even losing his mental balance in his distress.

Example: Cardinal Richelieu (Sun's degree).

N.B. Richelieu built castles and palaces and heaped up riches which were fabulous for his time; twenty million francs cash,

120

equivalent to some billions today. At least twice in his career the cardinal gave up everything in utter despondency and was raised up again by others nearly in spite of himself. The two events were *la journée des dupes* and the defeat at La Corbie.

18° Virgo

Symbol: A hardy, century-old oak in the middle of a meadow, its boughs full of nests, and new sprouts bursting forth from its root. A herd of swine is grazing in its shade.

A great vitality; a paternal, obtrusive, autocratic spirit..Patronizing love of the little and the weak, sympathy for the populace, leniency, even excessive, for everything that has not yet been evolved or spoiled by so-called civilization; fondness for the country, for trees and life in the open. But little or no respect for the ones deserving it. The native will refuse stubbornly to admire the worthiest, will misuse his people's affection and devotion, and will refuse systematically to take even his wisest and truest friends' advice.

In less good horoscopes, indulgence toward the ignorant rabble might stray into base pandering of their tendencies and might degenerate into acceptance and support of bad taste. The lack of regard for others might be coupled strangely with a need to be understood-hence suffering at being misunderstood. Besides, contempt for so-called civilization might be perverted into dirtiness or even smuttiness.

Nevertheless, the native's knowledge is wide, his technical skill high, his mind deep.

19° Virgo

A rugged nature, satisfied with little, hard-working and averse to sweetness and niceties, but not devoid of imagination. Physical nature is sturdy and fecund, with features of roughness and even dirtiness. There is an absolute need of freedom, of elbow room, of ease of movement, and there is a strong resentment of any social code. This leads to the greatest outspokenness. The native is certainly not tongue-tied, and his criticism might prove harsh, his sincerity brutal.

Should the subject be born on a higher than proletarian level and therefore be in for a higher than primary education, he will feel inclined to choose a branch of studies allowing him to deal with the country or with the sciences related to it. He might become an excellent farmer but also have the makings of a good agricultural expert or penologist, and he might be proficient in any other subject connected with the products of the soil. As a lawyer, he might specialize in agricultural law, etc.

In any case he will love nature and perhaps become a passionate hunter and, as all sportsmen, point his gun at the living beings he is so fond of.

20° Virgo

The native is not utterly devoid of fairness but unfortunately he cannot afford to live at peace with those who hold views different from his own. A very courageous being and one conscious of his own strength, he is not so happy in victory as in the fight. Shunning a quarrel would be dishonor to him. If a brawl is in the air, he cannot even wait for the probable opponent to attack him first, and is bound to provoke him. He seems especially keen on picking quarrels with foreigners. While ignoring the meaning of such an expression as "getting round obstacles," he nearly always succeeds in overthrowing them.

A good tradesman and mathematician, wakeful and brimming over with initiative, he might become rich thanks to his intelligence and courage, but will not be able to escape mishaps, sometimes serious ones. For all his watchfulness, which might drift into suspiciousness, he will be beset always by lowly and despicable foes, who will lurk cautiously in the dark, but refuse to disarm.

Examples: Charles VI, the mad king of France (Moon's degree). Here also is Marshal B. L. Montgomery's Mars, in trigonal position with his Ascendant.

21° Virgo

Symbol: A large, showily dressed man, his hands full of tinkling coins; golden in his right, silver in his left hand

The native will be born or will become rich. As do all rich people, he will stick to his money, hug it and greatly fear to lose it. Money will be the only standard of his behavior, the common denominator to which he will reduce all problems of his existence. He will be a schemer even in the paltriest trifles of everyday life. Relying on his scent for bargains, he will be ever ready for sale to the highest bidder, with utter disrespect for ideals, friendships or extra-juridical promises. It is not to be ruled out that he may have to suffer losses, even heavy ones if portended by other factors in his horoscope, but never owing to lack of financial skill, this being, on the contrary, his strongest point.

As to his other fields of activity, Phaedrus's verse hits him off: *O quanta species, inquit, cerebrum non habet!*

Behind a show of lordly self-satisfaction and high falutin' conceit there is no substance at all: a hare's heart, a chicken's brain, a weathercock's character.

22° Virgo

Symbol: A naked lady with a lamb and a kid on her shoulders

A sensuous and strong character, she is brutally sincere with herself and others. She knows what she is aiming at and states it with a self-possession bordering on impudence. Yet in spite of all this the native's silly vanity plays her into the hands of anyone who knows how to flatter her.

Should other components exclude the danger of irreparable scandals, stem the erotic trend of this degree, or diverge its forces to a spiritual plane, the native's charm may make her into a guide of society; in what direction or which flock is likely to be led, only the whole of the pattern may decide; other pointers shall show whether it is toward good or evil.

Most of what I said about 24° Aries applies to this degree as well.

Examples: Caesar Borgia (Ascendant's degree); Oscar Wilde (Ascendant's degree).

N.B. Caesar Borgia has Mercury and Pluto conjoined with his Ascendant. As to Pluto's full meaning, see Brunhubner's work *Pluto* (published in English by AFA, Tempe, Arizona).

23° Virgo

Symbol: A man on a sailing ship in the middle of the ocean

There is an irrepressible need of evasion in time and space. A nature ablaze with enthusiasm and fantasy, which will chafe if fenced in its birthplace and the mentality prevailing there.

This influence will not supply the energy needed to prevail on such mentality and reform it; hence the need of escape. Disregarding the other astrological factors, it can be said safely that the native's success depends on real journey and migration. Any evasion into daydreaming will result in failure, since thirst for new experiences is the only real thing life can offer but may lead the native dangerously astray. Passion for the sea is a natural consequence.

Examples: Thomas Campanella (Sun's degree); Humbert II of Savoy, king of Italy in May 1946 (Sun's degree); Hirohito, Japan's emperor (Moon's degree).

N.B. While a prisoner of the Spanish Inquisition in 1602, Thomas Campanella (1568-1639) wrote a book entitled *The City of Sun,* wherein he advocates ideal social and political conditions on a Utopian background. It is interesting to note that Campanella based his description of the legendary city on an imaginary skipper's tale.

24° Virgo

Symbol: The scene of "Loneliness" which Richard Wagner has taken to the stage and musically describes with a leitmotif known as "the theme of loneliness" (Tristram, Act 3); on the ramparts of a castle rising on the ocean shore the exile lies alone, nailed to his sickbed by a deadly wound; not far away, on a lofty rock, a shepherd sits surrounded by his flock and, scanning in vain the desolate skyline, blows from his flute an infinitely melancholic tune.

Should the native be able to sublimate into lyric or musical effusion the plaintive dejection drawing him aside from his fellow beings and shutting him up in himself, and should he find an outlet to his desperate mood in melody or verse, he may become a successful, a famous, and-as an ironical luck would have it-even a popular artist.

But he will not be rich. The contrivance of life does not leave him any time for moneymaking, and something binds his hands when it comes to shifting from a contemplative to an active life. Optional or forced exile awaits him, perhaps even jail.

Steadfast and stubborn even at the risk of his own undoing, endowed sometimes with real inspiration but nearly always devoid of true intelligence, predisposed to sedentary life, materially or mortally short-sighted if not shady, the native will not be loved by his children and may die as lonely as a dog.

Examples: In this degree (exactly 23°01') is the Ascendant of the Italian Republic. The omen of exile can as usual refer to the individual founders and leaders of the Republic, as well as by transfer to the form of government itself, which runs the risk of being banned from the country.

25° Virgo

*Symbol: The emblem formerly employed in the Royal
Italian Army to show promotion for gallantry on the
battlefield (nicknamed "the crossbones" by the rank and file),
and consisting of the royal crown surmounting two swords
placed in the shape of St. Andrew's cross*

It is a degree of daring. This may come to light in any of its forms: heroism and aggression, self-effacement and recklessness, high-handedness and quarrelsome-ness, military gifts fitting a partisan or a *sabreur* rather than a real leader, more a pirate than an admiral, sooner a commando chief than a commander-in-chief. Whatever his profession, the native is farsighted, can plunge headlong into the scuffle and grab winged victory by the forelock. His character, or the deepest of his heart, may harbor something secret or mysterious. In spite of this, a charming personality. If he is a warrior the native will be able to carry his followers off their feet to do or die. In any case the native's friends will be as plentiful and as powerful as his foes.

Victory is likelier than happiness. Public rather than private luck will crown the native. There may be a taste for art, perhaps on the macabre side.

Examples: Queen Elizabeth of Great Britain (Sun's degree); Raymond Poincare, president of the French Republic (degree of the Point of Equidistance).

N.B. The more effective the rule, the closer the karmic ties are between ruler and ruled. In this sense Elizabeth Tudor is a case in point. A liberal queen toward her Protestant brethren, she executed Mary Stuart and persecuted the Roman Catholics nearly as much as bloodthirsty Mary had persecuted the Protestants. She connived to—or rather approved of—the piratical war against still neutral Spain and, after the outbreak of war, could see the enemy's naval might destroyed, practically without engaging in major battle. It is still debated today how far the love experience of the "Virgin

Queen" reached; it is certain, however, that if she loved, she never knew the joy of love. During her age, tragic poetry attained its full bloom in England.

26° Virgo

Symbol: Two elderly bespectacled friends walk and talk confidentially together.

A profound mind able to foreshadow ages to come but not to lay concrete plans for the morrow. Very remote events seem to be within its ken, yet no light helps it to see nearer things on which it may stumble at any step.

Any arbitrage or game of hazard is a sure trap for the native, who will, on the other hand, succeed with certainty in all undertakings ruled by national logic and method, but not by accident, blind fortune, or the imponderable of existence.

A courteous, friendly, likeable talker and a persuasive reasoner, he will inspire devoted affections and especially sincere friendships. The disinterested support and loyal cooperation of others, rather than his own methods by wingless and excessively long-sighted intelligence, will allow him to reach his aims, at least after going through some ordeals.

As to his private life he will be happier in ripe age than in youth and will close his days surrounded by his children's obedient affection and unanimous solidarity. Physical sight might be weakened by hypermetropy or precocious long-sightedness.

Example: George Clemenceau, twice premier of France, during and after World War I (Sun's degree).

27° Virgo

A rather undefinable character, brisk on one hand, lazy on the other. I believe its essence consists in thorough passivity. But the whole of the horoscope must. indicate its results. Passivity may be

127

taken merely to affect material work (as a sluggish disposition) or the struggle for life (cowardice or fear, unjustified resignation to being taken in by others' wiliness or crushed by their overbearingness); it may be neither psychical nor physical, but spiritual, etc. But whether hard working or lazy, the native has certain gifts and a remarkable skill in business, and a lively, subtle mind, however sluggish his movements and idle his hands. He may even be thoroughly happy, if born in an affluent or rich family, but he is likelier to tend toward despondency and gloom.

In a feminine horoscope there may be difficulty in securing a husband. On the other hand, another woman (mother, sister, colleague in work or the like) will play a great role in her life or destiny.

28° Virgo

Fullness of life, work on a large scale, activity supplying many with a livelihood and the native with well-deserved and better spent wealth.

The intelligence is above normal and bent on fruitful and industrious work. There is reserve but generosity. Many people (children or more distant relatives) will live on the native's income. There will be many friends and beneficiaries around him. The subject's powerful activity may extend its wholesome influence to all mankind. On the other hand, he may feel bound to his work as a convict to his chains. The whole of the pattern must not be lost sight of. The sprockets of such a mighty machine may even fail to catch.

29° Virgo

A great insight, a quiet, smooth sway over oneself and others; a deep religious sense of life and work. The native's foresight will border on prophecy. In all he undertakes he will be led by great sudden rushes of light, like a poet's flashes or a seer's visions.

Driven by an unshakable faith in his future and by perfect self-control, the native's smooth ease will not hinder his liveliness. He will act with lightning-like swiftness but without hurry. He may, therefore, seem heady but will never prove untimely. His liveliness may make his manner blunt but never rough and, even less, coarse. His sensuousness, however powerful, will not interfere with his professional work, which will go on smoothly and successfully in spite of a certain taste for exterior ceremony and formalism.

The native is very unlikely to avoid taking an attitude in front of religious problems. A Roman Catholic or a Protestant, a Christian or a Jew, a freemason or an active supporter of the Church, he must believe in something.

Examples: Francis I, king of France (Sun's degree); Pope Paul V (degree of the Point of Equidistance); Lord Kitchener (degree of the Point of Equidistance).

30° Virgo

Sincerity and love of truth as implied by this degree can belong only to an irresponsible being or to a great sage. While talking, the native will tell anyone the truth and will consider no price too high when it comes to discovering it. The price may even be mental sanity.

Work is done by leaps and bounds; overwork is not shunned and, as others throw themselves headlong into pleasure, the native may go into spells of meditation for whole nights or may even undertake risky experiments in witchcraft or yoga or that modern form of necromancy which is today blasphemously labeled as "spiritualism."

Should the whole pattern show balance and self-control, this bold explorer then would have access to the mysteries of true spiritual science, or of the so-called official sciences. His intelligence is sharp, his character melancholy but smooth, his habits secretive and lonely. The need to avoid mental overstrain must be borne in mind.

On the contrary, other factors point to a less sound whole, wounds in the head, cerebral hemorrhages followed by palsy, manic depressive folly, deafness, dumbness or neurasthenia are to be feared. Unenviable or dangerous strains like extravagance, light-mindedness and irresponsible absent-mindedness may show up in the character. These are certainly extreme cases, which had however to be prospected, as caution is never too great when health is at stake. Should the chart portend death due to judicial sentence, the guillotine is to be feared.

LIBRA

01° Libra

*Symbol: A man brandishing a sword in his right
hand and a dagger in his left*

Warlike but hypersensitive, hardly regardful of other people's prejudices and feelings, yet strictly just and tidy; strong and active but impatient, the native appears self-contradictory and hard to understand.

On one hand he is martial, even quarrelsome, ever ready to face danger, heady in everything he does; he will crush the obstacles in his path, break his way open and tread it in spite of anyone. On the other hand he will sincerely regret his being at dagger's point with his neighbors and surroundings, though failing to understand why, and will not swerve an inch from the right path in what concerns debit and credit. He is not inclined to marry; his fiery recklessness will rush him headlong into trouble; his hands are liable to get hurt.

This first degree of Libra clearly admits, among the features peculiar to this sign, cult of justice and love of art, along with other strains jarring with Libra's general influence.

Examples: Albert of Waldstein, generally known under the name of Wallenstein (Sun's degree).

N.B. Compare 19° Scorpio Point of Equidistance, and 07° Capricorn Moon; Sir Ernest Shackleton, Antarctic explorer (degree of Jupiter, ruler of the Ascendant).

131

02° Libra

Symbol: Raffaello's St. Cecily

A musical disposition. A great intelligence, thirsting for hidden truths, keen on fathoming the mysteries of the universe. A very kind and humane soul, an exquisite tact, a generous heart, a fine insight.

These gifts do not seem to be matched by a sufficiently hardened character. Hence perhaps a bent toward a deep melancholy. Faced with human wickedness, this soul will take refuge in God. Such a religious feeling may lead the native to the sacred orders and may as well drift into a craze, according to the other astrological components.

Example: Cardinal Newman (degree of Uranus, ruler of the sign intercepted in the house of personality).

03° Libra

Mit der Dumheit kampfen Cotter selbst vergebens . . .
(Even the gods fight stupidity in vain).—Schiller

A titanic intelligence in a weak, sickly, powerless frame; a mind apt to master the most baffling physical laws, chained to a body subject to the meanest physical miseries, and probably exposed to the persecution of ignorance, local patriotism and prejudice, all coalesced on a common front. Its slogan may well be *spiritus promptuo caro autem infirma.*

A forerunner of things to come, the native will strive to conform to his own principles—whether scientific, religious or artistic—but his uncompromising purposefulness may stray into self-centeredness and misanthropy, giving way to a repulsive hardness of heart.

Of the whole horoscope alone we must ask if the native's knowledge will conquer human ignorance or be conquered by it, whether his toils will yield riches and welfare or suffering and fam-

132

ine; in a word, if glory or banishment from home or, even worse, the workhouse or the lunatic asylum or a jail will fall to his share.

Example: Here is the MC of Eugene of Savoy who was notoriously rickety and crippled.

04° Libra

Symbol: A man tilling with a horse-drawn plough

This degree is, so to speak, tuned in to the dissonant harmonies of a fundamentally aquiline feature. As a result, there may be missed vocation or the native may be left suddenly in the lurch by fortune when, after clearing the first hurdles, he is just about to enjoy the fruit of his work.

Apart from this, the one hundred eighty-fourth degree may bestow different gifts leading to seemingly divergent trades, whose common feature, however, proves on closer scrutiny to be somehow connected with skill in cutting. Therefore, according to the other stars in the nativity, we may expect skill in the arts of wood carving and engraving, in a tailor's or a tiller's trade, or in a successful surgeon's career.

On the whole, two features stand out: the native's uncommon taste-even if he does not blossom into an artist-and the fact that as a farmer he would do better business for others than for himself.

05° Libra

Symbol: An albatross with glaring red beak and claws

A winged, impulsive, enthusiastic nature full of lofty aspirations but impatient to see its dreams realized and chafing at obstacles. Hence a tendency to impose one's will violently without an adequate psychological approach, overlooking and skipping the logical proofs of one's conviction and neglecting the cogent force of one's arguments. This exuberance may give rise even to physical dangers; the native will have to check his gestures and actions if he is to avoid harm from iron and fire, without, however, using violence.

The native is an essentially fiery and martial being, born to fly and bound to reach his goal with one great heave of his wings. Should he set foot on the ground, *ses ailes de geant l'empechent de marcher* (his huge wings sweep the ground and hinder him in walking.—Baudelaire, *Les fleurs du mal: L'Albatros).*

He is born to wage a titanic struggle with himself—whom he constantly sees reflected on the oceanic mirror of conscience—and against the opponents of his ideals rather than of his own person. The small skirmishes of everyday life do not concern him at all.

Nothing would be so pitiable as the life of such a being if he were chained by fate to a humdrum existence, as every step would cost him an effort not in keeping with the tangible results, which would sap his energies and shorten his life span. Strange as it may seem, this influence may induce stoutness or other bodily ailments hampering walk.

Examples: Henry III, king of France (Sun's degree); Pope Paul V (Sun's degree); King Louis XIII (Sun's degree).

06° Libra

Symbol: An old sapper busy digging

This degree exacts a hard, patient, endless labor, possibly a serfs work, certainly a very tiring one. A just but belated reward will follow.

Old traditions and antique objects are cherished or—as the other stars may bear out—the new is opposed on principle and there is an inordinate fondness for worthless old junk.

There may be a critical sense but hardly any inner balance.

Example: Sir John French, British commander-in-chief, 1914-15 (Sun's degree).

07° Libra

Symbol: Mary Magdalene at Christ's feet in the house of
Pharisee Simon, who is scandalized at the sight.

Wherefore I say unto thee, her sins, which are many, are
forgiven, for she loved much.—Luke 7:47

Need I say that love is the keystone of this degree? However, as some obvious features may escape many a reader, I shall dwell on some apparently idle details.

The symbol does not of necessity imply that the male native is a superhuman being or the female native a repentant sinner. On the contrary, it does imply a divalent influence acting on the plane of love.

Such a force may—as in many other significant degrees—raise one up to saintliness and apostleship; or rouse scandal and lose one's soul; or revile through worldly love and then redeem and purify through real love. All this more or less independently of the native's sex but in accordance with his or her other stars.

Some patterns may even bear out the figure of the prudish pharisee who will not only refuse to forgive the sinner but will curse the flesh and go so far as to ruthlessly and indiscriminately persecute love in all its aspects, even the legitimate ones. Here too, though negatively, love is the revolving point.

Yet there is undoubtedly something prophetic or messianic about this degree, and such a feature may sometimes come to light in the oddest ways.

08° Libra

Symbol: A young lady silently weeping by a bed where a patient
lies on his back giving no signs of life

A sensitive and melancholy nature apt to love silently and

135

passionately. Whether her inborn inhibitions, mournings or ailments, or anything else, is at the root of her unhappiness, karma threatens loneliness from her very youth. The native may even have to wail over her unsatisfied love throughout the rest of her life.

Example: We found this degree to be a knot in the pattern of a lady who had married a man sick with pox and had then sued him for divorce on this ground.

09° Libra

Symbol: An old warrior in full battle harness
raising his sword in token of victory

The noblest manly traits. The native worships freedom and is ready to forsake life for this ideal. He couples the keenest courage with an utter sincerity, a ready and precise wit, and a sharp, nearly unerring critical sense. But all these virtues open as many pitfalls.

Love of freedom may straggle into waywardness, daring into reckless aggressiveness, frankness into libel; the critical sense may be warped into the peevish pettifogginess of one keen on taking everyone to task and reveling in endless faultfinding. Even his loftiest motives may lead the native to a blind ambition that may prove his undoing.

He must be trained to respect other people's freedom as much as his own, to understand how frankness ought to go arm in arm with kindness, and to realize that daring cannot go without wariness and magnanimity.

Examples: Paul von Hindenburg, German field marshal, 1916-18, later (1925-34) second president of Germany (Sun's degree); Mahatma Gandhi (Sun's degree).

10° Libra

Symbol: A marabou

(The marabou, alias "the philosopher" is a kind of stork, very frequent in Eastern towns and performing of its own accord a scavenger's work by swallowing any kind of refuse. Its name is due to the bird's solemn and nearly thoughtful attitude, the word marabou [Arabic *marabu*] being the equivalent of the Indian word *yogin.)*

The native's work is indispensable to society's bodily and mental healing, but he must have the stomach for it.

The native is likely to be a profound thinker and to have a serious, dreary, ceremonial outward attitude. His garments are likely to be more slovenly than niggardly, perhaps downright grubby or, if well groomed, he is likely to show a definite partiality for black. If smart at all, the native will be so in his style rather than in his dress.

All this is more or less probable. But only the nativity as a whole will be able to tell us whether we are faced with a great philanthropist so engrossed in his study of the most hideous social evils as to forget his own outward aspect altogether or, with a public man who, even if honest, meddles with the loathsome ordure politics mostly consists of; or with a swineherd, a humble sweeper, or an even humbler scavenger in a backward hamlet.

Freedom and life itself are open to risk of a kind varying according to the subject's social status and special activity. When harmful influences are together at play, he can turn out to be nothing but a dirty pig, a regular, authentic, unadulterated swine.

In higher nativities this influence may induce an arcadian strain, a taste for domesticated nature.

Examples: Joseph Mazzini (degree of Saturn, ruler of the Ascendant); Palmiro Togliatti, Italian communist leader (degree of Saturn, ruler of the Ascendant).

11° Libra

Here is such an outspoken dualism as to make the influence difficult to define. However, it is certain that, like the previous one, this degree has something arcadian–pastoral too—although the native can hardly be said to strike a pose if he fosters a longing for the freedom of country life or for a shepherd's wanderings. He may be a shepherd himself, and not only of sheep but a pastor of souls or the leader of entire peoples as well.

The horoscope studied in its entirety will have to reveal the calling or point to the mission to be carried out; however, the native himself is sure to be outside the fold of common mankind. In his being there is something lordly or beastly, super- or sub-human, led by divine inspiration or atavistically instinctive and cruel; the twain are unlikely to co-exist in one soul, as this degree portends a divalent, self-contradictory, jumpy and jerky nature.

There is a sharp and bright mind, an assured practical intuition, a wide knowledge (provided social conditions warrant schooling). Although the native may be slow-witted in certain things, he is usually quick in the uptake. Unfortunately there may be that lower by-product of intelligence that goes under the name of cleverness and may be warped easily into cunning or hypocrisy. The native may be fond of hunting, riding and all strenuous sports.

Examples: Catherine de Medicis, queen of France (Moon's degree); Jerome Cardano (Sun's degree); Cardinal Bellarmino (Sun's degree); Francesco Crispi (Sun's degree). Here the Ascendant of the United States is to be found.

N.B. Robert Bellarimino, S.J., was beatified in 1923. He was one of the judges who sentenced Giordano Bruno to be burned alive at the stake.

12° Libra

Symbol: The callipygian Venus of the Naples Museum

This degree favors only women and harms the other half of mankind, as the only gifts it vouchsafes are good looks, smartness, and formal courtesy. But it nearly always gives a frivolous character, vain to a degree, fond of leisure, and likely to do a good deal of looking around, and looking at herself, without achieving either prudence or moral consciousness. No useful lesson will be drawn from past mistakes.

And these are not her worst defects: the real drawbacks of this degree are effeminacy and impotence. This latter may affect the mind or the virility; and may be partial, rendering thought, or the semen, sterile *(impotentia generandi)*, or the impotence may be total (producing idiocy or *impotentia coeundi);* and may strike the male or the female husband. Where other astrological components offset this and stress a powerful manliness, a productive mind, a practical sense and the like, this influence may turn to impairing one's health and warping the sexual urge, without excluding the power, thus leading to narcissism or onanism in its widest sense.

(Onanism is a word which means self-abuse. It is traced to Onan, whose misdeeds were, according to the Bible (Gen. 38: 6-10) smitten by God's wrath as, while lying with Tumar, he behaved in such a way as to avoid impregnation; as it were, malthusianism *ante literam.* Later the meaning of this word was extended to cover any fruitless sexual aberration. Most of those who term themselves Christians seem to ignore how serious Onan's crime was according to theology.)

Example: Eleonora Duse (Sun's degree).

13° Libra

*Symbol: A man and a woman spitefully turning their
backs to each other*

This influence will benefit only the mind or, rather, one of its faculties—presence of mind. Affective life is a failure; marriage will almost certainly result in divorce, friendships in disappointment; there will be disagreement with everyone and, as a consequence, misanthropy.

The native's trouble may be boiled down to an excessive fondling and pampering of the ones he loves, so that the other partner

139

will feel smothered with love and hardly be able to breathe.

Example: George Sand (degree of Uranus, ruler of the Ascendant).

14° Libra

Symbol: A fox and an ancient theatre mask (from one of Aesop's fables)

O quanta species—inquit—cerebrum non habet!—
Phaedrus, 1, 7

It is a degree of theatricality, implying cunning but an otherwise dull mind. The native's whole life is on the stage. An empty being, dying to play a role and able to put such an apparent life in his personage that he will deceive himself before taking in others. The pattern of his acting may change with circumstances.

All this assuming the best. In other cases there will be self-conceit coupled with the most abject toadying, a mixture of priggishness and pandering; bluff and treacherousness; should the worst come to the worst, there might even be obsession or devilish possession. (Anyhow, mediumship will be a constant danger to be duly considered; even the native's mere presence at a necromantic invocation—the so-called spiritualist sittings where children masquerading as grownups play with fire—may be a peril in itself).

Among the less serious strains, coquettishness—and not only in female natives-is a normal feature. Equally normal are pseudo-classicism, worship of a manneristic Hellenism or a pasteboard "Romanity," love for the *beau geste* and a flamboyant style, propensity for dazzling pageants, void and bombastic rhetoric.

Such rhetorical trash may obviously sublime into dramatic skill or stage ability. But the star, whatever its sex, is unlikely to be very intelligent.

Example: The Fascist regime (degree of Saturn, ruler of the Ascendant).

15° Libra

A merely instinctive life. Laziness and lack of ambition dampen an otherwise worldly, fribbling, shrewd, untrue and courteous temperament. The native is selfish and has no backbone, but after all he is harmless and has some common sense.

For him the main problems are those touching his inner man; once his appetite is sated, everything is all right. For the rest, his weakness of character borders on total lack of will power and delivers him into the hands of others.

A lowly sensualist, the native may get into trouble on account of love affairs or sentimental entanglements; he may even be the victim of magic ensnarement (what the French term *envoutement* and the Javanese mean by *guna guna)* or other similar filth.

Example: Louis XIII, king of France (degree of the Point of Equidistance).

16° Libra

Symbol: A camel speeding along

A rugged physique with an unusual turn of speed; endurance to fatigue, cold, hunger, and thirst; an ability to stand any hardships; a body fully responding to will power.

A brisk, daring, firm, lively will; a far-reaching imagination but wayward rather than original, a more showy than profound mind; and more pluck than independence.

Inborn ambitions are faraway travels and the army, though the native strikes one as more an organizer or a technician than a fighter. Anyhow, he would have no luck fighting for his country on the front line as, barring strong components of luck, any enemy grenade falling into a trench would surely have his name on it. Electrical engineering would be a calling for him.

Should other stars grant the native an original and independent mind—which this degree falls just short of bestowing—the virtues mentioned above would come into full light and allow self-assertion, success, and even renown.

Example: Marshall Bernard L. Montgomery (degree of Uranus, ruler of the sign intercepted in the house of personality).

17° Libra

Symbol: A sweetly chirping starling

I do not feel like being fenced in within these four walls.—Cardinal Sarto's words before being elected Pope Pius X

A musical soul, gifted for tuning together human voices more than instrumental voices, and more for solo singing than polyphony.

A perennially youthful spirit, a born enemy of the powers that be, irrepressibly poking fun at traditional taboos. According to other astrological factors, the character may tend more to good-natured joking than to cruel jesting, to a cheerful unconcern rather than to bitter faultfinding, or vice versa.

In either case, critical sense and dialectic fluency are first rate but may degenerate into a childish desire to demolish and contradict, into an idle quarrelsomeness that looks for trouble and may land in it for no reason. Even if other aspects and a suitable upbringing instill the most gentlemanly and the politest wittiness into the native, he would still be very unlikely to use it opportunely.

The native's drawback is an ingenuous belief in abstract logic and Goddess Reason. He cannot find it in himself to admit the existence of such a thing as a mentality.

As the mind, so the native's body will stay nimble, lithe and youthful till late years. The snag about this is that youth's passions will lose little of their fire and will be hard to check. Such a glut of physical energy will need a life in the open to find its proper outlet. There is a great fondness for horses and riding. However, this breezingly irreverent Till Eulenspiegel often will run the risk of losing his freedom, through either reprehensible light-mindedness, the uncalled-for heroics of an improvised revolutionary, or simply the crime of having slighted the undisputed sovereignty of philistine tradition. All that is likely but not certain. Widely different reasons may lead the little bird into a gilt cage.

Examples: Joseph Mazzini (degree of Uranus, ruler of the sign intercepted in the house of personality); Giuseppe Verdi (Sun's degree); Pope Pius X (degree of Saturn, ruler of the Ascendant).

N.B. In order to appreciate fully the above examples, one ought to bear in mind that Verdi had in Virgo his ruler of the Ascendant (Jupiter); and that both Mazzini and Pius X had their Ascendants in Capricorn, which is revealing in itself.

18° Libra

Symbol: A lordly villa in the open country, its inner walls decorated with encaustic tiles or trimmed with engravings

An outstandingly good influence for home life, which will be happy and quiet in spite of the great number of friends the native's hospitable nature will have within his house's walls. His open and fair character will win the hearts of both friends and strangers, and the favor of stars, which will grant him happiness and wealth.

A profound psychologist, he may excel I»- outlining with a few lucky strokes or, as the case may be, stigmatizing anyone's character. This will be the greatest merit of his works, if an artistic career is borne out by other stars, which will then have to determine the kind of art to which he is destined.

19° Libra

Symbol: A magnificent castle on top of a mountain

Living humbly as a thane. / In his heart dreaming of reign.—Manzoni, "The Fifth of May"

This is one of the most remarkable among the degrees portending rulership, another one being 13° Scorpio. The human being hallmarked by it is born to rule out of his own power and, barring indications to the contrary, will be endowed with lord-like manners, strength and good looks; an indomitable character, a cold-blooded and wary courage. On the other hand he will be overbearing, selfish, heartless. Should the nativity point to any criminal tendency, he may even not balk at intentional murder.

At variance with his native surroundings, he will strive to reach higher and higher, coolly assessing and lining up the means necessary to work his way up. But he will go too far in his efforts, leaving nothing to chance or to the flash of the moment to decide, thus exposing himself to disappointments and hardships.

He may prove thankful to his faithful followers, seldom to his supporters, never to his equals. Purpose, not feeling, will make him lenient or ruthless. Mistrust of others will harden him into a haughty attitude of self-reliant impassivity, and will isolate him spiritually. Sparing and hard working by nature, he will, however, love pomp and will not be loath to patronize arts. These conflicting features will puzzle his contemporaries. But within himself he is clearly conscious of his aims and will, if by devious paths, steadily and stubbornly pursue the high goal he set his heart upon.

But he is no cynic. On the contrary he sets a great store by other people's good opinion and is too shrewd a schemer not to back his bid for success with the support of public opinion as well.

If favorably aspected elsewhere, he will overcome all his enemies and end by holding undisputed sway. Even if he is not going to rank among the rulers of Earth, he is likely to reach the top-flight of any given career, and will make his authority felt, much to his dependents' dismay.

Examples: Benjamin Disraeli, Earl of Beaconsfield (Ascendant's degree); George Clemenceau, alias "The Tiger," French premier during World War I (degree of the Point of Equidistance).

144

20° Libra

Symbol: Around an altar, on which the fire of sacrifice is blazing, the priests lay the sacred meal.

An outstanding personality, inwardly filled with light and warmth. There is a sincere religious spirit, exclusive of hypocrisy but not of earthly pleasures, prominent among which is enjoyment of good food. The other factors have to show whether this pious strain is likelier to inspire an ascetic or a sensuous mystic. In either case the native may enter the clergy or, as a layman, lead an apostle's life.

Either in a cloister or in the world, the native's ecclesiastical or worldly career stands under good auspices and even may prove very fortunate indeed, if backed by other indications of luck. The support of highly placed people and the sympathy of learned persons will bring forth the native's otherwise unmistakable gifts, and his presence will appear indispensable to others.

Examples: Count Cavour (degree of the Point of Equidistance); the Right Honorable Ramsay McDonald (Sun's degree).

21° Libra

This nature shows some undeniably positive features and bright gifts, or even magic abilities. Yet it lacks some practical faculties needed to make one's way in everyday life. The native will have to work in someone else's employ, which he can do without debasing himself, as service does not mean servility to him; he can keep his self-respect even in the humblest positions, and is apt to resent the slightest encroachment upon his free will.

Unfortunately the native is likely to stick to absurd fads and to tread ways leading him nowhere. The greater his stubbornness, the more cruel the disappointments fate has in store for him. He will not make any headway but will see all his plans crumble and his alleged friends turn their backs on him.

Example: Marie Antoinette of Habsburg, queen of France (degree of the center of the Moon, whose brim overlaps into the following degree).

22° Libra

Symbol: Two saddled horses

You cannot hold your foot in two stirrups.—popular Italian proverb

Here is another inconsequent degree, pointing to an inwardly split nature. There are side by side wisdom and recklessness, good-heartedness and haughtiness, earnestness and light-mindedness, stern justice and guilty self-indulgence, absolute sincerity in some things and double-dealing in others, deep pondering and illusory daydreaming. Great plans and aspirations yield paltry results, perhaps as a consequence of wishing too many things at a time.

The native may be advised to use more firmness and a measure of self-denial, to be less vain, to stop lulling himself into a deceiving sense of safety, and to step boldly into real life. Thought and will create, whereas yearning and daydreaming only destroy.

Examples: Lord Byron (degree of Neptune, ruler of the sign intercepted in the house of personality).

N.B. In the nativity of unlucky Queen Marie Antoinette, part of the Moon's orb juts over from the former degree to cover the first minutes of this.

23° Libra

Symbol: An old physician intent to a urine test

The native is a tireless researcher who will inquisitively pry into nature, snatch her secrets, analyze them and methodically pigeonhole the results. A restless urge to change subject and shift his grounds of observation will make him loath to stay put, so that even when penned within four walls he will try to change his room from time to time. He may be fond of journeying to unexplored countries and will certainly worship knowledge. The branches most congenial to him seem to be chemistry and medicine (this one perhaps in a spiritual sense). Occultism is not to be ruled out in branches akin to the ones quoted: viz., alchemy, the mother of chemistry, and pastoral medicine.

Success ought to crown his efforts; public recognition, though belated, may ratify his discoveries. Either for this or other reasons there will be a certain self-assurance, a somewhat consequential mannerism in his speech, as if he were delivering abstruse truths to a large audience.

Attention is to be paid to the urinary system. On the other hand the whole organism is subject to precocious decay, either owing to the stuffy laboratory air or to the unhealthy atmosphere of close rooms.

Examples: Friedrich Nietzsche (Sun's degree); Paul Ehrlich (degree of the Ascendant).

N.B. Ehrlich developed tuberculosis during lab research.

24° Libra

Symbol: A satyr strikes a dragon with a stick

A tall, sturdy and handsome physique, great sexual vigor and inordinate lustfulness. A fierce character, more likely to prevail upon others than upon himself. A sharp wit, inclined to good natured irony or to bitter sarcasm, as the case may be. Self-confidence in even too large a measure. The native's high ambitions will shut him off from the common fold and inspire him with a pride verging on haughtiness. He will be fond of hunting.

The native is exposed to ambushes and foul play at the hands of his opponents and may collapse when he least expects it.

Whatever kind of gambling he may try his hand at, bad luck is certain to crush him.

Examples: Henry IV, king of France and Navarre (degree of the Ascendant). The bulk of the Moon's orb of King Louis XIII is in this degree, its center being at 23°52'43", yet the influence of the following degree (passivity and love of justice) could already out-shine more than one feature of 24° Libra's sexual power, fierce-ness, independence).

25° Libra

Symbol: A pea fowl

A pride that can be sublimated into the noblest sense of hu-man dignity or debased into vanity rather than haughtiness, into a tendency to strut and show off, either materially or morally.

On the other hand, kindness, equability, poise, tidiness, love of justice and harmony are inborn virtues. Yet these in their turn may induce a too yielding, dull, helpless and fickle disposition. The native thus may fall easy prey to flattery, or to his own desire to appear obliging. A contrasting strain of jerky impulsiveness will seem not to fit in with the whole.

In the main a nice—even charming—personality, a graceful and probably good-looking figure, a great career, a happy life.

Occult initiation cannot be excluded but may certainly be hin-dered by vanity.

Examples: Louis XIII, king of France (degree of part of the Moon's orb—see preceding degree); astride this and the following degree is Eugene Savoy's Sun.

26° Libra

Dieu et mon droit.

A firm and generous heart, jealous of his own rights, an un-daunted courage, a fighting spirit not devoid of wariness and pru-dence, a warm patriotic feeling. A sturdy and aristocratic phy-sique, very keen senses of sight and hearing; an emotional, perhaps oversensitive temperament, open to danger of jumping to extreme mental attitudes.

A two-edged fortune; great chances of victory in the struggle for life, and danger of losing all of one's property.

Examples: Eugene of Savoy (Sun astride this and former degree); General Dwight Eisenhower (degree of the Point of Equidistance).

27° Libra

Symbol: A great eucalyptus in a garden

A vital force spreading its wholesome influence on all surrounding beings, a healthy spirit radiating around itself. A charitable, hospitable and fatherly nature, love of home, a taste for comfort and coziness.

A strong but limited intelligence, as the native's mind can do only one thing at a time and does it with all its might. There is a cool courage and sudden spells of fury on a background of impassiveness. However, if deliberately planned, this wrath will explode blindly. Lack of moral and physical suppleness; the native is unwieldy and nearly horny skinned; not springy; slow-witted and slowly aroused.

Few will be able to see through the apparent contradiction of this over-sensitive, close soul, gifted with imagination, but loath to conceive certain ideas.

Example: The *coup d'etat* of July 26, 1943, in Rome (degree of the Ascendant).

28° Libra

A self-conflicting influence; human dignity and bondage, aristocracy and menial work, gallantry and lack of initiative, a sensitive soul and a limited mental range. I think the keynote here is resignation, in both good and evil senses. Therefore, ambition is totally absent, even if the native's karma leads him to occupy ruling positions; whatever the status, his patience is boundless, his view confined.

The drabness of such a narrow horizon will be borne with ease and taken for granted by this unhinged mind, prone to find any wider ambitions abnormal.

29° Libra

Although the native has moral principles, he will put up with anything for the sake of peace. An intellectual mind, gifted for literature and art, and likely to dodge his enemies' underhanded plots.

Should the nativity bear out fatalism rather than ambition, the subject would be a crack shirker, a likeable sluggard, a pleasant daydreamer, whose life will risk flowing on uneventful and dull without an ideal and with the sole aim of shunning effort. Most of the intellectual flotsam of the modern middle class is under this influence; their only ambition is some obscure government job, where they can dig in and bend their backs, ready to stick anything provided it wards off hunger.

On the contrary, where other forces at work supply the native with a bare minimum of initiative and self-respect—which this degree in itself neither gives nor denies—there could be real courage and firm principles behind the outward softness of manners. Such virtues must be developed by manly training, enabling the native to weather any storm and to take life like a man. Then the native's twist toward cunning can be turned into wisdom, and culture and good manners will confer great charm. The rest of the horoscope must show what the native is driving at.

30° Libra

Symbol: Deluge's end: the Ark is stranded on top of Mt. Ararat, and the raven flies over the expanse of water. (Gen. 8:1-7)

150

Quando in domo tua nigri corn parturient albas columbas, tune vocaberis sapiens.—An alchemic devise engraved on the "hermetic door"—the run of an alchemic laboratory in Rome—between the Symbols of Saturn and Mars

This degree may see any occult disciple through some stage of the Great Work (the raven), but is ominous to anyone else insofar as it hinders the establishment of a correct relation between the human being and its surroundings.

It is as if the sprockets of the native's wheels could not engage with the links of the outside world. If he is not endowed with the kind of faith that moves mountains, he risks growing fearful and reckless, humoring his own weaknesses without understanding the weaknesses of others. Shy of human society, he will feel safer among dangers; absolute faith or blind recklessness? Danger of accidental death or murder? To the stars the answer to those questions, although it will never be stressed enough: *inclinant non necessitant* (they predispose, never compel).

SCORPIO

01° Scorpio

Symbol: Othello

(Attention should be paid to the Shakespearian character's nature, not to the story of his marriage to a gentlewoman much younger than himself.)

A fierce, daring, snappish and high-handed temperament; an altruistic, generous, impassioned and unrestrained nature, brimming over with bodily and mental strength, led into endless strife by the wayward quarrelsomeness; impatient bluster; frantic outbursts of wrath; high-strung lustfulness and fitful jealousy. With all this the native is most likely to stick to someone unto death and to let himself be unconditionally ruled by the person loved.

In less developed beings, the lack of restraint in anger and lust may drift into delinquency if other astrological factors concur. Anyway, there will be quarrels, break-up of friendships, duels and the like.

Example: Marie Antoinette of Habsburg, queen of France (degree of the Point of Equidistance).

02° Scorpio

Symbol: An elephant

Essential elements of this personality are strength, sturdiness, wide mental range, ponderation and slowness in everything.

A detailed description, taking bodily features into account, will point to a tall and stolid frame, a large nose and small, lively eyes; an individually marked character, a strong soul, gifted with sharp and deep judgment. The native has not only a mentally great head, much humanity and plenty of power, but is cautious, reserved, unprejudiced, either evenly melancholic or fearlessly confident in the future. Though he is normally easy and self-controlled, his wrath will know no bounds if he is roused. His memory is exceptionally retentive of both good and evil; his grudges can hardly be smoothed over.

Sturdiness may lead sometimes to stubbornness, the huge strength may stray into high-handedness; in particularly ill-aspected charts, greatness may induce a swelled head. Less seldom, the native-basically sober as he is-may develop an unnatural taste for the macabre and may be obsessed with the idea of death. This in its turn may be sublimated into a surgical talent or into mystical contemplation of the next world.

03° Scorpio

Symbol: A meditating ascetic, squatting in a yogi's posture, head and chest upright, and palms turned forward

This degree is oriented toward a contemplative life and bestows such a depth of thought as can become an abyss. Whether it shall be an abyss of evil or of good, the whole of the nativity has to decide. The Powerful One, having overstepped the limits of sense delusions (what the Hindus called *Maya*) is rid of the bonds and ties hampering earthly beings, which is a danger in itself.

This ought to be enough. Outwardly the native is silent, close, lonesome and shy of human society and fellowship, but others sooner or later may be compelled to acknowledge that, though he spoke not, he had his way and left a very conspicuous mark where he trod.

It cannot be ruled out that, in particularly ominous horoscopes, lamentable travesties of true yoga and mystic pilgrimages are staged: the idle beggar stationed at a street corner; the vagrant wandering aimlessly through the world.

04° Scorpio

Symbol: A zither

Art, harmony and merriness are the hallmarks of this degree. Merriness: a sparkling fullness of life, a freedom from worry, a lively cheerfulness utterly exempt from coarseness; happiness or, at any rate, contentedness and luck. Harmony: an agreement of the soul with the innermost self and the surrounding world, creative balance, inner peace, lord-like generosity toward one's neighbors, faithfulness to the ideal of the chosen career, apt to reward the native with renown or, at least, success. Art: lyrical art in its widest sense; poetry, theatre, particularly music; or, at least, refined taste and feelings.

Should the whole of the pattern bear the mark of spiritual pursuits, the native would be a follower of the mystic school leading to union through love, and to the attainment of one's highest aims through an inharmonious correspondence with things rather than through a harsh self-conquest. On the other hand, where the stars purport a feeble character, or an inner spirit, idle propensities and a trifling disposition, this degree but heightens such vices and does not bear any of its above-mentioned fruits.

05° Scorpio

Symbol: A man maimed in his lower limbs, stands in the middle of a plain, while a storm rages overhead.

Miscarriage of any undertaking, lack of any constructive capacity, powerlessness to carry anything to its end. A volcanic and bungling mind, apt to set hand to a thousand and one fine things without being able to see a single one through. The resulting extravagant waste of energy is crowned by complete failure.

This is no doubt a reckless, brutal and ravaging nature, a real hurricane incarnate. The body actually may be crippled, perhaps in the legs. Yet, should the native be open to highly religious and spiritual ideals—not incompatible with the features mentioned above provided the rest of the nativity confirms it—he may be of some use to society by shaking slumbering consciousness and giving an impulse toward good, which then could be carried out by others.

Examples: Timur Lenk (Timur the Lame), emperor of the Mongols (degree of Saturn, ruler of the Ascendant); Charles VI, the mad king of France (degree of the Point of Equidistance).

06° Scorpio

A real worker, the native will easily put up with hardships and think little of himself. In spite of a great sense of duty, there is an inner split, which could result in gossipy duplicity or even pervert modesty into dissembling servility. Though patient enough, the native will carry out his task bluntly rather than further it actively and steadily; he does not put enough zest into his work. An appropriate training will have to supply him with the necessary share of stead-fastness, or he will risk stopping in the middle of any undertaking.

If the will power can be educated at all, the native's limitation will not exclude success, as his painstaking care of details will be appreciated. Ups and downs can be expected in his social status, but if he is liable to fall, he is as well apt to rise again.

07° Scorpio

Symbol: A treasure

The symbol conveys its meaning clearly enough, but it may help to remark that this influence can work on different planes. It may refer to the native's precious gifts as well as to something outward that destiny has in store for him as a surprise; in this latter sense the Symbol may be taken literally or metaphorically. None of the foregoing interpretation bars other ones; as usual, things are to be looked at within the frame of the whole astrological picture.

Now for the details: Inner treasure may be taken to mean wealth of feelings, ideas or other forces of the mind. The element prevailing in the nativity will show the right sense if the houses and the aspects also are taken into account. A material treasure may be collected as a result of commercial dealings; or, whatever the success, the native's lot may be to deal in jewels or rare objects. Otherwise he may be born to dig out mineral ore (gold, silver, etc.), archaeological remains, or to perform fruitful research journeys. In some cases the native may be singled out by destiny to be, spiritually or technically, the leader of an entire people.

Apart from all this, we may add that the native is a tireless worker and that he is liable to show some childish features even in adult age; at the same time there is something royal about him, and his fortune holds something unexpected—and illogical—in store for him. Whether these are all to be pleasant surprises must be left to the pointers of luck in the chart to decide.

This much can be said with assurance: the native has some karmic mysteries in his path, before which the average mind will feel thoroughly puzzled.

08° Scorpio

Symbol: A huge cock with a dazzling tail

An original, fighting, generous and unprejudiced nature. A writer's talent, a demonstrative, enthusiastic, buoyant and sprightly character, thoughtless of the morrow, capable of the most intense activity and likely to reach distinction through some outstanding feat. These are the assets.

Now for the liabilities! An extraordinary light-mindedness, an unaccountable splurge and waste of energy, a random existence, a ceaseless and aimless whirlwind of activity, an extravagant or scandalous life of perpetual hustle and bustle. The native knows no self-restraint and is driven to monopolize everyone's attention and to be the cynosure of all eyes. His sexual urge will be raised to a principle inspiring his behavior. He will dive headlong into love affairs, intrigues and adventures, with a haughty disregard of consequences and a defiant contempt of custom. There will be an unruly foolhardiness; squabbles will occur over the paltriest trifles; where lust is at stake, the native will not balk at crime.

Example: James Casanova de Seingalt (degree of the Ascendant).

09° Scorpio

Symbol: A child in a tub

It is a degree of childishness. Spiritual development will be lopsided, and therefore incomplete, during childhood. Early suffering. (The two things do not hang of necessity on the same thread, though it may be assumed that they do.) The following may be reasonably expected to occur: either the child will lose both parents at an early age, or lose one of them and be neglected by the survivor, or neither of the parents will die, but the child will feel or believe itself neglected or misunderstood, and therefore will waste its days sticking to the skirts of an old charwoman or to the overalls of an old workman of its father's. Allowance may be made for other cases as well; the scholar will have to find them out, taking the other features into account.

The keynote of this degree consists in its exposing childhood to the risk of an irregular development of mind and character. The whole of the horoscope will have to show whether men or events are to blame, whether the reasons for this are to be sought inside the native in an inordinately developed ego, or in the outside world. The possible consequences of this influence are twofold: either an unmanly sagging and flagging of the mind, or an exaggerated reaction resulting in a superiority complex.

Whatever the truth, the native will stay long unripe and childish in his youth after having had an insufficiently youthful childhood. Restless, hypercritical, irreverent and ingenuous at the same time, he may, however, blossom into a useful member of society; when he reaches a higher position than his limited mind would purport, and thus shows a positive reaction to his early discouragement, he may even develop materially humanitarian tendencies. I say materially. In the spiritual field, ungenerosity will be the rule.

10° Scorpio

Malice ranging from witty joke to coarse treacherousness. A lightning-like presence of mind and intuition; in stupid natives, cunning. A mathematical mind. In lower beings, a scheming brain, a soul that can exploit to the utmost the sympathy it awakens in others. The greatest faculty of dissembling and surprising, a marked political, talent. In contemptible beings, double-dealing. In all cases the character will be close, silent, sphinx-like, fond of secrecy.

There will be journeys, perhaps scientific discoveries.

Example: Philippe d'Orleans, regent of France during the minority of Louis XV (degree of Jupiter, ruler of the Ascendant).

11° Scorpio

In the foreground, a son's love and solidarity with one's native clan. On the reverse side of the shield, lack of measure.

Lasting affections, inability to live without love; faithfulness and jealousy. Contrast of daring and shyness, of headiness and yieldingness. Lack of balance in front of life's dangers and ambushes, unnecessary alarm and neglect of the most obvious precautions, implicit faith in those who do not deserve any, and injurious suspicions; fear of imaginary risks and blindness before real risk, useless wariness and silly rashness.

Examples: Marie Antoinette of Habsburg, queen of France (Sun's degree); Warren G. Harding, president of the United States (Sun's degree).

12° Scorpio

One virtue is outstanding here: prudence. The word is to be taken in its widest range of meanings: wariness, ponderation, wisdom, foresight and, above all, the highest ability to ward off one's despicable but sly and numerous foes.

A resourceful mind, an individually marked character, reserved manners. Such virtues, however, border on the corresponding defects: cunning, selfishness and, perhaps, devious ways.

The sexual urge is strong and could induce lustfulness. Longstanding angers, leaving behind muffled grudges. There may be real ill will. The native's karma is bad and will force him always to keep on the lockout.

Examples: Francois Mario Sadi Carnot, president of the French Republic at the time of *boulangisme,* fallen victim to an attempt (degree of Saturn, ruler of the Ascendant).

13° Scorpio

Symbol: A lonely stronghold on a high mountain top, a veritable eagle's nest. The place is fortified by nature itself rather than by man's hand. It is the key-point of the region, and its possession grants sway over the neighboring states.

Whether the native is high-born or a self-made man coming of an obscure family, fate certainly has earmarked him to occupy an eminent, independent position and to hold sway over others, owing to his inborn inexhaustible force. To obey him is a matter of course, nearly of necessity.

An untiring, hard worker, he is fully confident in himself, and his firmness of purpose borders on stubbornness. Laconic, or even

160

silent, he can scan and pierce everything around himself at a glance without betraying any of his feelings. Close but long-sighted, strong but on his defensive, cunning yet intelligent, he has fortune on his side and all the good or evil qualities needed to assert oneself and achieve success, his main asset being an iron will, unshakeable and undaunted; his main defect, a selfish, despotic, scheming ambition.

When other aspects point to a liking for the career of arms, this degree will bestow the gift of strategy. Should the stars point to agriculture instead, the native would be a great organizer and manager of farms.

Examples: Napoleon Bonaparte (Ascendant's degree); George Clemenceau (degree of the Moon; compare 17° Leo and the accompanying note); James Ramsay McDonald (degree of the Point of Equidistance); Raphael places here the Ascendant of Sir John French, British commander-in-chief, 1914-15.

N.B. Napoleon's Ascendant is closely joined with Jupiter in 16° Scorpio.

14° Scorpio

Many would be the native's likeable sides if only he had some character, but he is very unlikely to have any should his Ascendant (or Point of Equidistance, or Sun) happen to fall on this degree. Anyhow, his best features would be openness, directness, innocence-all virtues which, to be realized in practice, would need such firmness, energy and self-denial as are certainly conspicuous for their absence here.

Moreover, the native is more hearty and impulsively courageous than cool-minded and clear-headed, candid rather than reserved, modest rather than discreet.

In spite of all, people will like his genial, hearty open comradeship, his loving kindness toward his friends. Though he may be harmed by other people's (if not his own) indiscretion, he is no

161

fool and can gauge human characteristics in their whole, if not through a minute test of their details.

15° Scorpio

It is a feminine degree. It bestows remarkable beauty, a debonair character, a probably strong physique or, at any rate, one that can stand pain, hardship and hard work; but it tends to exclude any spiritual kind of religion. Its essential feature is an absolute fatalism which, according to the marshaling of the other influences, can produce two different effects.

In a noble native there will be a tragically deterministic view of the main problems of life, a mechanical conception of the universe, leaving no room for any religious faith or anything transcendent; a stoic acceptance of any sacrifice-nay, a need to sacrifice oneself, even groundlessly, as a kind of mental masochism, without any enthusiasm or joy for the hardships withstood, which may really have cost a great self-denial.

On the other hand, a much coarser being will not be an atheist but a fetishist, a bigoted clericalist or the like. He will be utterly devoid of any stoical spirit and apt to let his fatalism or determinism—no longer a purely sentimental or speculative leaning—weigh heavily on his practical life and work. In this case the native's main feature will be a slothful passivity, which may border on idleness or cowardice. Should a fillip from outside or an inner impulse rouse the sluggard to some work, he will fling himself blindly into it, but his labor will risk being wasted, and his body being crippled in the process.

One result is common to both types of native: he will not be able to taste the joy or the pleasures of life.

Example: Madame Curie (Sun's degree); this degree was rising on the horizon of Damascus at the solar noon of July 14, 1949, the day of the *coup d'etat.*

16° Scorpio

Symbol: A knight of the Holy Grail

Per manum benedicentem maledictus adumbratur.—
Mediaeval slogan of occult meaning

*In fernem Land, unnahbar euren Schritten liegt eine Burg,
die Monsalvat genannt.*—Wagner, *Lohengrin,* Act 3

An ancient Christian legend tells how, when Lucifer was flung down from Heaven, a jewel fell from his crown. From this jewel a cup was carved in which, on the day of our Lord's passion, Joseph of Arimathea gathered the blood flowing from crucified Christ's five wounds. This chalice, luciferic by origin, divine by destination, is named Grail. Its wardens are knights enlisted into a military order having its headquarters in a mysterious and impervious place by the name of Monsalvat. Hence the knights set out to bring mankind the medicines it needs, to defend the oppressed, and to redress down-trodden rights. But not all the knights have stayed faithful; evil forces try to win over as many of them as possible, and the ranks of deserters form the army of Monsalvat's bitterest foes.

This legend's secret meaning does not concern us here, but only such hints as are necessary to explain the Symbol, whose essence ought to be clear by now, consisting in a spirit of Christian charity and mercy served by an enlightened mind and a chivalrous and enthusiastic heart. A knight errant may not tell a lie; formidable as the foes may be, a righteous one cannot be conquered in an ordeal, a merciful one cannot but be human and kind, a Christian hero cannot but be lovable.

Whatever the moral height of the native, foreign is the country where he is called to act, his outward appearance is nimble and attractive, his wedding princely. Should other components allow, he would belong either to a secret sect or to the militant Church.

Examples: Cardinal Mazarin (degree of Saturn, ruler of the Ascendant); Wolfgang Goethe (degree of the Ascendant).

17° Scorpio

Symbol: A deer

He who takes no risks, takes no rusks.—Italian proverb

This degree would greatly favor a military career if it had not a great drawback—the total absence of even the slightest amount of civil courage. To be more accurate, that slightest amount would have been no moral virtue but merely a show of some political value, so that the absence of even that much results not only in cowardice but in imbecility as well. The native is weak toward himself, his opponents, life; though a line must be drawn between private and professional life. Outwardly the greatest gentleman, he is punctual at work, scrupulously honest and accurate, always smart and proud, and will enjoy the sympathy and esteem of all. At home he is ruthlessly selfish and torn by the craving for new sensations and lusts. Rather than reckless and dishonest in love, he is unprejudiced and shameless and will be naturally enough worshiped by representatives of the opposite sex.

Will that universal esteem or this widespread worship amount to anything? Hardly anything at all; if it comes to a fight or to the slightest show of manly pluck, the native will stage a dignified withdrawal, lordly and cowardly beyond belief.

Therefore, unless favored with a great amount of luck from other stars, his life will be a failure or, at least, a great disappointment as he always will consider discretion the better part of valor and will end his days in misery.

Voyages are better avoided.

18° Scorpio

A strict sense of justice, a liking for aimless leisure, unlucky love affairs thwarted by jealousy and mistrust (whether the native or the other partner is jealous, the whole of the horoscope must tell), an absolute lack of autonomy, a life weighed down by an excess of sloth. The native seems to lay little store by his own word, as he thinks little of entering an engagement and even less of subsequently breaking his pledge.

Courage to act openly is conspicuous by its absence, and there is just enough courage to bear the consequences of one's flippant fickleness or follies and to accept any sacrifice. Love for art, especially music, is deep-rooted. But one who has no character is unlikely to succeed unsupported in such a field, and there is no trace of any moral force here.

19° Scorpio

Symbol: Cerberus

(Cerberus is a dragon with three dog-like heads. The Greeks called it "Taenarius snake" and placed it in hell as its doorkeeper. Dante places it in the infernal circle of the gluttons and tells how Virgil managed to pacify it by throwing it a handful of mud to eat.-*Inf.* 6, 13-33. Traditional comments ta Dante's poem rate Cerberus a dog. Where is this written? Dante's monster has but a dog's barking. Dante ought to be read more attentively before coming to sweeping conclusions. Her terms Cerberus a "cruel and multifarious beast.")

As watchful and wary as anybody, the native is far from being a daredevil and seldom has real courage but looks as if he were always angry at everything and everybody, or nearly so, and his threats frighten numberless people. A fighter with words, he will display a bugbear's grim-faced bluster but seldom attack, and never in front; if assailed, he will fight back with unequaled doggedness, and his bites will leave their mark.

Faithful in friendship and enmity, very exacting, quick-tempered but stubborn, inexhaustible on the battlefield, inexorable in victory, his Achilles heel lies in his unappeasable greed for material pleasure, sexual and convivial. He is, on the other hand, an excellent trencherman and could do justice to a gargantuan meal. At

165

table he is nearly affable.

Where other aspects of the nativity indicate a spiteful and treacherous character, this filthy reptile will be a curse and a scourge for his fellow beings, as his is a heart of stone. Why do all too human beings acknowledge subconsciously this slimy being as their own master, even while hating him with all their soul? Is the reason to be traced in the destiny of all sensible things—and of them alone—to fall sooner or later into the dark god's power, or in the power of his earthly representatives, as mud belongs to mud?

Anyhow, Cerberus will destroy whatever he lays hands—or better, paws—upon, and cannot build anything. But he knows a thing or two; he has an assimilating, wary, manifold, prompt mind, and a gift for languages, but is never either consequent or original.

Examples: Albert von Waldstein, better known under the name Wallenstein (degree of the Point of Equidistance); Benito Mussolini (degree of the Ascendant). In the fascist dictator's horoscope, Jupiter (18°34') is in exact trigonal position to this degree, which scarcely needs comment.

20° Scorpio

This degree favors social advancement and success in one's chosen career, but it assures neither stability in it nor firmness of character. Where other factors concur, the native may attain to renown or glory which, though, never will rule out ups and downs.

Success is within the native's reach on account of his courage and his spiritual height, supported by a rugged yet pliant body, and in glaring contrast to his unbridled lustfulness. Few people will be such an easy prey of women, gambling and wine; on the other hand, few can stand hardships so well as he can. But his balance could drift into inner split, his force into quarrelsomeness or love of word fights, or into aggressiveness altogether.

Travels, probably east, will play a remarkable role, and during his wanderings the native is likely to make discoveries or important researches. A potentially unlimited intelligence lit by spiritual hope.

21° Scorpio

Symbol: A steppe of northern America at the beginning of the eighteenth century; herds of bison and wild horses gallop on the prairie. Tribes of Indians live freely on hunting and fishing.

A savage or primitive nature longing for freedom and champing at the bit of restraint. A great but undisciplined moral force, a courage ready to stand any test. A probably wild or downright ferocious character, knowing no inhibitions. At the same time, simplicity and naiveness; a love of childhood is apt to drive the native so far as to make him take part seriously in children's games and to look a child among children. Fondness of horse racing.

A hard destiny: acts of self-denial and heroic struggles in defense of one's independence, with a constant threat to this and to freedom itself.

Example: Napoleon III (degree of Saturn, ruler of the Ascendant).

22° Scorpio

Symbol: A waterfall driving an overshot wheel which engages no contrivance and whirls aimlessly in the air

It is the degree of random impulses and haphazard resolutions, after which one is forced to reconsider one's plans and to retrace one's steps. Restless, thoughtless and therefore ignorant of danger, the native is apt to lose his head and even to prove a coward when forced to face the situation brought about by his own foolishness. He then will back out as hurriedly as he drove forward. He will repay himself for such drawbacks by taking advantage of those weaker than himself, with the overbearingness typical of cowards.

Life will be hard on him, so that after a succession of ups and downs he will find himself in a blind alley from which he will not manage easily to escape.

Attachment to home is the only redeeming feature.

23° Scorpio

Hopefulness, often unjustified confidence, certainly more luck than deserved typifies this degree. Unrealizable plans prevail—plans around power and wealth, which are squandered. Love of arbitrage and trade at large. A taste for paradox, which the native will mistake for originality; a contrary and spiteful nature. There is no firmness in decisions, and the will power is jumpy and shaky.

Example: The Third French Republic (degree of the Ascendant).

24° Scorpio

Symbol: A woman spinning with the rook and distaff

Many a feminine virtue; a sensitive, modest, earnest disposition, a great love of peace, of the family and of home. There is a deep-seated sense of duty and above all a real passion for work applied to useful and concrete things. Few have such practicality. A firm and sedate character, an extraordinary self possession, as the native never will lose her composure and is perhaps even too cocksure.

Nor is this the only defect. There is too much thrift, which can stiffen into close-fistedness, too much reserve, which may lead the native to shun society. The tragedy of life is so deeply felt that a pall of constant gloom is likely to set over the native. Every family mourning will leave lasting traces.

For all her thrift, the native will stay poor, or nearly so, but will manage to have a house of her own, will be esteemed for her virtues and is not unlikely to leave behind not only an honored but a famous memory, provided that the rest other pattern bears it out.

A partiality for black, and dull or sedate colors.

Examples: Giovanni Pascoli (degree of Venus, ruler of the Ascendant); Arturo Toscanini (degree of Saturn, ruler of the sign intercepted in the house of personality).

25° Scorpio

Symbol: A wolf carrying away a goose

A very undesirable influence, leading to trouble and even to crime. A life of strife and sorrows, misery and wrangles, adventures and ephemeral conquests, cheerless victory over one's foes followed by bereavement of the fruit thereof; abandonment, probably treason by one's oldest friends.

A silent, greedy, unscrupulous, gruff and unsociable egotist, the native will be given a wide berth by all and will nevertheless pick quarrels with everyone. Little as other pointers hint at dishonesty, this degree will make the native into a criminal in the technical sense of the word, a thief, a murderer, a sharper.

Strongly beneficent influences may neutralize or balance this one, sublimating into lofty aspirations and high-spirited rebellions those psychic forces which, in a less noble horoscope, would have come to light as antisocial tendencies. Then the selfish curtness becomes lord-like reserve, ascetical isolation, inner quietude, but this case is very rare.

Example: In this degree is the MC of Marshal DeRichelieu, whom his soldiers nicknamed *petit père La Maraude* on account of his embezzlements of the property of the conquered. The marshal had Jupiter in sextile with the MC and in trigonal position with the Ascendant, the Sun in trigonal position with the MC and sextile with the Ascendant; which is quite enough. Yet in spite of his gallantry and intrigues, he was forced to leave the army.

26° Scorpio

A very marked personality, a resolute and deliberate character, both shy of publicity and contemptuous of public opinion. Courage driven to the utmost of recklessness may bring the native into danger.

There are two possible cases: (1) An honest and human nature, whose loathing of the pick of society and of the smart military set will turn his feelings into sympathy and love for the needy and the destitute. He will courageously go out of his way to succor this undeserving flotsam of society who has been disinherited and left in the lurch by the highbrows. But he will get the usual reward of benefactors: "ingratitude more strong than a traitor's arm" will overpower him. (2) The native has no moral principles whatsoever. Then hatred of mankind will strike root and sprout in him. He will lurk in the shade, plotting against human society, a thief or even worse.

27° Scorpio

An inborn authority; a gentle way of getting things done; ambition and sense of duty, gift of gab and literary talents; great courage and great dangers to face. In such a horoscope as to exclude public life, eloquence may sheer off into balderdash or gossip (as the native is a very sociable being, fond of festivity and entertainment) and political skill into double-dealing. Anyway, the native has a powerful and adaptable mind, a deep-rooted sense of responsibility and a greater prestige over others than logically purported by the social position, whatever that is.

Others are unlikely to acknowledge they are under the spell of such a prestige which, in some cases, may become great indeed.

Examples: James A. Garfield (Sun's degree); Admiral Ernest Kin (degree of the Point of Equidistance); Arturo Toscanini (degree of the Moon, which, however, already skims over the following degree). Here is the MC of Marshal B. L. Montgomery.

28° Scorpio

A faith ready to stand any test is the keynote of this degree, where the word faith may be taken to mean anything within the limits of the meaning conveyed by such an extensive word. In a good sense, this will be faithfulness to a religious ideal, apt to create perfect human relations. Were it bad faith, this would turn into lasting grudges and ill-will, or into treacherousness in trade; viz., cheating; and it may bring about an accomplice's solidarity and a tendency to stick together in crime.

Certain virtues, however, are sure to be there: scrupulousness, reserve, earnestness and firmness in purpose, consequence in one's views.

Whether honest or dishonest, the native is of an austerity bordering on prudery; he will appear sometimes priggish but always will make a thoroughly spiritual impression. Therefore his trespasses are so much more dangerous, and his crimes so much more intentional.

29° Scorpio

Symbol: An elderly man, draped in the regalia of old universities, sits at a table, a book unfolded before him. On the wall behind, hunting trophies.

Fondness for learning, aptitude for arts, and scientific gifts. A creative and original mind that can reach the height of genius, if the other stars bear this out.

Inner nobility and humane feelings.

A sedentary life on work days, sport in the open on holidays; fondness for hunting, success in shooting at stool (clay) pigeons.

On the whole, good luck, even a very good one, if it did not keep the native waiting too long.

30° Scorpio

Symbol: A very large-headed snake

Wariness, wisdom and skill in the highest measure, which can be sublimated into the cardinal virtue of prudence, and as easily swerve into ignoble cunning, sneaking toadyism, venomous treacherousness.

The native will exert the greatest influence on his neighbors through his mastery of words, which will enable him to hold a nearly irresistible and hypnotic sway over others with the greatest parsimony of sentences. Should other aspects concur, he would have an uncanny knack of shifting any argument onto ground most favorable to himself, and of cunningly turning the debate in such a way as to let the opponents dig their own graves with statements jeopardizing their own case. This would make him highly danger-ous if he were, as he is likely to be, a double-tongued trickster.

Unusually enough, to his gift of gab and to his moral and bodily supple-ness, the native will join a true warlike spirit and other gifts that may stand him in good stead both on the battlefield and in a barracks; he will be able to alternate the use of a stirring word with the display of a combativeness that sometimes can reach heroism, but will oftener make him harshly and aggressively unpleasant to anyone not under the power of his magic spell.

With these gifts, the military and political careers are obvi-ously open.

In spite of all, the gifts mentioned above are capable of subli-mation; one should not forget that this degree stands under the symbol of a snake, whose meaning is well known to the initiates.

Example: General De Gaulle (Sun's degree).

172

SAGITTARIUS

01° Sagittarius

This degree confers an unruly imagination that may run away with the native at times, but it will give him a keen and ready insight as well. He will not avoid trouble, but his scent will be so delicate and his wits so piercing as to enable him to take off at a glance the most entangled situations and to tell accurately truth from falsehood, right from wrong.

Freedom is for him a proud and jealous possession. There will be a sensitive, easy and natural disposition, a simple, somewhat unprejudiced and whimsical spirit.

The greatest danger is a tendency to get into scrapes through association with reckless people. Where other astrological data fit into the picture of a rebellious and knavish character, this may go so far as to mean penal condemnation, even capital sentence as a result of conspiracy and murder, provided that laws warrant capital execution. In charts evidencing that kind of legalized villainy—the birthmark of cops and detectives—there will be obvious risks attending upon such professions. In an honest and law-abiding nativity, danger will derive from other people's light-mindedness (like serious losses, incidents harmful to one's body, etc.).

Anyway, it will be a life of distress and hardships and of such continuous efforts as to tax the endurance of the strongest. There will be a religious sense and a certain philosophic wisdom even in the bobby, lightening the burden of life and suggesting ways of making the best of it.

02° Sagittarius

A warlike and aggressive nature. The native may be as well a romantic *Stummer und Dranger* as a quarrelsome swashbuckler, ever ready to engage in brawls and therefore exposed to the risk of violent death. Anyhow, he cannot put up with the dullness of a humble middle-class life. The unknown calls him, and a craving for wonderful adventures possesses him.

Example: Admiral Ernest King (Sun's degree).

N.B. Compare 05° Virgo (ruler of the Ascendant) and 27° Scorpio (degree of the Point of Equidistance between Sun and Moon).

03° Sagittarius

A self-contradictory character: on one hand gentle and sensitive, on the other mettlesome, combative and even aggressive. His sense of charity and altruism can lead him to the hardest sacrifices that border on absolute self-denial, yet there will be something mean in it. Psychic and sexual fecundity, love of family, home and work; an aptitude for arts, engineering and perhaps architecture, though the skill in planning to the least detail be transferred from the field of material buildings to the one of feelings and induce a petty scheming and plotting mentality.

People may like, love, even adore, the native, but the concourse of other astrological factors will be needed for this.

04° Sagittarius

Symbol: A grated window in a mediaeval manor

The native's warlike and impulsive nature will stay hidden till drawn out and revealed by circumstances apt to produce an outburst of rightful wrath or ambitious fury. Till such time, the native will look like a good-natured man, rich in deep-felt affections but full of reserve; not submissive but unassuming and self-contained;

174

kind, correct in business, sensitive and watchful, with a slight hint of tameness but ready to defend himself.

On the contrary, when the bugle has blown, there he will go, leaping out of his den to do or die, a hero or a villain, violent and ruthless, a real daredevil.

05° Sagittarius

Symbol: A woman in mourning clothes rocks a cradle and sings a lullaby.

A dull voice, apt to induce drowsiness. A melancholic and re-signed nature, perhaps content in her suffering or downright de-lighting in her grief. Lyrical, sentimental but muffled outpourings. Passion for art, aesthetic refinement or fickleness of taste, continu-ous wavering between two opposite artistic tendencies or schools of thought. A humble attachment to one's work and to the hard tasks imposed by fate, a scanty aptitude for life's struggles, sympa-thy for the needy and the undeserving poor, and powerlessness to help them as one would wish; a permanently shilly-shallying and wavering nature.

A lonely and confined life, danger of widowhood. The soul's silence and solitude are broken only by a muffled song "reaching no further than two steps away." (Pascoli, *Imbrunire*, "Dusk").

06° Sagittarius

Symbol: A many-homed ox

An even too soft character. A manifold mind, inventive and resourceful, fond of study and work. But all this will turn to the benefit of other people who will exploit the native's work and will ill-use himself. His destiny is to serve; whether the servant of one or of many masters, whether on duty for his country or subordinate to mankind's interests, neither his life nor his work ever will be in-dependent.

A pun may express this rather well: when the native does not work in the service of others, his work is of no service, of no use: all his efforts for his own sake will stay fruitless. Strangely enough, this seems to suit his boundless vanity, which is nearly ridiculous for a man; he will think of himself only as in a show-window, and all the mental work he reserves for his own personal benefit will only aim to make himself admired. He will not dream of his own independence, or at least he will not think seriously.

Example: Wolfgang Goethe (degree of Pluto, ruler of the Ascendant).

07° Sagittarius

Symbol: An idle woman

An uneventful life. Ambition is absent, patience borders on inertness, inactivity verges on sloth. There is no lack of self-control, but mental habits tend toward a settled and unruffled life interwoven with steady domestic joys and intimate bliss. Barring pointers to the contrary, marriage will be happy, and luck in general will not be too bad.

08° Sagittarius

Symbol: Two men playing dice

Alea jacta est.—Words ascribed to Caesar on crossing the Rubicon

The native will tend to have all his eggs in one basket, and may risk everything on one throw when his very life is at stake. If he wins, success or even glory is his; in case of defeat there is no further chance, as he has burned his bridges. Usually Fortune will smile upon such confidence in her favors, though this will not always be the case.

The nativity taken as a whole must point out whether we are confronted with a great man's deliberately planned gamble, or with a game operator's or betting addict's random shot; we hardly need say that the latter is more frequent. Therefore, unless well aspected elsewhere, the native cannot rely exclusively on the blind Goddess' smile to balance his accounts, and he will risk failure at the slightest wink of ominous stars. He then will have to put up with the lowest jobs and bear the humblest fatigues. Yet even in this case his buoyant cheerfulness will stay untarnished and the faith in his own star unshaken; this loser's mem-ness may even spread around him like wildfire, and he will take a hand-to-mouth existence in his stride, waiting for Fortune's wheel to give another half turn.

Example: Eugene of Savoy (degree of the Ascendant).

09° Sagittarius

Symbol: A blazing pyre

Fire, either in a real sense or in the figurative ones; the fiery element takes a hand here.

Literally it may portend a work connected with fire, or an accident due to the same.

In a figurative but still material sense, it may point to fever, to physical consumption due either to the flame of a too-lively passion or to lack of balance between the rush of a spiritual surge and the body's limits of resistance, or to financial ruin and swift destruction of one's substance.

In a non-material sense, fitful and restless yet aimless activity; enthusiasm or stubbornness, or both together; inspiration or a fanatic's visions; feverish, driftless and fruitless work, scatter-brained eagerness and precocious exhaustion of one's energies; sacrifice of anything else, provided one's ideal—or point of view—carries the day, with exactly the same chances of falling flat.

Burning pains: life's battle will be ablaze with searing fire which, however, will cast its glow on the native's personality. Even if destined to an early death, he will have been prominent and may have chosen such a career as to bring him to the limelight. The career itself, whether literary, political or forensic, will have to be determined by the chart as a whole.

Example: Rudolf Steiner (degree of the Ascendant).

N.B. Remember how the first Goetheanum, all built of wood, was destroyed by fire.

10° Sagittarius

Destiny singles out the native to defeat his competitors and to come off with flying colors in his career. He has the makings of success; a way with people, a manifold and assimilating mind, handiness and skill in general. Should these peaceful gifts not be enough, he will show his claws when the occasion calls for it, and will appear quarrelsome and aggressive. Whether by hook or by crook, he must reach both a renown and a position above his mental powers, which can be a genius', but never will be original. Whether by birthright or by professional earnings, welfare and riches must either accompany him or meet him on his way. This far 10° Sagittarius. Now, what^do the other stars say?

Example: Gustav Adolph, king of Sweden (degree of the Ascendant). The Sun was here when Monroe proclaimed his doctrine.

11° Sagittarius

Symbol: An ape riding a wolf

This degree will favor a military and a political career. It confers all the virtues of a noble and fearless heart and all the vices of a sly, dissembling and unscrupulous mind. The native is glib enough to defend the noblest cause, resorting to the underhand tricks employed to bolster up a forged and exploded cause. Strong favorable aspects would strike off the craftiness, whereas concurrence of evil features may taint the nobility of the cause.

178

The native will win many friends and make many enemies; and his life, after seeing him through many perils, may have a sudden end.

Example: Mahatma Gandhi (degree of the Ascendant).

12° Sagittarius

Only a comprehensive glance, taking in the astrological picture in its entirety, will enable us to judge whether the features of this degree are vices or virtues. There may be love of home or selfish attachment to one's comforts; a faithfulness to habit implying a methodic mind, as well as the utter powerlessness of one chained to his customary routine; a self-containment suggestive of a wealth of pent-up energies or betraying sheer impotence to act.

A strong lover, the native may lavish his affections on his lawful wife, or have many erotic ties at the same time, the only clearly emerging feature being sacrifice of other—however eager—desires to the flesh.

He will be kind and affable with his neighbors. Yet in talking he may display a self-contradiction apt to annoy his interlocutors.

The excess of lust may involve him in all kinds of trouble and may wear precociously his bodily vigor, thereby increasing his congenital slackness.

13° Sagittarius

Ye cannot serve God and Mammon.—Matt. 6:24, Luke 16:13

This degree glaringly denounces the greed of filthy lucre. In order to achieve wealth, the native would gladly tread over his father's corpse (which is hyperbolically expressed but may literally come true, as the native's career may well drip blood, even the gore of mass murder).

But we must not lose sight of the result. Ill-gotten is ill-fated. The wrists of the worshiper of the golden calf risk becoming too well acquainted with shackles or strait jackets. Unless powerful stars come to his help elsewhere, moral decay, bodily contagion or the breakdown of his reason will take the poor wretch to jail, the isolation ward or the lunatic asylum.

14° Sagittarius

Symbol: A master holding an open book in a very untidy but not uncomfortable room

The native will set his shoulder to the wheel in anything he undertakes and will be able to give his intelligence the full support of splendid gifts, though intelligence itself is not specifically bestowed by this degree, which will grant only endurance in mental pursuits and eagerness in learning. This will be crowned by an excellent memory, a creative and harmonious imagination and a fine literary style. Little as other aspects hint at an outstanding mind, the native will emerge as a master in his own line, even a great master. There might be a suggestion of stiffness about him, something dignified and formal which will impair his popularity. But there will be no pettifoggery in him; on the contrary, there will be an outward carelessness and an inward bent to enjoy the robust pleasures of life.

In less developed beings the transcendent features of this degree will produce superstition or witchcraft. Departure from the beaten track may be a cause of unpopularity for the professional writer, which may apply to the non-writers as well.

Examples: Francis I, king of France (degree of the Point of Equidistance); Armando Diaz, Italian commander-in-chief in World War I (degree of the Sun). Compare 09° Taurus, where he has Pluto as ruler of the Ascendant, and read the respective note.

15° Sagittarius

A wild growth of images and a sharp intelligence. The native may be passionately fond of sciences—especially astronomy—and slightly clairvoyant. An even character with a slight touch of laziness.

Still in his prime the native may see all his ambitions satisfied, but he will face disappointment in his riper age if he cannot turn into a steady flow the energy that pushed him forward in leaps and bounds during his youth; one never ought to rely on one's flying start to take him all the way up to his aim.

Example: Gabriele d'Annunzio (Moon's degree).

16° Sagittarius

Symbol: A narrow, dark and deserted blind alley, littered with broken toys.

An evil influence. The native's utter lack of practical skill will prevent him not only from leading anything to completion but even from getting down efficiently to any task. His plans will be made of thin air, his action will bear no other fruit but mistakes and mishaps, misery and ruin.

17° Sagittarius

An original mind and an outstanding personality. There is a great faith in God, a strictly religious mind without taint of puritanism, an open and honest heart, a free and easy temper.

On the reverse side of the shield we find that the native's merriness betrays a childish strain, that his carefree and frolicsome craving for amusement sometimes runs away with him and stops him from doing any real good. His too-marked personality may, in spite of his generosity, isolate him or cut him off altogether from human society.

The native is sensitive to cold and needs warm garments. His life will be long but not prosperous-therefore too long. Some reckless acts may land him in endless trouble. The shakiness of his position will sour his ripe age and bring about an old age of hardships and toil. Abandoned by his neighbors, the native will find no refuge other than prayer. May God lend an ear to his wishes.

18° Sagittarius

Symbol: In full daylight Diogenes, clad in rags, goes around with a lighted lantern. In the background is the cask where he lives.

The native is raving mad and driven to further excesses and absurdities by each of his impulses. He not only loves a rustic and sparing life but goes out of his way on an endless search for self-imposed hardships. He will not work, though he subjects himself to an unceasing and aimless toil. He is wayward rather than original; his planning is but castle-building. He cannot be denied a certain cranky and crotchety genius, but he is thoroughly off balance. A scatterbrained madcap and a dizzy cloud-dweller, he never will be able to get on in this world. He will only rouse a sensation. The failure of his hard efforts may even bring about real madness.

19° Sagittarius

Symbol: A house on a holm whose bushy banks are wrapped in flame

Fondness for boating, a taste for art; a nimble mind and a lazy disposition; a subtle but crooked intelligence, a passionate and touchy character, endless worrying.

The native is crazy about water—not at meals—yet he will have to go through fire. Whether this is to be taken literally or figuratively, whether real fires, war conflagrations or searing moral pains are in store for him must be left to the rest of the horoscope to decide.

At any rate, something will have to be thrown overboard in order for him to escape, and the burns will leave permanent scars.

20° Sagittarius

This degree will grant gifts referring to three different branches of life: society, art, and medicine. The word society must be taken in its widest sense. The native will be as sociable, cordial and merry as anyone else; he seems bound to win many friends, to enter lucky business associations with many of his acquaintances and to have a crowd of admirers. He takes passionately to social problems and joins political propaganda and party struggle with the zeal distinctive of scholars and the fieriness of a partisan, sometimes with a sectarian's stubborn cantankerousness.

For art he has good taste, perhaps artistic and decorative gifts; certainly a love of beauty. Nor are his gifts for medicine negligible.

This native is surely a tireless and manifold person. The whole of the horoscope will point to the activity he must choose, though the three do not exclude each other, as the medical scholar may write treatises going down to posterity as masterpieces of art, the artist may choose subjects with a sociological background, whereas the sociologist may have to delve deeply into problems of sanitation and health.

The whole of the theme may indicate also whether there will be genius or amateurish shallowness, a manifold mastermind or a brilliant dabbling, thoughtless zeal or fruitful activity.

Examples: Gustave Flaubert (Sun's degree); Karl Marx (degree of Uranus, ruler of the Ascendant).

21° Sagittarius

Symbol: The six-pointed star, or David's seal

In a certain sense, David's seal is synonymous with the Cross, as both represent the divine order, the cosmic balance of the four contrasting elements. Apart from this the two Symbols differ: The Cross—and it only—representing Our Lord's passion, and David's seal picturing in the most dramatic way the endless dualism of matter against spirit.

This two hundred sixty-first degree clearly attunes the contrasting forces of man's upper and lower being; it gives self-mastery—a balance between spirit and matter. Any balance may be dynamic or static; whether the former or the latter is to be realized here is up to the whole horoscope to tell.

If there are pointers of initiative, decision and liveliness elsewhere, we may conclude that the native can admirably exploit the uncommon energy God has granted him; he will thirst for truth and justice, and his judgment, his self-possession, his wisdom may make him into a Guide for mankind and he may well become an Initiate.

On the contrary, should other aspects in his chart show a resigned, dull, unpractical mind, the influence of this twenty-first degree of Sagittarius then would turn to harm insofar as it enhances the native's irresoluteness and renders him suspicious of all and everyone.

22° Sagittarius

Symbol: Two men engaged in a deadly fight

Here is the perfect embodiment of stubborn and relentless dissension; should other aspects fail to soothe this influence, the native would be an unmitigated faultfinder. To listen to him, current public opinion is nonsense (and there is something in this); the established order is unjust and absurd—nay, this is the worst possible world (which is slightly exaggerated); whatever idea is conceived by others can be but worthless trash, if by no other reason, because it crossed someone else's mind and must be condemned without trial. Here the native's spirit of wanton denial reaches the freakish height of its childish hideousness.

At the bottom of all this there is an unavowed thirst for applause and a total lack of the constructive gifts leading to recognition; the native must therefore fully exploit the only weapon still at his disposal-applause of his critical thrusts against other people's buildings. He will tirelessly throw stones at others, polemicize, heckle and run down their works. Still, when milder stars do not interfere, he will be in for quarrels, brawls, squabbles, lawsuits for libel, well-deserved boxes on the ears and duels, which will be his dally task. Death on the dueling ground cannot be ruled out.

We spoke of the politician. Should the native not be one, I should be at a loss what other profession to advise. A look at the whole may help in any event. Where this shows evil moral features, theft and murder must be feared, or death in a scuffle or on the gallows.

23° Sagittarius

Symbol: Mortal row between two women

Blind and impulsive passionality, cruel disappointments, frenzied jealousy, danger of murder committed in hot blood where the native easily could be the victim if other astrological factors consistently point at lack of violence and portend murder at the hands of a man. The native woman would nearly always be wrong in confiding in someone and is invariably wrong when she is in love. Lack of return will stow a bitter resentment in her soul, which may find its outlet in bloodshed or turn into sour misanthropy. In a man's activity these and other omens may refer to him or to his woman.

This degree carries the mark of jealousy and excessive suspicion. Jealousy means mistrust of everyone and everything, hidden watching, stealthily rummaging the beloved one's papers, spying and lying in ambush to follow with the eyes from afar, taking other people into one's confidence and ending in being double-crossed by them, torturing one's beloved and especially oneself.

Heart ailments are not unlikely. If not the mind, the nerves are certainly unhinged.

Example: The supersensitive planet Lilith was in this degree when, on July 14, 1949, the nationalistic *coup d'etat* executed the Syrian government.

24° Sagittarius

Symbol: Suicide

A gloomy spirit obsessed by the idea of death. The symbolic image may come true literally or metaphorically, or both together. Anyway, life will be short arid dreary, death sudden and perhaps violent; but the native himself is responsible for—if not the author of—his own mishaps. His ambitions are wrong, preposterous or fruitless. He cannot win friends and establish business connections. His life will be marked by a quick succession of accidents.

The symbol also may mean departure without return, like emigration, relinquishment of an entire world, etc., or more simply, faraway travels and even gain through foreign trade but. in this latter case, income will be desultory and uncertain.

25° Sagittarius

Misuse of pleasures, of mental activity and of manual work; a freakish coexistence of the loftiest longings with a glutton's dreams. Intoxication of the mind, alcoholic drunkenness, an orgiastic temper in everything and the attending danger of bodily or mental fuddle.

Hard ordeals are ahead. If the native knew moderation and could rhythmically alternate work and rest, pleasure and duty, success would be within reach.

26° Sagittarius

Kindness, faith, trustworthiness in friendships, a helpful,

merry and playful nature, attractive manners, a likable personality.

The body will be light and nimble, the movements supple and precise; there will be skill in handling weapons and a sense of rhythm. The native is one of those few people who can use their hands and can above all imitate their neighbors and counterfeit them strikingly. Should the rest of the pattern support this, there would be great scenic gifts—whether tragic or comic, will have to be decided by other features.

A bad nativity may pervert art into mummery and the harmless jokes into dirty tricks. The nimble person, mastering his own body with matchless skill, may turn into a clown or be warped into a quicksilver. Anyhow, it ought to be borne in mind that a soul nobler and deeper than expected hides behind those outward striking and likable features. Few will notice it.

Example: Mary Stuart (Sun's degree).

27° Sagittarius

Should other stars support this, the native would be a man whose mind and activities stand out for all to admire, but he would be morally poor unless other aspects greatly improve this point. The native does not know what he is driving at, has no moral backbone and cannot stand upright under destiny's blows; he is, in a word, characterless, and on top of this seems to have his hands bound for one reason or another.

His speech will be persuasive, his nature sociable, likable, attractive, even charming; he will be irresistible in love. If you add to all this a mastermind, genius, the peak of greatness and glory is sure to be reached, even through stumbles, wanderings and waverings. But the position thus reached will not be stable and safe, as the envious will refuse to lay down their arms—nay, will never feel secure till they have thrown into disgrace or ruined the native who will, therefore, have to be cautious in things political.

Sudden death may sever the thread of career and work at their climax. Examples: Gustav Adolf of Sweden (Sun's degree); Percy Bysse Shelley (degree of the Ascendant); Arturo Toscanini (degree of the Ascendant). In Jerome Cardan's nativity cast by Morin de Villefranche, according to the Rudolphian tables, the native's Point of Equidistance is in this degree.

28° Sagittarius

The very embodiment of patience; slow but stubborn and tireless, the native will get on thanks to his steadfastness. A silent, close, somewhat bent and precociously aging being, he has something tragic about himself as tragical will be the ordeals and even the slights he will bear without batting an eye.

In spite of his hardships and of the burdens laid on his shoulders, notwithstanding the crushing weight of a huge task to fulfill and the attempts to check his progress on his opponents' side, he seems destined to success.

I said he seems, not he is, as a sudden death, perhaps a violent one, may snap his career. Will this mean his own death, or death of a protector or an inspirer? The answer is to be sought elsewhere in the nativity.

29° Sagittarius

Physical fitness, skill in scientific work, love for precision, muscular ruggedness and moral uprightness; psychological insight and a talent for physiology, surgery and medical sciences at large.

Unfortunately these gifts are spoiled by lack of courage of one's own opinion. Not that the native is a coward, but he is surely a sluggard. He is particularly timid, even morbidly so; morosely mistrustful and constantly on the alert.

He has no poise, no pivot. His very honesty, straightness and intuition are not those of a wise, sound and experienced human being. On the contrary, they bear dreadfully naive and childish marks. Restless, and as reckless as the timid usually are, the native may easily head for a fall, and some mental or bodily illness may lame him for years. Nevertheless, if favorably aspected elsewhere, he may expect a measure of luck, but the whole of the chart must be referred to for the exact balance between bad and good luck.

A peculiar feature is his fondness for a soft and snug bed with sheets of fine linen.

30° Sagittarius

The native is a misfit in his times. He may discover some of the most jealously guarded secrets of nature and be a forerunner of times to come; and may as well bring again to the light things long forgotten and buried, thus reviving the past. Whether the former or the latter, he has a mission to fulfill and possesses the force of character and the sharpness of mind life demands of him. A naturalist or a mining engineer, a pioneer, an archaeologist or whatever he is, he is born to discover, to innovate, and to be misunderstood and bitterly fought. He will have to suffer but will be able to overrule the intrusive advice of the zealous. Should the other aspects not rule out a measure of luck. he may well end by carrying the day.

Example: Benjamin Disraeli, Earl of Beaconsfield (Sun's degree).

CAPRICORN

01 ° Capricorn

Symbol: A couple of twins

This degree is in partial contrast with this whole sign's influence as it tends to weaken, if not entirely to blot out Capricorn's main features-that outer isolation and that inner feeling of seclusion from the rest of mankind.

The native's essential trait is a close tie to another human being, possibly neither a lawful nor an unlawful marriage partner; the whole of the pattern will have to specify which kind of bond this is. All suppositions are admitted; the subject may have a twin brother or sister (the extreme case being Siamese twins) and that may have a decisive bearing on his or her existence; he may have a kind of spiritual brother or brotherly twin ray, as the legend has it of Orestes and Pylades. In a thief's pattern, this influence will tend to establish a criminal partnership to be dissolved only by the gallows; in a degenerate's pattern there may be a homosexual tie of durable character.

In all of these cases the answers to such questions as whether there is any reciprocal affection, which of the two brothers is the other's succuba, are to be sought elsewhere.

Other features: a great—nay, exceptional—versatility for a Capricornian, a certain intellectual merriness wiping out altogether or dimming the sign of the rampart's usual rampaging character; a diplomatic gift easily perverted into double-dealing and treachery, which can, however, lead very far either in an ambassador's or in a consul's career, or in that of a trade commissioner, or in cultural exchanges.

The typical self-assurance of Capricorn is stronger than ever in this first degree; the faith in oneself and in one's cause is driven to its utmost.

02° Capricorn

Symbol: A weather cock on top of an old steeple

The lack of character, of constancy, of steadiness, perhaps of resolution, are this native's heel of Achilles, who would otherwise hold the best trumps to win at the gambling table of earthly life.

He never will be at his wits' end; he will be rich in initiative, will guess the right angle of each problem, will have a penetrating mind and possibly a gift for architecture. In his thirst for sublime things he harbors a deep respect for everything sacred and ancient. Yet his intellectual powers risk fruitlessness in spite of the most strenuous efforts, as these will be inconsequent and jerky.

03° Capricorn

Symbol: The copper snake raised by Moses (Num. 21:6-9).

Whoever knows the secret meaning of the word snake will be able to adduce from the Symbol itself the occult possibilities of this influence. Even outside the sphere of the supernatural, the native is heir to an exceptional force and ascendancy. He is brimming over with vitality, will valiantly withstand attacks of both enemies and illnesses, and will show an outstanding faculty of recoupment after repelling the assaults of fellow beings or of bad health. He is wary, wise, possessed of extensive and deep knowledge, of a subtle mind, of an immediate intuition of truth and of the ability to strike successfully with lightning-like timeliness.

Should the pattern at large point to a perversion of those gifts, we might be confronted with a nearly morbid distrust and a nearly complete lack of dignity and sincerity. Driven to the limit, this would mean perjury and treason promoted to life rule.

Many careers are open: natural sciences (especially medicine), arts, and literature; diplomacy and politics in general. A long life and nearly certain success may be expected unless other threads in the pattern point to the contrary.

Example: Henry IV, king of France and Navarre (degree of the Sun).

04° Capricorn

Symbol: A decorative design representing either a couple of combs or of rakes

A mind endowed with exceptional discrimination or insight. Cleanliness and accuracy. In all the rest, a two-edged influence.

A strong will power, focused by the native with the help of all his resources, exactly on the aim to reach, saves him a useless waste of energy in the pursuit of glory. The sign does not tell us, however, exactly where this aim will be set; the native has a fine sense of beauty which may work in any of the following ways:

His love may be bent toward sensuous beauty, or may lead his gaze to rest placidly on nature as grown and tended by man's care, so as to bear his dominical imprint, as in cultivated parks, grounds, villas, and fountains; the subject may be a worshiper of art for art's sake, or may toy pointlessly with the shallowest vanity of outward elegance. His will power may be focused toward good as well as toward evil. In extreme cases, we shall have on one side the great initiate, or on the other the arch-criminal, the organizer of black masses and orgies reserved to a very select circle of refined addicts; or we may have the gambler or the rake.

05° Capricorn

Symbol: Two open doors

It is a degree of hospitality; home and heart are open to all. A jovial character, a generous and unassuming nature, marred by imprudence in word and action.

The native's lack of reserve will give fuel to other people's slander and, coupled with his sometimes reckless hospitality, will lead to material theft and plagiarism of ideas. The native will look upon all this with unheeding light-headedness or at least excessive leniency. He is conscious of his productive—nay, creative—power and does not pay too much attention to the earth's material wealth or moral misery. He is independent or, at any rate, self-sufficient by nature and tends to tolerate his neighbors' failings and to neglect their vices in order to focus his whole attention on his own inner world and to enjoy the work of his own mind.

06° Capricorn

Symbol: A shepherd sits among his sheep and dogs,
while a wolf lurks in the background.

Either a good shepherd or a wolf; either somebody who is as innocent as a lamb and as faithful as a dog, an affectionate, confident being, ready to sacrifice himself for those he loves and to be disappointed by them in the end, or somebody driving his cunning and cold-blooded ferocity to such a length as to sacrifice everything to his own selfishness. The stars will have to point which of the two Symbolic figures is to come true; they even may co-exist in actuality.

Shyness does not mean cowardice; a lamb's disposition does not bar courage and, on the other hand, a wolfs nature clearly bears it out. On the other, hand, there is an extraordinary power of psychic concentration. Therefore, unless unfavorably aspected elsewhere, success ought not to fail the native, who could even become a pastor of peoples if Jupiter and the Sun are well posited.

Examples: Tamerlane, emperor of the Mongols (degree of the Ascendant); Louis Pasteur (Sun's degree).

N.B. The native's surname seems to be unaccountably—but not through accidental coincidence (there is no such thing as accidental coincidence for an occultist)—connected with the image in the symbol. In some families certain astrological factors are hereditary, and the surname is a constant reminder of them. It may be noted further how the scientist's fate brought him again in touch with dogs and wolves, and herds' milk, all shown in the symbol, as Louis Pasteur's greatest glory lies in the discovery of the treatment of rabies, as his name is constantly mentioned on milk bottle labels. His link with herds is especially apparent through the clamorous Arbois "flocks challenge," his first official victory.

07° Capricorn

Symbol: The Sphinx

Seer Charubel gives the labyrinth as a symbol, which is as good an image. The whole of the sign Capricorn is in fact a labyrinth, of which this degree especially stresses such scientific and engineering skill as to be really worthy of Daedalus, and drives to their utmost its defects of puzzling and selfish secretiveness.

A labyrinth: Will the native be its maker or its victim? Or, like Daedalus, both at the same time? A Sphinx: Is the riddle in the native's self, or waylaying him at a bend of the road he is to travel? And will the riddle be of a material, intellectual or spiritual nature? Will there be political, or feminine, intrigue?

The Sphinx would rather not be asked questions. She is to ask them herself. As usual, the whole of the nativity will have to help formulate the answer.

If woman, the native would likely be a crack at the game of holding more than one suitor at a time by his heartstrings, twisting them around her little finger, and exasperating the jealousy, the male vanity and the curiosity of each in turn. She is whimsical but sparkling with wit; scheming but frolicsome. Many a man whom his fellows respect or fear will fall into her snares. Some, driven crazy with jealousy, may risk their lives at this game, some may lose their reason or their freedom.

Should the native be a man, and he be involved in political intrigue, there is sure to be a woman somewhere. The native may fly high or land in jail, may be exiled or die a tragic death. It is the end that counts.

But the man is not by all means to be an Oedipus, nor is the woman, whether a winner or a loser, to be a sphinx. The riddle may belong to the domain of science, and the sphinx watch the secrets of the physical world or the threshold of the world beyond. I shall not tire of repeating that only the chart in its entirety can supply the key, as the parts fit into a whole, but the whole gives them a background and a meaning.

Example: Albert of Waldstein, popularly known as Wallenstein (Moon's degree). If the registrar's data are correct, Hitler's Moon ought to be here as well.

N.B. Kepler cast his famous horoscope of Wallenstein assuming the birth hour to be 16:30 real time, and placed the Ascendant at 10° Aquarius and the Moon at 07°03' Capricorn. I suppose that Wallenstein was born a little earlier and I place his Ascendant in Capricorn and the Moon within the Seventh. Whoever disagrees may skip this.

08° Capricorn

Noble in nature and mind, full of self-respect or self-conceit, but content with, little; apt to let his fantasy run away with him into the realm of wild dreams, but endowed with endurance and horse sense; peaceful but fond of hunting; the native inclines toward a misanthropic pessimism getting more and more acute as the years go by and letting the events of his earthly life look drab and boring to him. Anyone else would consider them breath-taking.

196

Example: Emperor Charles V (Moon's degree); Woodrow Wilson (Sun's degree).

09° Capricorn

Symbol: Via Crucis

But rather seek ye the Kingdom of God, and all these things shall be added unto you.—Luke 12:31

In a spiritual nativity this degree could carry a very high reward for the native's sacrifices. These will be superhuman, and the prize not of this world. Down here this prize will take the same shape as it took in Solomon's case: wisdom, as this degree by itself will not grant any earthly happiness.

If the horoscope therefore—far from conferring spiritual gifts or spurring toward lofty goals—grants only a craving for earthly pleasures, the native could reap only unhappiness therefrom, even the more so as his oversensitiveness will dramatize every failure into a tragedy. Even in the sexual field he or she may be struck with impotence (if only momentarily owing to excessive sensitivity, the so-called lover's impotence); but apart from this, danger of collapsing under the cross and being unable to go on is an ever present one.

The virtues here are a great humility before God and a dignified reserve before the. world. The native ought to face and bear his karma with quiet courage, without trying to dodge it, as he would only risk losing his reputation.

Example: Rudyard Kipling (Sun's degree).

N.B. Remember the famous poem "If."

10° Capricorn

The native is wise and learned, oversensitive, melancholy or pessimistic, sometimes gloomy, but always self-possessed, fair and lord-like; a defender of the week, but watchful and wary. He is a keen hunter and, like all true sportsmen, very fond of the game he kills. He may be an occultist, perhaps a seer; certainly a pursuer of studies too profound to be accessible to the middle class.

Nighttime dangers are to be taken into account, deriving perhaps from magic.

Examples: Prince Bismarck (Moon's degree); John Pascoli (Sun's degree); Sir Richard Quain, famous anatomist (degree of the Point of Equidistance); Victor Emmanuel III, king of Italy during the whole of the first decade of this century (degree of Saturn, ruler of the Ascendant).

11° Capricorn

Symbol: A king wearing the crown and seated on the throne receives an envelope from a messenger or an ambassador.

This influence will help those aspiring to power, to a position of high political authority, to a diplomatic career or any position at court, whether high or low.

On one side, all the moral or immoral traits required are at hand, such as secrecy, reserve, cautiousness, world wisdom, cunning, diplomacy and, if needed, double-dealing. On the other hand, there will be the favor of high-placed, or even top-flight people, whose importance and the brilliance of the native's career will be determined by the rest of the chart. This applies to the measure in which those virtues or vices will come to light as well.

A minor feature of this influence is fondness for horsemanship. In the middle ages, squires, esquires, marshals and the like must have been born in this degree.

Example: Lloyd George (degree of the Point of Equidistance).

12° Capricorn

A knack of getting work done with a lively and nimble rhythm, without a hint of routine, but with a harmonious sense of time and space; a brisk activity, a springy energy closely adhering to things.

A great—perhaps excessive—reserve. There is a depth of feeling tinged with melancholy. The native loves life in the open, is fond of trees, worships the quiet of the countryside, adores walking across the moonlit fields. Though unaware of it, a dash of gentle blood may run in his veins.

On the reverse side of the shield, if blighted by pointers of unfairness elsewhere, that realism may induce unscrupulousness, those deft hands may become crafty, in plain words, slick and thievish. The man's rhythmic insertion in time and space then may become skill of getting within an inch of trespassing and into close shaves with penal law. Neither do those romantic feelings bar lustful-ness, and that reserve may be warped into sharing crime in secrecy and putting up a poker face before justice. Even cruel people—such are human nature's contradictions—may be born under this degree.

The risks the native is up against range from voluntary exile, meant to foil justice, till flight and attempted evasion and even till jail. The Vatican's thunderbolt—excommunication—may be in the offing as well. Another peril, threatening even a straightforward commoner (especially if stressed by other stars) would be losing one's inheritance at the hands of a usurper. The native may even fail to know his own birthright.

13° Capricorn

Symbol: A Tartarian archer drawing an incendiary arrow

A thirst for absolute power; a tireless and sleepless activity; a tendency to burn one's bridges behind oneself.

An heroic courage, which is never an end in itself, as all energies are subordinate to the aim in sight. Such a character is ready to go to any lengths in order to secure his aim. He will draw the line at no extremities, never withdraw before personal danger, even impassively watch bloodshed, refraining, however, from flinging himself into useless risks. In spite of what the victims of his boundless ambition may think, he is not bloodthirsty by temperament as, on the contrary, he has a keen sense of honor, but is driven and burned by an even keener thirst for superhuman honors.

Chaste, or at least sober, in his enjoyments, fond of art, perhaps a proficient scientist, the^native seems born to destroy rather than to build. As an archaeologist, either in Europe or in the Far East, he will plunder the picturesque and venerable ruins of ancient cultures to amass their spoils in the dusty, sleepy and already laden shelves of museums. If a diplomat, he will serve his own thirst for power rather than his own country; if a chief, he will love the people as the rider loves his horse.

The fullest measure of success will crown such an ambition provided the native knows where to stop.

Example: Napoleon I (degree of Pluto, ruler of the Ascendant).

14° Capricorn

Symbol: A gardener tidies and trims a splendid park which has lain abandoned for years; uprooting the weeds, pruning the withered or blighted twigs, felling decayed trees and the like.

Here we are confronted with a first-rate critic and polemicist, a revolutionary innovator. He is not of necessity to be a politician or a journalist; whatever field of action he chooses, the native will fight a successful battle and end by disposing of the mentality his circle had inherited from the previous generation as a useless burden.

In this light he will be helped by an inborn irony which will at times take up a tinge of humor, at times acquire the edge of cruel sarcasm against the opponents of the idea he stands for. A past master in the art of unmasking other people's hypocrisy, he will ruthlessly lay bare the most hidden recesses of human mentality, but will spare the populace's superstition rather than the smart set's prejudices. His crude realism does not in the least exclude sincere devotion to an ideal. He may even be an artist; landscape painting exerts a special fascination over him.

Such a fighter will seldom become universally liked, but he will be admired and he certainly will be feared. The most congenial professions are medicine (neurology or psychiatry) and ethnology.

Example: Hirohito, emperor of Japan (degree of Jupiter, ruler of the Ascendant).

15° Capricorn

A degree whose nature is hard to define, as it can bring either good or bad luck, both peace and strife. I should be tempted to say that everything depends on the native. This much can be said anyhow: there is a lot the subject can do, but it will be no easy task.

A man worthy of the name will not stoop to the tactics of a despised enemy; the foes here are overbearing and sly and draw the line at no weapon.

Personally the native may well count his blessings; he can make himself very much liked; if he only wants, his inborn nobility and sweetness of manners may win him many sincere friends; his intelligence is open to truth, and the seeds of hope and faith in God lie deep in his soul. The native must surrender himself entirely into His hands to get the necessary protection and justice. Should other components bar faith, let him then rely on the measure of protection that the powers that be go out of their way to grant him. He must not let human wickedness intimidate him, but he must keep his eyes wide open and be watchful and firm. Let him be above provocation and not stoop to squabble with those unworthy of him.

On the contrary, should he prefer to react violently in word or action, or to oppose cunning with cunning, he would only incur the dislike of those who otherwise would have been willing to protect him; but he never will be able to outsmart or to overpower his despicable opponents.

16° Capricorn

Symbol: A man riding a reinless horse

The symbol is divalent. It may imply that the rider control the horse without the help of material means, acting, as it were, magically through sheer will power; and it may mean as well that this soul is carried off by a subhuman energy over which consciousness has no power. The horse is usually taken to mean the three lower vehicles of man, and the vehicle *par excellence* is certainly the physical body, its unbridledness being a transparent token of unleashed lustfulness.

One may wonder how the two divergent constructions can be brought to an agreement, but this is hardly necessary as the stars will leave place for only one. Moreover, one and the same person is not at all unlikely to hold an irresistible sway over others while at the same time being ruled and led by lust. The answer, as usual, must be sought in the whole of the chart.

Should the pattern be generally good, grant a strong character without barring good luck, and show favorable aspects of Jupiter and the Sun, the way then would be open to highest distinctions for the native.

At the outside, this degree would produce the Master, the man of God, the Great Initiate, the Anointed One. In any event, there will be independence, faraway travels, and such features as to make life appear like a novel to others.

In unlucky themes, great undertakings imply dangers corresponding to the daring; short of a lightning-like intuition, luck, or the support of long experience any enterprise will come to grief. Where other pointers of sensuality concur, there will be a carefree epicureanism forgetful of the morrow; concurrence of sportsmanship will lead to horse racing or riding.

Example: Woodrow Wilson (degree of the Point of Equidistance).

17° Capricorn

Symbol: A dog-headed man

A barking dog won't bite.

A very human character, showing all the higher features of its animal part. The native's dog-like, all-out fidelity will be put to many a severe test. He will have a grumbling, growling, quarrelsome, nearly always harmless spirit; at the same time, the friend of mankind's docility and admirable reasonableness. The temperament will bear the marks of the utmost decision, but of steadiness as well, and the intelligence will be above the native's rank.

Hallmark of this humane mind will be the most persuasive eloquence, a cogent logic, a suggestive expression, an artistic if not poetic style, a well-pitched voice and an inborn musicality.

Such a gift for music and poetry could make the native into a true artist if an excessive accuracy of detail does not pinion the wings of inspiration; his exactitude will be driven to the limit of punctiliousness. The native will have a craze for analysis. Astrology and instruments of precision, and any work he does will bear the marks of such a tendency. In art, therefore, he may go so far as to become a faithful and likable executor, but hardly a creator.

Outside the artistic field he may well become the herald of new scientific doctrines or philosophical systems, which, however, must be borne out by the rest of the horoscope.

Luck may smile upon him more as regards associations than affections. He may be successful at the bar, in diplomacy or politics.

18° Capricorn

This is hardly a good influence, and little as unfavorable stars concur, it may prove altogether evil. Its redeeming features may be its utter refinement (provided it does not become warped into ostentation or even worse) and that minor gift of the mind-promptness.

The other features, good as they may appear, are all negative. The native will dare public opinion, but without deriving from this eighteenth degree of Capricorn a sufficiently good reason to do so; viz., that independence of thought and character which confers upon a man worthy of the name the right and the duty to rebel against society's idolized fallacies and organized wrongdoing.

Here is no trace of courage, but an aggrieving and cowardly effrontery. There is no independence, rather a peevish tendency to be at cross purposes with one's interlocutors, sheepishly sponsoring the diametrically opposed point of view even if blatantly wrong. A blustering and chicken-hearted liar, erratic and stubborn, he will waste time and money on arbitrage, gambling and racing, shirking work with all possible means.

He may become a croupier or a bookmaker if favorable aspects concur. Should the stars endow the native with political opportunism as well (which does not exclude contrariness in other fields at all), he may prove a perfect *agent provocateur* or, even better, a regular Vicar of Bray, a champion of that political double-dealing which the Italians practice with such gusto.

19° Capricorn

Symbols: (1) Mucius Scaevola in Porsena's tent. (2) In the night of August 31, 1706, while the French break into the underground of the Turin buttresses, Pietro Micca sets the powder afire which will blow up both parties together.

Squareset and steady in front of fortunes blows.—Dante, *Par.* 17, 24

The native's defect is a tendency to speak or to act out of turn in whatever he chooses to do. Other contrasting factors, will power, and suitable training may well blunt this edge, though they are unlikely to knock it off altogether. The native will dash forward when it would be wisest to stay put; much oftener he will rather bide his time when the occasion calls for action.

His virtues are as firm as a rock; an unshakeable courage which may become real heroism at times; an absolute autonomy and a deep self-reliance. Very original and endowed with a sense of truth that seldom fails him, the native; knows what he is driving at and does not lay too great a store by what others choose to think; should the tide happen to flow the same way he is going, he may find himself having the lead; should the waters ebb the opposite direction, he would be ready to stand their rush, even to fight against it with unruffled coolness. A victor, he will not misuse victory. To break him, a foe will have to deal him an unexpected and smashing blow, as he is easier to annihilate than to conquer.

Apart from life's struggle, explosions and collapses are materially to be feared. The native may own a mine or have to work in one.

Example: Admiral Stepan Makarov, whose ship was blown up by a mine in the Russo-Japanese war (Sun's degree).

20° Capricorn

Symbol: A monkey and a mirror

A very versatile but altogether unoriginal mind; mimetic faculties may come to light as a merely perfunctory assimilation of foreign doctrines, or in the arts of dance, pantomime and burlesque.

A nimble body and graceful ease of movement. Adaptation to the most different environments and points of view comes to such a character and, unfortunately, to such a conscience as a matter of course. Yet the native remains an insufferable crank. Physical vanity will be bottomless and, in a woman, will go hand-in-hand with a wanton coquettishness. Where other factors help, there may be good taste in dressing, and the native may turn into something of a fop or a Beau Brummel, as the case may be.

As to money, the fruit of his labor will be belated, even if he works hard; whereas he seems to be in for luck in love.

21° Capricorn

Symbol: A master holds open between his hands an ancient book in Hebrew characters.

Profound studies, a really great knowledge. Chemistry seems the most congenial line. A supple and manifold mind which can be kept at more than one work at a time; an original intelligence apt to revive—if helped by favorable stars—currents of ancient lore, or to create fresh theories and to found new schools of thought. In this case success will exceed all hopes, but in any other case the native's mighty work will serve the needs of progressing mankind more than his own personal interests.

With the concurrence of suitable components, this degree may purport initiation, alchemy rather than chemistry, the Great Work more than great works; in other words, will produce a master rather than a teacher.

22° Capricorn

Symbol: A man engaged in deep spade work

This image can be taken both literally and metaphorically. In the former sense it will point to a heavy, steady, drudging work; obviously this work will in all likelihood be mining, digging up archaeological remains, and the like.

The latter construction of the symbol would by no means bar the former. It points to a sharp and piercing mind, to a profound spirit, eager to pry into the unknown, and perhaps to a fondness for mystery. According to the different temperaments, there can be a religious sense bent on the esoteric, the study of abstruse sciences like archaeology, dead languages, paleontology; or a strange, undecipherable, hermetic temperament.

At any rate, either with his brawn or with his brain, the native will have to work hard; will be patient rather than stubborn, or vice versa, as the other factors purport. As to his tools, he will be an extremist in either sense, will either put up with the roughest, nearly antediluvian, equipment, or will exact the most up-to-date outfit modern technique has evolved.

The obstacles to clear will be great, but he will face them courageously, and luck will smile upon such strength of character and such unflinching will.

Example: Russia (Sun's degree and the Midheaven).

N.B. The movement of equinoctial precession has taken Russia's meridian from Capricorn into Aquarius (now seventh).

The shift from the one to the following sign roughly tallies with John the Great's advent to the throne in 1462.

23° Capricorn

Symbol: Two people of different sex dine alone at a luxuriously laid table. The room is lit by a profusion of tapers. There is a sacred image on the wall.

Recourse was had to Law as a control. A King was chosen, who could steer the course of realm, his gaze fixed on a holy goal.—Dante, *Purg.* 16, 94-96

A bright but rash mind, an utterly jolly temper, on the main more or less forgetful of the boundaries set by thrift, law or custom, not of those set by manners; a hospitable, generous and winning nature, but reckless and inordinate in love matters. Sentimental entanglements can bring trouble or worse; lavishness, extravagance, foregone conclusions and overhasty decisions can produce financial losses, failures, even complete breakdown should the stars be particularly evil. Overindulgence in food and drink are not unlikely. A leading hand, wise and firm, seems nearly indispensable.

Earthly affections may sublimate into God's love and Christian charity; where other factors point the same way, the native may become an ascetic, even a saint but, too often, earthly and holy love will co-exist side by side and will induce a typical Freudian complex of sensual mysticism. Should the horoscope as a whole point to neuropathy, erotomania or the like will be the result.

Charubel maintains that if the Sun is southeast of the pattern, trouble will be limited to the former half of life. He goes on to say that the physique will be of a sanguine temperament, which reminds me of an old distich I heard attributed to the Salemtian school, though I cannot guarantee its authenticity:

Pallide virgo cupit, rubicunda dat, alba recusat; sed tota in Venerem nigra puella ruit.

Example: Marshal de Richelieu (see Ascendant of 24° Pisces and accompanying note).

24° Capricorn

Symbol: A potter's wheel

What one may incline to call a head. An eminently constructive brain, an intelligence open to truth and at the same time bent on things of practical use ;a mind where, in spite of its manifold gifts, tidiness and order prevail. A leaning toward medicine, applied or pure, toward chemistry, physics, engineering, arts and crafts, for trade at large and the purchase and sale of wine and oil.

Self-mastery, character, straightforwardness. The native is as good as his word, sturdy, unfaltering; as most sincere and open-hearted people, he lacks diplomacy and abhors what he cannot see through; he will break, not bend. Therefore, the earthen pot ought not to enter competition with pots of iron.

A plebeian temperament; simple tastes, sound instincts, heady passions, though curbed by will power, a leaning for the people, though the native strives to reach higher and higher to make headway.

Either literally or metaphorically, the native may run the risk of drowning (in a stream or in debts); the chart as a whole will have to tell in which of the two senses the omen can be taken.

One ought to bear in mind that the wheel is also whimsical Goddess Fortune's tool.

Example: Woodrow Wilson (Moon's degree).

25° Capricorn

Symbol: A fair lady riding and holdings gerfalcon on her fist

The native reaps where others have sown. An unquestionably gentle and demonstrative but fickle and shallow person, given over to fun and enjoyment, and fond of frills and frolics, the native will be but an amateur in everything; yet, barring a sudden accident, she will have luck on her side.

Unless, as I said above, a sudden accident hits her; the position of Uranus in the pattern has to be considered.

Example: Marshal de Richelieu (degree of Saturn, ruler of the Ascendant). (Compare 24° Pisces and the appended note.)

N.B. Mars was exalted in this degree when Great Britain and France declared war on Hitler's Reich. Uranus was depressed but in a trigonal position with Mars; Neptune was in exile but in a trigonal position with both. It would lead us too far to follow all the mental associations arising from this.

26° Capricorn

Symbol: A tropical forest

A rich nature, sweet when in a good mood, becomes stormy and cruel when aroused. The native would rather have peace but prizes his freedom above anything else, and it would be foolish to think of taking it from him. Perhaps the same cannot be said of the freedom of others, as the native seems rather meddlesome.

There is a great fondness for nature, travel, and things out-landish. A musing mind, tending to delve deep into thought, able to rise to genius with the help of other factors.

A pitfall of such a nature lies in its rank,, luxuriant, unruly un-dergrowth, in its lower impulses bent on lust and thirsting for stim-ulants if not for dope. Should the native yield to this, there would be no stopping him, and the way to any kind of perversion would be open.

27° Capricorn

The native is a kind of good-natured curmudgeon or gold-hearted savage, a strong, rugged, rather awkward and bearish being, remarkable for the ups and downs of his temper, as well as for his kind soul.

Fit as he is, he may take to sports and games, but the most con-genial work will be tilling the soil or running farmed country, steering clear of those intrigues of society his straight and open character abhors. He may be weak in front of human wickedness, but is certainly naive, often skittish, never thoroughly polished, much as those in charge of his breeding may have done.

Where this omen is not offset by other influences, harm or ac-cidents in travel are to be feared. One hardly need say that he is as fond of nature as he is shy of human crowds.

Example: Lloyd George (Sun's degree).

N.B. Once more the Example shows how one single feature can get its full meaning only when connected to the whole. Lloyd George's Point of Equidistance is at 11° Capricorn (see) and his Ascendant is at the beginning of dictatorial Aquarius (after Ra-phael, in its second degree). Venus, the sweetest of planets, is in conjunction with his Ascendant (6° Aquarius); in quadrature with Mars (02° Taurus), meaning inner conflict; in sextile Neptune (02° Aries), the planet of crowds and popularity. Uranus, ruler of his Ascendant is in sesquiquadrate with the Ascendant, portending more inner strife; it is in the sign of social life (Gemini) and precisely where the capital of England's Ascendant is placed (18°). Moreover, crafty Mercury, placed in the house of personality, is in the degree where London has its MC (13° Aquarius), and it is widely known that the best political prognostic is a close connection between the main feature of a politician's horoscope and those of his country's capital.

28° Capricorn

Symbol: Atlas carrying the world on his back

This is a divalent symbol, as it may mean huge wealth as well as an unbearable, crushing burden. Spiritually this may be brought into agreement, as wealth is tantamount to a millstone around one's neck, and the serfdom of the poor is no less a chain than the rich man's swollen purse.

Intellectually, the Symbol means geographic, nautical sciences and the like; exploration of the globe and travel at large; indirectly, astronomy and mathematics. If other aspects help, there may be a vast intelligence; less good components make for what is commonly termed a blockhead or worse. Anyhow, whether bright or dull, this is a methodical mind, with well-defined ideas and rigorously logical reasoning.

Whether rich or a slave, the native is sometimes driven by immoderate ambition, the slave craving a position not only of absolute independence but of lordship, and the rich never setting a limit to his yearning for new wealth. Ambition, however, does not bar righteousness and chastity; slavery—or what is felt as such—does not exclude an honorable or even a famous name; and lucky components may make the native into a pillar of society, either in a moral, scientific, political or financial sense. The relations of the parts to the whole of the pattern must determine this last point.

Example: Both the Communists and their opponents may be shocked to learn that the Sun of the Soviet Union is here.

29°Capricorn

This is one of the finest degrees of the whole zodiac and bestows even physical beauty, but its highest prize lies in the inner stillness and, enlightenment it confers. The native has such a wealth of spiritual resources as to enable him to, preserve an unruffled self-assurance under any circumstances. Even if poor and uneducated, he will draw from an inborn, instinctive wisdom, an unerring insight into nature, its beings and its laws; if in a position to learn, he will delve deep into the knowledge of such laws and will be led to discoveries that will raise him into renown; but in any case, whether famous or obscure, he will prefer inner meditation and silence to the fuss of the teeming human masses.

Other components, in contrast with the spiritual nature of this one, may let love of nature and animals drift along utilitarian lines and result in the trade of a dairy farmer, a cheesemonger, or a beemaster.

30° Capricorn

Symbol: The cylindrical part of a shrapnel

Something fatal, the highest prestige, art or even power to sway over others but not to rule himself.

Power of concentration, inability to alter the direction of one's inborn impulses. Lightning-like promptness and discontinuity in action. Lofty ambitions, huge hopes; an extraordinary energy; often foreign to the native himself, but anyhow likely to boost him very high; but he may dash along like a fiery meteor, whereas the results of his actions will disappoint everyone as the power propelling him toward the goal may let him overreach himself and go astray.

The horoscope as a whole will tell what kind and what amount of luck he will get; surely, should the native make a mistake, he cannot rectify it or retrace his steps. On the other hand, the propelling force is an impulse, a dash and not a constant drive, and tends

212

to sink to naught through friction, wear and tear, so that either the goal set to him is reached within a certain time, or utter failure has to be faced.

The native's career will resemble a parable in its broad outline. Example: Napoleon I (Moon's degree). Here also is the MC of Frederic the Great, the inventor of modern artillery.

AQUARIUS

01° Aquarius

Embarrassment of riches. If other components enable the native to make up his mind without delay and stick to his decision, he will be in a position to enjoy the fruit Providence has strewn in plenty along his path. Faith in God and contempt of hackneyed ideas and prejudices are supported in him by a creative imagination and a fair intelligence, but those faculties may drift easily into fatalism, self-centered haughtiness and idle daydreaming.

Yet the real danger lies elsewhere. Should the pattern fail to show any trace of resolution which, as stated above, the native even too badly needs, the very favors of fortune would be wasted on him. Many an occasion will pop up and slide away before he has found it in himself to grasp it. His rightful place in the world may be taken by the first comer, even by someone less intelligent and scrupulous than himself.

This degree rules the hands; favorable aspects give ambidexterity, whereas harmful ones make every gesture of the upper limbs awkward and clumsy.

02° Aquarius

An outstandingly powerful and manifold mind, capable of probing deep and ranging far, keen on scientific research and philosophical musing (each of which does not bar the other); apt to fathom the unknown and to improve on the known; independence in character and scientific methods; a great handiness.

215

03° Aquarius

As the olive, when broken in the mill oozes sweet oil, so let your broken heart bleed a song that redeems, uplifts your will.—D'Annunzio

It is a degree of action closely following thought; there is love of art, mastery in one's chosen art or profession, courage and combativeness. The head or the legs risk being affected by numbness, illnesses or wounds. Pain in general casts its shadow over the native's karma, but a stalwart will power enables him to bear it like a man. There may be disappointments, sorrow, dissolution of bonds, perhaps grief over the loss of dear ones.

Victory is likely to crown the native's steady daring, but it will be as splendid as fruitless. The native has a mission to fulfill and is not supposed to fight for his own sake. Occult initiation is not unlikely.

Examples: Lord Byron (Sun's degree); Gabriele D'Annunzio (degree of the Point of Equidistance); General de Gaulle (degree of the Point of Equidistance); General Eisenhower (degree of Jupiter, ruler of the Ascendant).

04° Aquarius

Unpopular authority. The native is likely to be misunderstood, but will be held in esteem by those in power and may be entrusted with delicate, sometimes very important, tasks. The most congenial field of action seems to be diplomacy in general and politics in particular, but any activity connected with travel and negotiation is possible, a typical example being trade, either on one's own or as a representative. It goes without saying that the whole of the pattern must point this way.

An oversensitive temperament, jealously close in self-defense and liable to have its purposes misconstrued. Inborn authority is strangely coupled with some puerile traits; e.g., a liking for flashy and liveried attire. The character is unsteady but, at the same time, likely to offer the toughest passive resistance. This last feature may decide victory.

Examples: The Third Reich, or Nationalist Socialist Germany (degree of the Moon, ruler of the Ascendant). Catherine de Medicis' MC is to be found in this degree.

05° Aquarius

The native will be weak with himself and his sexual urges, but self-assertive, even too much so, toward others; he will leave a marked imprint on his own surroundings. An engaging, though selfish, lively, prompt and precocious being, he will show a marked artistic talent since his green years, which can thin out into good taste, or can gain volume and ground and can blossom into creative power.

But his existence is threatened with untimely death, and luck is undermined by all the trouble the native will call down upon himself through his sexual urge, either as love of the opposite sex or as exhibitionism, narcissism and worse, I

06° Aquarius

Symbol: Wagner's Sixtus Beckmesser

The typical figure of the peevish, stubborn, ambitious, envious and cantankerous critic. He is devoid of neither taste nor of finer feelings; as he is something of an artist himself, his eye will at once detect a breach of the rules of perspective, and his ear will be keen enough to perceive the tiniest intervals in sounds and to denounce the slightest off-key note. Artistic technique will hold no secrets from him. But he is a slave to school precepts and prejudice, his jealous god is method, and he subconsciously strives after an unearthly perfection. He never will be satisfied with what he knows or possesses, hankering as he does after things he can improve upon and picture to himself as beautiful as his heart can desire.

He has no sense of measure. Though he is fond of practical jokes and lively verbal fencing, his humor lacks the human touch. A pliant and hard-working pupil and later an outstanding professor, he ought to get through other stars the winged stroke this degree in itself cannot bestow, in order for him to become a real master. He will strive subconsciously to fill up the vacuum with travel, which can play an important role in his existence.

Outside the artistic and teaching field, he may gain some repute as a speaker. As a priest, he would emerge as a preacher, and his services as a director of conscience would be in great demand. All this is likely if other strands in the pattern bear out a great eloquence, lead toward the sacred orders, etc.

In a more modest nativity, artistic leanings may pave the way to humbler activities and may confer the makings of an outstanding craftsman; on an even lower plane, it may lead to a juggler's sleight of hand.

I think here are all the prerequisites for a good chess player: a sharp eye, a grinding criticism of the opponent's moves, an agnostic and methodical spirit.

07° Aquarius

Dangers deriving from sudden impulsiveness, indiscretion and stubbornness. Greater offensive than defensive aptitude. Oh the other hand, the power the native is entitled to would be greater than the one he groundlessly insists on wielding in another way. A sharp psychologist, just and objective toward others, he cannot either probe into himself or cling to his own principles, and will be satisfied with a lower status than due him; at the same time he will squander his forces in mean squabbles and pointless strife from which only danger can accrue.

Example: Warren Harding (degree of the Point of Equidistance).

218

08° Aquarius

Symbol: A man with a broken chain hanging on his foot

Here is certainly a sincere thirst for freedom. The native's defiant, brisk and masterful character will endow him with growing efficiency as more and more of his energies are released by his conquest of freedom. But his karma is certain to bring him either moral or physical chains, and he himself is likely to tend unconsciously to chain his neighbors. Therefore, the hidden aim of this degree will be the release from bondage. One's bondage will in its turn warm to respect the freedom and dignity of one's fellow beings.

Kindness and love of justice are not wanting. The sense of justice may not be enough, as there is too much self-centeredness, leading the native to look at things from a too-strict personal point of view. This applies to the mind as well, as the individual flight into new and unfenced territories is held back by the fetters of logical reasoning.

Should the native be able to break his chains, his thought thus freed might soar beyond the Threshold.

09° Aquarius

Symbol: St. Paul struck by the lightning flash of the
Spirit on his way to Damascus

A huge inner power, immense mental horizons. A courage exempt from earthly ambitions, the utmost physical or mental combativeness; an orator's, a polemicist's, or a critic's temper; brisk and watchful brains and nerves, capable of the timely and quick execution of any task.

The native is likely to embrace religion, turning his back to the atheism or agnosticism he formerly professed, or to convert himself from a lower to a higher form of faith; and then it will just fit his nature to try to convert others, to become a missionary or to preach in his own country. However, he is certain not to get at truth gradually but by a sudden flash, and he is apt to get down at once to the task he feels himself entrusted with, as resolutely and firmly as his fiery personality bids him.

The physical organ of sight is extremely sensitive and therefore vulnerable. Examples: Gustav Adolph the Great, of Sweden (degree of the Point of Equidistance); Charles George Gordon, the hero of Khartoum (Sun's degree).

10° Aquarius

Symbol: A beheaded man

The native will either be a scatterbrain or will risk bodily losing his head to the executioner's ax, or will face maiming, laming, or invalidity.

Apart from this, the influence is divalent if not altogether contradictory. Experience can teach many things, can drop a pinch of salt into the native's head and inspire him to a fondness for archaeological or historical research and even, at the limit, can make him into a good organizer of other people's activities. In this last case, however, the sense or polarity of such organizing is not revealed by this degree and must be sought elsewhere in the nativity, as it may tend toward evil as well as toward go6d.

Anyhow, such a gift will be the exception, the rule being still dispersal of energy. A gift for managing and ruling is, as I said, a limit; even if the native gets his mind under control, he will use it only to sink back into memories of his past, whereas in the present or in the future his plans will stay just as fruitless as will his sexual power.

The early or efficient cause of these evils may be traced back to his having been exposed, orphaned or neglected, and therefore, inadequately brought up in childhood or in his early adolescence; hence the waste.

11° Aquarius

Symbol: A headless man, whose body is in full battle harness

Warlike, rushing and forcible, outwardly splendid and inwardly noble, the native seems to have no bearings and no aim. Reckless—nay, altogether blind—he will be destitute of any authority; his victories and his possible popularity will be short-lived. If a winner, he will not know how to exploit his victories and will leave his shoulders undefended for his opponents to hit back; if a loser, he will wander about as luck would have it. In a material sense, there is a real danger of wounds, mutilation, or death sentence.

Example: Paul Doumer, thirteenth president of the French Republic, fallen victim to a political attempt (degree of the Moon).

12° Aquarius

Symbol: Lese majesty

(A pictorial image of the symbol may be supplied by Molingue's celebrated painting showing Etienne Marcel as he covers the French Dauphin with his cap in sign of protection, after having had the marshals of Champagne and Normandy killed before his eyes. On a higher plane, a case in point may be the figure of Beethoven crossing a group of emperors and archdukes in the Schönbrunn Park, his head high and his hat on.

Can a man born to rule find his feet in a world where even the lords do menial work and live like slaves? Craving liberty and being proud, strong and resolute, he has such a high feeling of self-respect that he cannot allow others to presume to have him at their beck and call, or to exact—or even to expect—homage or salute from him. Free from lip service as well as from inferiority complexes, he is, however, still swayed by his inner feelings and endeavors to stem and hide them; but the harder he tries to confine them, the harder they bite him.

This is not the only weakness of such a strong mind; unless favorably aspected elsewhere, he will be haughty and devoid of human sympathy; he even may trample upon his inferiors and prove wicked and crafty at the same time.

Bad aspects may earn him a sentence for rebellion, insubordination, resistance, or outrage upon armed hirelings, and the like; he may be compelled to beat it or to cross the border for a certain time. Other, less unfavorable stars may force him to champ at the bit for awhile in bondage, or on one of those ignoble duties going under the name of civil service or military career.

It may be remarked, by the way, that in ancient Egypt the scribes were slaves and there were no misunderstandings about this; the juridical figure of the public servant exactly corresponds to his moral function.

Examples: Nicolas Fouquet, finance supervisor under Louis XIV (degree of the Point of Equidistance); Franklin D. Roosevelt (Sun's degree).

N.B. The renown of Dumas' novel *"Le Vicomte De Bragolonne"* dispenses me from commenting upon Fouquet's example, though a less-known detail may be of interest; his bearing was *quo non ascendant.*

13° Aquarius

Symbol: An array of mediaeval knights; shields, doublets and shabracks are showily trimmed with each warrior's own heraldry.

Attachment to one's own interest and to the interests of one's family and clan; combativeness in all fields, from literary polemic to real weapons. Fine manners and quick action.

All these features may sublime into the highest virtues-watchful and selfless daring, love of one's home and ancestry, human solidarity, noble pride—and may ebb into the correspondent vices—unscrupulous and reckless aggressiveness, a decayed gentry's pride and prejudice, a gangster's solidarity with crime, conventional formalism.

The native will have to be on the lockout if he is to avoid destiny's unexpected blows, and he will have to respect his neighbors if he wants to be respected himself.

Example: Tradition places the city of London's MC in this degree.

14° Aquarius

Endowed with a poor memory but alive to the slightest impressions of pain, the native will, right in the middle of his earthly life, face sudden disaster, as injury to life and limb, financial breakdown or any other accident. Such a mishap will prevent the native from getting on in one of his activities, in which he is unlikely to pick himself up again. From then on, should the interrupted work have been his main one, the native's future will really be in God's hands.

15° Aquarius

Symbol: The Statue of Liberty (in the New York harbor)

An all-round open mind, an enterprising character, an ambitious and adventurous spirit; the native's country is the whole world, as he feels at home everywhere. In his native country he will associate happily with congenial cooperators and he will do excellent business abroad, profitable both to himself and to others.

Fluent in speech and articulate in writing, possessed of a sharp insight, pleasant and easy with everyone but far from submissive, the native will build himself up into a splendid financial position if other stars lead him to trade or to other lucrative callings. On the contrary, should he take to purely intellectual or altogether spiritual activities, he would enjoy a transcendental intuition enabling him to perceive the spiritual reality underlying this world.

16° Aquarius

Symbol: Vulcanus forging Jupiter's thunderbolts

I am come to send fire on the earth; and what will I, if it be already kindled?—Luke 12:49

A fiery will, a stormy ardor; immense, often inordinate, aspirations, boundless phantasy and enthusiasm, a nearly always unhinged and jarring mood; in a word, a volcanic character.

There usually will be a modest career not in keeping with the size of the native's ideals or with the power of his constructive mind. A rough and tumble life, full of surprises and ups and downs, is not at all unlikely. The profession or trade may be bound with physical fire or glow with the flame of Spirit, normally symbolized by fire. Let this be a warning in both senses, as playing with fire is usually dangerous, and one can easily come off with ugly scars.

The native is likely to have the god Vulcanus' bodily defects.

Examples: Richard Wagner (Moon's degree). Here I should place Lord Byron's Ascendant (which Beer sets at 04° Cancer and Sepharial places somewhere in Scorpio). The poet's Jupiter is at about 17° Gemini and his Venus in 25° Aquarius.

17° Aquarius

Symbol: A sick woman in bed

It is one of the worst influences, as it can lame the body, pervert the soul, poisoning both at the same time. Idiocy also can fall to the native's lot.

18° Aquarius

Symbol: A perched-up owl

Woe to him that is alone.—Eccl. 4:10

Wickedness and gloom. Shyness and sensitivity, a shunning

of company that may drift easily into misanthropy. In spite of the native's sexual power, marriage is unlikely. Sex will come to light as a selfish, sustained and cruel coquettishness, a fierce jealousy not exempt from envy.

Unless excluded by the rest of the pattern, such a influence can lead to sexual magic; many a witch and sorceress will be born under this star.

As sex is marked, so also is the character. There will be sensitiveness to cold and danger of harm to the lower limbs. Barring pointers to the contrary, life is full of mishaps and grief, the greatest being the progressive estrangement of relatives and friends as the years go by.

19° Aquarius

Symbol: A head severed from its bust is held high by
someone and still goes on talking.

The native will go far. A man of many parts, he may, however, dangerously skirt light-headedness or amateurishness. He is not independent, but wields a measure of authority that may make him feared. He will love his lord as faithfully as did Pilades love Orestes, or as Kurnewald loved Tristram.

All these features may be marked enough, but they do not reveal the key of his personality, lying in a formidable either psychic or bodily strength, such as to enable him to survive catastrophes apt to shatter lesser men. Vulgarly he would be thought to possess nine lives, as is said of cats. Just in the nick of time, when everything seems lost and any further hope of rescue would sound absurd, a providential intervention allows him to survive. Usually this will come as a deserved prize for the faithfulness mentioned above.

Will it be faith in one's lord or in the Lord? Here the rest of the horoscope should supply the answer. At the limit, the Symbolic image recalls the miracle of St. Denis, who, after being beheaded, rose and picked up his head again. At the opposite limit, the native would be an executor of Justice's dire retribution, and would show the populace the culprit's severed head.

20° Aquarius

Symbol: Hermes invents the zither.

(Remember how the God of Wisdom built the first stringed instrument by fitting two horns to a turtle shell, thus making up the resonator.)

This degree denotes skill either in art (music in particular and, more especially, stringed instruments), or in industry, medicine or science at large. An everyday philosophy, much fondness of work, a great handiness, a patience apt to stand the stiffest tests, and an even excessive prudence.

By this I do not mean either tearfulness or sloth; the native treads with leaden feet like a tortoise, keeping, as it were, to the Italian proverb, "What is done accurately need be done but once."

Fenced in by a nearly hermetic reserve, he enjoys his neighbors' esteem, though he holds aloof from them, engrossed perhaps in planning his future welfare. But anyhow, he seems unaware of the outside world. The astrological picture in its entirety will have to say whether such a prudence will sink to cunning or sublime into a noble equanimity.

Barring pointers to the contrary, life will be exceptionally long. The native's face, however, is liable to appear precociously lined and shrunken, but his die-hard physique is likely to lack real ruggedness.

21° Aquarius

Symbol: A monk lying face upward on the naked earth

This influence strongly reminds one of the three hundred seventeenth degree. Yet this three hundred twenty-first degree offers one way out: the cloister, provided the prior has some grit and will prevent loafing.

22° Aquarius

Symbol: The sirens

Enmities but luck. When not altered by other components, the female native, or the male native's mate, will postpone any affection and any ideal to the care of her person. Her physical appearance will be a matter of taste and will appeal especially to those fond of lusty roundness, apart from the real beauty of her complexion, hair and eyes. Her disposition will be less appealing, being a mixture of cunning and violence, of unbridled passion and cool scheming.

As beauty is not rated an asset in a man and excessive personal grooming is a morbid symptom of narcissism, this influence will lead a man nowhere. In a man, beauty will be an excuse for that fitful impulsiveness and that loss of self-control in anger which in a woman are usually blamed on the weakness of her sex. If stressed by other malignant stars, those sudden surges of wrath can lead to hideously brutal acts and can transform the woman into a termagant and the man into a murderer.

Should other factors supply those inhibitions which this degree by itself fails to grant, the blind urges may be checked and bent, so that violence may turn into manly resoluteness. But too much would be needed to sublimate the cunning selfishness, the wickedness and the turbid flow of passions which make the native into a hated, though perhaps feared and even admired personality.

23° Aquarius

This is one of the best zodiacal degrees as it bestows a strong and merry, active and tireless, faithful and sturdy nature, an industrious intelligence, a constructive mind, capable of creation and execution at the same time; a knack for trade and, usually joined to it, artistic taste. Where other factors concur, it may bestow genius.

This degree's most beautiful feature is the cheerful eagerness with which the native carries out his work and gives it the finishing touches; humble as his work may be, he plunges into it as enthusiastically as if it were a feast. Any advice as to the most congenial profession would be wasted on him, as he instinctively knows what he must do and does it well.

The crucial point of this degree lies in the province of social life, as the native's relations with his neighbors will have a decisive; influence. If the horoscope shows favorable features in the sector of trade and of the outside world (the non-ego), the fruit of his personal initiative will increase an hundredfold through intelligent association. On the other hand, bad components in those aspects will hinder success, arouse redoubtable rivalries and unfair competition, and threaten loss of the deserved profits.

Example: Thomas A. Edison (Sun's degree).

24° Aquarius

This influence confers a bright mind, but carries something tragical in itself and spells mishap. The rest of the horoscope will have to say whether the native is himself the author or the victim of such bad luck. But whether evil or ill-fated, the native will be an unhappy being anyhow, unable as he is to grasp the meaning of his own actions. According to what the stars say, he may lack partial or total moral sense or prudence. He will get into trouble unconsciously in any event, and will realize his plight when it is too late.

The physique inclines to weakness, as does the mind. I said there is a remarkable intelligence. I may add, this is not in keeping with all the rest. However, the chance of distinguishing oneself in some branch of science is not ruled out; the native is even likely to attain renown, though it may be in a good or bad sense.

Examples: Abraham Lincoln (Sun's degree); Louis Deibler, executioner (Sun's degree).

25° Aquarius

No lack of rational intelligence, but rather a lack of inner balance. Passion may blind and momentarily black out the native's wits, provided of course that other stars point the same way. (Mercury in quadrature with the Moon, Uranus or Neptune; Neptune with the Sun; Saturn in Scorpio and in the house of reclusion, etc.).

In such cases, the native is apt to fall in with the typical picture of the mad criminal, who believes that his moral duty is to kill, either to pacify the wraith of a revengeful relative or to restore the stained honor of a lineage. (Unfortunately, only lunatics believe that a family's honor resides exclusively in a woman's reproductive organs. Such ridiculous and revolting ideas are especially spread in the Mediterranean countries). Or he may kill on account of other crazes rooted in his psychical foreground and likely to invade gradually the patient's consciousness and to obsess him.

Neither the typical born criminal nor the passional criminal is excluded. Nobody can deny that the former is abnormal; the latter is only momentarily so, as long as it is enough for the flash of passion to dazzle his mind and to guide his hand to bloodshed.

Other factors must decide whether he is to be a harmless lunatic, a sham, or a regular criminal. Certainly if other strong components fail to neutralize the effects of this degree, he will be a pathological case or, at any rate, an unbalanced being. Such a lack of measure will leave a trace even in the good deeds he is quite likely to do if more benevolent stars lead his passionate nature to find an outlet there.

Example: Pope Alexander VI, Lenzuol y Borgia (degree of the Point of Equidistance).

26° Aquarius

Symbol: A water source spurts forth by a high mountain top and dashes down, filling its boulder-strewn path with hissing foam.

Among his neighbors, the native will stand out like a beacon, but his nature is as reckless, and his position as unstable, as water; the danger of tumbling is an ever-present one. His steadfastness is greater than his firmness, the elemental forces of the whole being are more powerful than limpid. I do not say that there is mud, but the purest source loses its transparence if it squirts out too violently.

As in other similar cases, the danger of tumbling may even literally come true; the rest of the pattern must throw light upon this as well as on whether that steadfastness is not to turn into a boring persistence.

Should other strands in the pattern offset the headiness of the temper and induce a certain order in the turmoil of ideas babbling up in his mind, the native could turn into a real master (initiatory components would make him into an occult master); on the other hand, baneful components may warp his recklessness into blindness (taken literally or figuratively).

Examples: Arturo Toscanini (degree of Jupiter, ruler of the Ascendant); Prince Bismarck (degree of the Point of Equidistance).

27° Aquarius

Symbol: A Renaissance castle

This is one of the most desirable degrees. The native is a highly aristocratic being in the fullest sense of the word, as he is likely to join refinement and splendor, generosity and prudence, kindness and reserve. He will be extremely liberal, and a conservative in the best sense. He is nobly proud of his house and lineage; he delights in remembering the deeds of his ancestors and, though reproving the bad ones, he nonetheless keeps as careful a record of those as he does of the good ones. He loves his country's soil as his own land, his nation as his ancient kin, and is as jealous of the national as of the familiar customs.

230

He is apt to couple the cult of the past with a keen sense of progress and evolution, and is likely to initiate reforms and to be the trailblazer of new ideas. Therefore, the die-hard gentry may consider him a revolutionary and the all-out Jacobins may twit him with conservatism. If the stars do not hinder his progress, such slander will not keep him from following a brilliant political career, if he should wish to. As a politician he will enjoy immense popularity and prestige, owing to his broadmindedness, his civic sense, his humanity, and especially owing to the instinctive liking that everyone will take to him.

He has a keen mind, perhaps an excess of inquisitiveness. Though he has a generous and hospitable heart, the sense of private property and of hereditary right is lively in him. His only real defect may be an unjustified cocksuredness, or an undue eagerness to defend himself and his own property.

Fortune conferred by this degree is really what the Romans called *Fortuna Major;* little as the stars smile on him, the astrologer may foretell the native, ". . . should you follow your star you cannot fail to land in glorious harbour." (Dante, *Inf.* 15, 55-56).

Examples: Napoleon III (degree of the Moon); Albert Lebrun, president of the French Republic (degree of the Moon); Sir Ernest Shacklefon (degree of the Sun).

28° Aquarius

Symbol: A man guzzling from a flask

The assets will be merriness, an absolute naturalness of manner, a direct insight into reality. This degree's besetting sin is a tendency to ply the rummer. There will not be bad manners; there will be no manners at all.

Possible vices are alcoholism, idleness, fondness of gambling, dissoluteness, a tendency to loathe both poverty and the means to keep it at arm's length. Any reflection upon the consequences is superfluous.

29° Aquarius

Symbol: A knight with a drawn sword

An heroic degree, but its chivalrous character may degenerate into quarrelsome-ness, or induce a destiny too bristling with frightful ordeals to be borne by human beings.

Should no other element point to recklessness or threaten hurdles too high to clear, we may foresee a degree of luck as high as the degree of daring, military and civil honors, the raising to the highest dignities, fame among contemporaries, and renown in posterity.

As the body is nimble, so the mind is swift, suitable for word fights as sharp as the sword. Military careers and the art of fencing, diplomacy and the bar ought to be accessible in themselves, but an eye should be kept upon the rest.

Example: Francis I, king of France (degree of the Moon, ruler of the Ascendant).

30° Aquarius

Symbol: A king on his throne, wearing the crown

This degree portends an all-round fortune, excepting perhaps only the faithfulness of one's marriage partner. The native himself—or herself—is faithful and sincere but lukewarm if not altogether frigid; hence the danger of marital unhappiness. This refers to a married person, but wedlock is far from likely as this degree suggests that smooth, self-possessed wisdom expressed in the Italian proverb "Better alone than badly matched." Unfortunately such an easy self-mastery may breed selfish isolation and, at the limit, misanthropy.

For the rest, this is one of the noblest degrees, a really royal one. It promises the subject, whatever his origin, undisputed authority, easy riches, and high feelings. The moral feelings are austere and inflexible in spite of ambition and even thirst for power.

PISCES

01° Pisces

Symbol: Goethe's Mittler in his work "Elective Affinities"

Concordia discors: a typically dualistic and divalent influence. The native is a live wire, and his main problem is how to deal with his neighbors in all senses from spiritual exchange to sexual intercourse. Whether he will eventually find his feet, or stay a misfit in his surroundings, will depend on the horoscope looked at as a whole.

In the former case the native will be an extremely sociable person and a useful go-between, intercessor and peacemaker. He will make a faithful and staunch friend, endowed with the gift of persuasion and of adapting himself to any environment. Marriage ought to be extremely lucky unless particularly unfavorable aspects bear upon marriage relations in the horoscope; ambitions ought to be peacefully satisfied.

In the latter, he will be a peevish, grumpy, inquisitive meddler, with an unpredictable and often snappishly short temper.

Exactly as in Goethe's character we chose as a symbol, the virtues and shortcomings of this degree may co-exist in a few cases (see Freud's theory of ambivalence).

The most suitable professions are those connected with the law: magistrate, barrister, solicitor, coroner, attorney, notary.

02° Pisces

The native is a good-natured, outwardly harmless scholar, but excessive negligence and inborn slackness prevent his being refined. Far from being rough, he is superficially very uncouth, a lazy, haphazard fatalist.

But an emotional, touchy, fitful and skittish, altogether choleric character slumbers under the surface, which one had better not rouse. The rush of self-willed fury of which He will then prove capable will be such as to smash and sweep away everything and everyone. A boundless ambition, which was dozing under the cloak of the epicurean student, awakens suddenly when the native realizes mankind's cowardice and its willingness to appreciate only those who bully it and brutally kick it in the pants.

In spite of this the native is unlikely to manage well what he has, or to acquire permanently new wealth, as his action develops by fits and starts and he does things only when roused. Once his fury has abated he is apt to wonder why one should act at all. Thus he may sooner or later find himself broke and forlorn.

This furious resentment may sublime into noble indignation, and ambition may purify itself into unselfish aspirations. Astrological components inducive of altruism may move the native to an heroic sacrifice for the benefit of mankind.

03° Pisces

Symbol: Through Jupiter Pistor's inspiration, the Romans, beleaguered on the capitol, throw white leaves to the besieging Gauls.

He is at the same time haughty and diplomatic, harsh and steadfast, fierce and hospitable, rough and generous—nay, lavish—to the point of squandering. A barbaric nature, coupling high spiritual gifts with a coarse, lusty, gluttonous grain. There is a peevish self-assurance and an unruffled self-indulgence, and also such gifts as to overcome the many enmities the native's rough manners may arouse.

Food problems are of paramount importance to the, native, who considers the art of cooking as the supreme art. He is therefore likely to find congenial employment in the trades connected with food (cook, innkeeper, baker, and the like); if rich by birth, he will delight in treating his friends.

Luck seems to top expectations. But if success is not apt to cost too high a price, lavishness and neglect on the other hand can cause trouble. Creed is like a powerful whirlpool, liable, as the Umbrian proverb has it, "to swallow a house up to its roof," and the evils that rudeness can work are but too well-known, as rudeness can cut people right off from human society.

Example: The Third Reich (degree of the Point of Equidistance).

04° Pisces

Symbol: A grave

The native's character will be as impenetrable as a grave, and may be as dismal. The nature is firm and fond of justice. Other factors will depend on their relation to the whole, like this degree's seemingly super-rational and potentially unlimited intelligence, to which, however, the rest of the horoscope must give a background and an outline.

Should the pattern indicate moral strength and not bar luck, the native may become a haven for the weak and the outcast, commanding at the same time the respect of those in power. A prudent, steadfast, self-sufficient personality, he may seem even more impenetrable and baffling to astrological research than to the vulgar eye. If helped by outstanding planetary aspects, this degree may give birth to a spiritual master.

On the contrary, in less lucky horoscopes this degree may produce mediumship, membership in a Masonic lodge or any other shamefully secretive feature. This sense of disgraceful mystery—may refer either to the super-sensible or to the lower human sphere, and may warp this degree's reserve into hypocrisy. But its justice and intelligence never will be blighted. This latter—something abstract in itself—may even appear admirable in a weak or wicked native.

Examples: George Washington (Sun's degree); Louis Deibler, executioner (degree of the Point of Equidistance). Here is also the MC of the French King Louis XIII. If the register has not been falsified, here is Adolf Hitler's Point of Equidistance.

05° Pisces

This influence has much in common with 30° Taurus (which see). It will give masterfulness and the accessory prestige over others in more or less refined utilitarian and earthly matters, lending toward enjoyment, though not exclusively material; its supreme pleasure is friendship.

But, for all his good intentions, the native, will) bring little luck to his devoted friends; however, unconsciously and against his own will, he will lead them to sacrifice, which he himself will not escape, as his inordinate and dissipated life will inflict a spell of ordeals and mishaps Upon him.

He is likely to get over it sooner or later. The pattern as a whole and a careful study of directions and of Uranus transits will have to show whether the beginning or the end of his life will be marked by bad luck.

Example: Nicolas Fouquet, *Louis* XIV's superintendent of finance (Sun's degree). Here is the degree of the Point of Equidistance of the Soviet Republic (Moscow, June 18, 1918).

06° Pisces

This degree tends to confer physical sturdiness and proportionate lust—or lusts. The craving for money is not the least of them. Whether he is compelled to hoard by a niggardly greed, or is driven to amass money by a reckless personal ambition aiming only at his own success, or in order to restore the level of his father's family up to the splendor of its gifts or its renown, the native seems to act on the firm conviction that one single lucky stroke—on the green carpet, at the races, or at the exchange-would manage to solve once and for all the twofold problem of food and the family's gilt edge. Yielding to this temptation would mean his final undoing.

The career of arms (not of the sea) seems to be the thing for him; a good marksman, an impenetrable character, a combative or downright aggressive person, a commanding figure, he has all the makings of a successful soldier or airman. And his power of concentration will fit him for different careers as well, according to the rest of the astrological data.

He is certain to set his aim high, and likely to attain it too, if he is as careful as he is ambitious.

07° Pisces

Symbol: The guardian of the Threshold

A hard trial to face; a frightful obstacle to overcome. In an otherwise irrelevant horoscope this degree will make the native into an usher, a doorkeeper, or, at best, a chamberlain. Where no other influences are at play, the native will be very keen on his own comfort and leisure, and this will make him dodge the obstacle mentioned above.

But little as the nativity swerves from the trodden path, here are the greatest chances of evil or good ever accessible to human beings, both of them in a mystical sense, with a deep religious feeling, or at least with a formal respect for rituals and ceremonies.

Where good factors concur, the way to saintliness is open to the native; or he can receive the highest initiation. He may become a church dignitary, or a valiant scientist, a profound thinker or even a remarkable/artist, but always on the plane of universal ideas.

237

A humble, but not bad, nativity, may bestow a lower degree in the ecclesiastical hierarchy (as a convent's guardian) or a low one (a lay brother, a sexton, or the like). On the other hand, a noble but rebellious theme will produce that amount of anti-clericalism that marks many a sincere follower of the church, or will lead the native so far as to oppose the church on behalf of a religious, or nearly religious, ideal striving to be more universal than Catholicism and to be worshiped more faithfully than Islam.

The concourse of evil components will lead to black magic, the practice of Satanism, possession or obsession, or in a humbler way, to witchcraft, shamanism, necromancy (so-called spiritualism) practiced as a ritual, etc.

The absolute absence of any spiritual component will lead to Goddess Reason's abstract worship in a more developed native, to non-initiatory freemasonry in an indifferent subject, and to sectarian partisanship in a poor devil.

In the field of affairs, of ordinary administration or even of everyday life, this influence will lead to heaping mistakes on mistakes. The native will have to pay more attention and to curb his absent-mindedness. Yet this is a remarkable mind with an uncommon steadiness in study.

Examples: Michelangelo Buonarroti (Moon's degree); Galileo Galilei (Sun's degree); Benedetto Croce (Sun's degree).

08° Pisces

Shiftiness and inner dissension, the co-existence of conflicting features such as, on one side, childishness or unripeness, lack of self-criticism, unfitness for independent life; and on the other side, a remarkable aptitude for business, practical skill on a small scale, bodily and mental resilience and fitness. Ability to do great deeds and to botch the simplest things. There is promptness and indecision, tact and boorishness, light-mindedness and immodesty, recklessness and at the same time naive cunning.

The brother or brothers have a great part in the native's life. Luck is ambiguous. There is a great love of water, which may grow into a positive danger if ominous pointers concur.

09° Pisces

Probably a long, certainly an adventurous life, with very unstable luck. The horoscope at large may tell us whether happiness or bad luck will prevail, whether trouble is to reach its peak in childhood, in youth, or in ripe old age. Certainly there will be hard ordeals to go through, leaving premature traces on the native's face and hair.

He will be able to change his ways and means all of a sudden, though staying faithful to himself; his religious principles will not prevent his being overcome and carried away by passion now and then. Nothing will either find him unprepared or throw him off balance and betray his feelings. He will be called rightly a man of character. Destiny bids him away from his country, on long journeys, and may sever his blood ties even in his adolescence. Other items in the pattern will give this forecast sharper outlines.

Example: Thomas Campanella (Moon's degree). (See note at 23° Virgo.)

10° Pisces

Felix qui potuit rerum conoscere causas.—Virgil, *George* 2, 490

Stubborn pursuit of the laws hidden behind nature's appearances. Hard and efficient work; an uncommonly sharp and analytical mind; practical sense, per haps marred by a certain routinism; a gift for exact sciences, especially physics and chemistry (or alchemy).

In front of strangers the native's behavior will be cautious and reserved. People's behavior toward him will be typical: he will be looked upon with that kind of uneasiness or mistrust that earthworms harbor in front of a really superior being, in whom they feel they might find their master. His teachings will be ignored rather than fairly discussed and openly fought. As to himself, he is so engrossed in his researches as to overlook such trifles; the deeper he delves into Nature's bosom, the more he loves her with a fervor which could be termed religious—even if he started to be a godless materialist. Willing to forego present glory, he works for those future generations who will in fact recognize him as a trailblazer. Barring harmful influences, his ought to be a long life, marked by a great magnetic force.

Examples: Rudolf Steiner (Sun's degree); Nicolaus Copernicus (Sun's degree).

11° Pisces

Another degree portending wanderings and gallivantings, its key lying, however, in the native's impulse to rear up and struggle against constraint.

His headiness and daring may border on foolhardiness; his fierce and defiant love of independence may strike as savage sullenness. Yet the spontaneous flourish of his speech, his frankness bursting forth like a force of nature, will make him liked in spite of his lack of measure. Luck is a decisive factor, but its sense will not be determined by this degree.

Sepharial suggests a career at the bar or with the pen. Both he and Charubel admit of priesthood. I leave them the responsibility for such statements.

12°Pisces

Gnoothi soauton . . .—Words on the lintel of Apollo's temple at Delphos

From the hub to the rim and back again.—Dante, *Par.*

14, 1

As he who looks back, back will have to go.—Dante, *Purg.* 9, 132

The problem of such an existence is how to insert oneself in the Whole, or, in other words, to find out where one's central point is. (Central, not middle, point, as hasty interpreters will have it.)

The way to one's own innermost core may prove an ordeal, taking up one's best years and further. At each crossroad the native may have to stop in utter puzzlement and retrace part of his steps. Like a wheel caught in the wrong contrivance, the native may go to pieces; or, like a sprocket wrongly fitted in its hub, he may skid off and come to grief; or even, like a wheel forever removed from any contrivance, he may end by becoming a pretty but useless trinket, an ornamental dead weight for himself and others. But once the hub is properly fitted upon its axle, the yield and the range of the native's activities can no longer be measured by conventional standards; his vitality is prodigious, and the depths to which his unfettered thought can reach are abysmal.. Thus the more dangerous is any aberration.

Examples: Wolfgang Goethe (Moon's degree); Sir Richard Quain, the eminent physician (Moon's degree).

13° Pisces

Subjected as he is to a divalent influence, the native will feel an urge either to help or to harm his neighbors, an alternative he will not easily escape. No living and letting live for him; his inner life does not seem to fulfill him, and his center of gravity seems to lie outside himself.

Here is the raw stuff to which only other pointers in the pattern can give shape. A nativity pointing to goodness or straightforwardness will make the native into an ideal marriage partner, an excellent cooperator, an exemplary citizen; one who will protect the oppressed and the poor, and who will spread his soothing influence on the surroundings where he lives. Yet, even in the best sense, he will have to meddle with other people's business arid will haunt them when they would rather enjoy their privacy.

If born evil, he will take tp black magic and will hurt others without afterthoughts for the sheer joy of it; he will oppress the poor, sadistically torture those who love him; in a word, he will be a devil incarnate.

An indifferent nativity will produce rather a pointless meddler.

14° Pisces

Energy, eagerness, steadiness, technical ability in performing one's task, which is more than likely to be heavy and at times long and hard. A slight fillip from other stars will be enough to make the native into a really talented engineer or pioneer; at the limit, a founder of colonies.

A healthy and rugged physique, a peaceful disposition, a simple and kind character. Luck and happiness, to which; the native is fully entitled, ought not to fail him.

Examples: Emperor Charles V (whose Sun is at 13°54'; therefore see the following degree as well).

15° Pisces

Symbol: Among the storm clouds in the heavens, an archangel appears, his sword drawn.

(I do not know if the archangel is Michael. He also may be the wayfarer's protector, Raphael (= God healed), whose weapon kills and recovers.)

Rational intelligence is far from clear if not downright blurred. But there is a great power of feeling, a bright, keen, piercing insight, whose edge is as sharp as a sword's.

242

Here are Seer Charubel's words: "Whosoever thou art, thou hast a mission to accomplish and thou wilt be armed with the necessary power and authority to execute that mission. Thou art a child of the Sun."

So far the positive side of this influence, which the nativity as a whole will be called upon to bear out according to Charubel's favorable construction. Yet one ought not forget that just and holy as that right may be, a sword is resorted to in its service, and that revenge does not behoove to men but to the gods. A grim, stormy, short-tempered, aggressive, even quarrelsome being, he will make many enemies without turning a hair, so sure is he of himself and of his aim, so unlimitedly does he rely upon his ambitions. Which may breed hateful superiority complexes or an utter inability to retrace one's steps, whatever the size of the mistake made.

A great love of travel; both literally and metaphorically, the native will make headway.

Examples: Michelangelo Buonarroti (degree of the Point of Equidistance); Louis Deibler, executioner (Moon's degree).

N.B. The executioner's example is revealing as to the principle I shall not tire of repeating: each degree can receive its right sense only when fitted into the whole. Deibler indisputably served justice, not handling its scales but its sword. Though he was of obscure birth, his mechanical skill led him far and he became *Monsieur de Paris*. Who was more feared, more hated than he?

16° Pisces

Attachment to one's family certainly is a virtue, and this native, who is very fond of his own, certainly has some redeeming features. Prudence he has galore, but his playing for safety, his inborn distinction, his fatherly love will not save him from strife. On the contrary, the quarrelsomeness attendant upon his life will, unless corrected elsewhere, make him repellent and widely unpopular. This is to be traced back to a stubborn, unbending, inexorable and not unsuccessful strain of ambition. His very excess of wariness will warp his prudence into offensive suspiciousness. Tenderly fond of his children, wards and pupils as he may be, he may, however, go so far as to be downright cruel with strangers, as a mere trifle is enough to arouse his anger.

Example: King James Stuart I of England and King James Stuart VI of Scotland (Moon's degree).

17° Pisces

Symbol: Headlong plunge

The native will fling himself headfirst into daring deeds before which others will think twice. Will those deeds be noble and heroic or will they be ambitious and foolhardy?

The pattern as a whole must reply. What seems certain is that, unless favorably aspected elsewhere, the drive pushing the native forward is but a momentary onrush, no steady urge. Moreover, it ought to be kept in mind that the native has set out alone; he cannot bank on anyone else's support, and his impulse naturally tends to run out. Then what can be expected?

No one is seen through to his goal by his more initial start. The native will have to expect from other factors the steadiness this degree seems to exclude, the prudence without which daring spells suicide, that sense of human fellowship and cooperation which ambitious people despise, though no lasting success can be achieved without them. Anyhow, the native will reach an essential turning point toward the middle of his life; any wrong move then will be liable to bring about his ruin, breakdown, bankruptcy, or the like. The symbol may be taken literally to mean drowning.

18°Pisces

Symbol: With lance at rest, two mediaeval knights, followed by their retinue on foot, ride against each other and the more gallant one throws his opponent.

(One has to bear in mind that the knight's word must be as straight as his sword, and that one single lie is enough to deprive him of his magic power—a thing which cannot be understood by those who fail to recognize knighthood's initiatory character.)

Man aride, death aside.—Italian proverb

An open, daring nature, easily led into contrast with the outside world, and into all sorts of danger.

The native is as unable to check his own passion as he is to enforce his will upon others. An outstanding organizer of collective undertakings, whether in time of war or peace, both in the political or industrial fields and in the artistic or religious ones, a brisk, deliberate embattled leader or chief; a formidable competitor; an aggressive controversialist, a lively orator, he will be ever launching all-out attacks both in real and in metaphorical wars. And it will be just this uncompromising resolve, this staking everything on one throw, this inability to retrace his steps, coupled with a passionate and at times unbridled nature, that may prove the undoing of such a chivalrous fighter. Love of violent sports still increases the chances of mishap. Horses are particularly dangerous.

Should the horoscope bear indications of a rebellious spirit, there would be danger of an open conflict with the law; whether the judicial, the ethical, or the religious law, the stars may foretell.

Example: Madame Curie (Moon's degree).

N.B. It is a case in point and it shows us that the omen can refer to the native indirectly, through someone to whom he or she is bound by affection.

19° Pisces

Symbol: A young man lying pierced by the thrust of a weapon

A keen, piercing mind, a critical and polemic gift, an inharmonious, aggressive, self-destructive nature; the temperament of a barrister or professional warrior.

A destructive nature does not necessarily bar practical sense or outbursts of enthusiasm. When these are spent, states of depression or suicidal ideas will crop up, the danger making itself felt especially during youth, as this will be affected by illnesses and many troubles. Ripe age will, on the whole, be less unlucky and, if helped by good aspects, may even be prosperous in spite of the lack of friends and the frequent quarrels and brawls.

Duels and strife will be hard to avoid; they will endanger physical integrity and threaten health and life itself.

20° Pisces

Symbol: Full Moon

Super-rational logic, or no logic at all. On a highly spiritual plane this influence will resolve itself into a stream of light. A noble soul soaring above the miseries of everyday life can expect many a gift from this degree. It may have to convey a message of love to mankind erring in darkness, and even may have inborn that imaginative consciousness constituting the first step of occult development. Beyond the range of any rational conceptions, the native's thought and behavior will be restored and prompted by lofty and dazzling imaginations.

On a lower plane this degree will breed public men. The subject then may be an idealist, but his activity, not a purely worldly one, Will never stumble on problems of consequence[1], he will let himself be led by merely political principles and will stick to empirical methods. In the light of such premises, it cannot even be said that the end justifies the means, as the end itself changes according to circumstances. Only that which proves useful for the time being is praiseworthy.

In an unlucky horoscope, castles will be built in the air, and the inability to have one's dreams come true will lead to changing one's opinions and to remolding one's random plans with the same casual unconcern with which one would change his shirt. Should

246

other such features concur, the danger of mental unbalance would set in.

21° Pisces

Symbol: Nightly duel of two ancient crusaders

My son, the cut was good, now think of the stitching.—Words of Catherine de Medicis to her son Henry III after the murder of the Duke of Guise

A very warlike temperament. Plenty of strife and struggle can be expected.

A rugged, proud and mettlesome individualist, daring and deliberate, ever ready to plunge into quick, efficient and even violent action. A supple and sharp mind, fond of peering and prying, a polemical spirit. There is a strong religious feeling, where, however, charity is not up to the level of hope. Conservative ideas, a respect for mankind's deep-rooted mistrust, and a dislike of novelty.

Combativeness may drift into brutal and bloodthirsty aggressiveness, individualism into fierce selfishness, conservatism into extreme reaction. Hopes can be fulfilled as long as speedy execution does not lead him to rash or reckless gestures. Darkness is harmful to the native.

Examples: Henry III, king of Prance (Moon's degree); Gustaf Adolf, called the Great, king of Sweden (Moon's degree).

22° Pisces

The native will play fast and loose with life, as it were, all his own show, and thus speed his ruin. In a female nativity this degree will promote immodesty if not shamelessness. For the rest, the native may well be harmless if the stars do not reveal other vices, but with concurring aspects he or she is likely to exert a more or less dangerous charm over everyone.

Wedlock obviously will prove a convict's chain to the native, which as obviously will not be the native's fault alone. The sector of marriage, its ruler and the Dragon's Head will have to be consulted.

Examples: Henry II, king of France (degree of Mercury, ruler of the Ascendant); Gabriel D'Annunzio (Sun's degree).

23° Pisces

Symbol: An old Frank in battle harness; his hair,
kept uncut according to the warned' custom, is wound
into a topknot from which it falls loose on his nape.
He hurls the double axe at his foe.

Here the axe blow of fatal determination is symbolized. Either the native's character is firm and manly, capable of initiative, certain of his aim and apt to snatch the right moment for action, or he is simply not up to his destiny and, high as his aspirations may be, he will shirk or rush through, give up before trying his luck, or waver, foam with rage or let things take care of themselves with a swaggering nonchalance for which there is not the slightest foundation.

Prophetic foresight is a feature, which may lead the native to try his luck at hazardous games or ruinous arbitrage.

24° Pisces

Symbol: A man and a woman lying together

The Symbol needs no further comment. It reminds us of Voltaire's fitting remark: Si *on ne marie pas les jeunes filles, elles se marient d'elles memes.* (See also 24° Aries.)

Examples: Marshal de Richelieu (Sun's degree); Paul Ehrlich (Sun's degree).

N.B. The sharper the contrast between the examples quoted, as obviously between these two, the more we can learn by setting them against each other.

Louis Francis Armand du Vignorod, Duke of Richelieu, ambassador, France's field marshal, etc., is famous for his victories but even more so for his love affairs. His utter unscrupulousness, both in harassing his defeated enemies and in jeopardizing the position of high-placed ladies, reached such a degree of wantonness as to shock even Louis XV's loose court. On two especially disgraceful occasions that foppish lecher, a past master at any kind of debauchery, had to be locked up in the Bastille, and twice a brazen Fortune set the brazen libertine free, whose prestige among the weaker sex grew accordingly.

Paul Ehrlich was a good husband and a good father. As a scientist, he is famous for his relentless fight against the most vicious among venereal infections-syphilis. To him goes the credit for the discovery of arsenical treatment of lues (Salvarsan). Which goes to show that there is no astrological influence that cannot be deflected to a higher plane; an idea which must become daily bread to the student.

In other words, like 24° Aries, so does this last but six zodiacal degree place the idea of sexual embrace above all thoughts; but nothing prevents this very idea from being faced scientifically rather than erotically. Likewise, the conjunction of Venus and Mars not only produces lady-killers and flirts, but can shift to the opposite extreme and give birth to puritans whose only worry is to prevent sexual gratification in others.

I shall not tire repeating it once more: it is the whole that gives a background and a meaning to every piece of the jigsaw puzzle; each element taken in itself means next to nothing. It could mean, anything.

25° Pisces

*Symbol: David about to sling at giant Goliath the
stone destined to kill him*

The native is ready to fight for victory and, in order to reach it, is ready to stand any amount of fighting. High as the reward may be, it is sometimes likely to appear inadequate to the native's heroic efforts. Driven by noble aspirations, as well as by lust, he will resort to any kind of assault. If attacked himself, he will drive the foe back with casual and playful self-assurance. Ready for the gravest decisions, he will go straight to his aim, even if this implies bloodshed. But he is likely to temper his aggressiveness with his sense of honor and to subordinate his tricks and makeshifts to the seriousness of his mission and to an unshakable faith in victory. A victorious fighter, he is more than likely to see that faith rewarded. Should he prefer a quiet life instead, the concrete result will be the more modest the less pleasant a peaceful life's task will have been for him.

26° Pisces

Symbol: Judith beheads sleeping Olophernes (Judith, 13-15).

Give me a cup, give me a stab, as in times past
In his immortal poem Alcaeus asked;
The stab he meant the tyrants' hearts to pierce,
The cup to drink and frolic on their hearse.—Carducci,
Giambi ed Epodi, 17

Unless provided with strongly opposing aspects elsewhere, the native will be a revolutionist, a tribune, a tyranicide. The woman native may turn a heroine, or a female gangster as well, as the rest of the nativity will have it. A man, the native ought to be on the lockout against the ambushes of the weak and of the weaker sex as well, as he can expect only trouble from that quarter.

Fearless and wary, strong and warlike, clear-sighted and a good organizer, he may tread safely his victorious path, as his friends' affection and his dependents' devotion will protect him from his foes. Against the little traitor, or traitoress, he is defenseless, a thing he ought to keep in mind in order not to let wine or love turn his head, or the dope of power let his watchfulness slumber. His downfall will spell ruin to the structure he has built and swayed.

Example: Maximilian de Robespierre (degree of Uranus, ruler of the Ascendant).

27° Pisces

Symbol: A naked man passing water

The positive sides of an influence bearing such an odd symbol are an absolute sincerity, an artlessness unhampered by mock prudishness, a free and easy way with people, which may win sympathy and friendships. But this degree is likelier to bestow the corresponding vices;'Instead of that lack of sham prudery, there may be real immodesty, cheekiness and brutal cynicism; instead of that free and easy demonstrativeness, a windy and empty verbosity with random chattering and unrestrained gossiping. In other words, a nature devoid of inhibitions and fond of scandals.

Nor is this enough, as especially weak natures are likely to be haunted by what so-called spiritualists call entities and could better be termed by the Christian word demons, their true name.

Total ruin threatens the substances. The need for prudence never will be overstressed; blind confidence never can be discouraged enough.

Bodily, the subject is exposed to bed-wetting; diabetes is not ruled out. A physical and psychic training is needed that does not overpower the nervous system, as any repression may engender Freudian complexes. Appropriate drugs may give back to the bladder the springiness it lacks, but green light baths are more efficient (sun baths through a colored glass slide, which can be applied directly on the organ to be healed). Time of the application should increase gradually .beginning with a few minutes on the first day.

Example: The Sun was here when the unity of Italy was proclaimed (March 17, 1861).

28° Pisces

Moderately ambitious, well-meaning, generous and amiable; uncommonly clever and fond of study, but led astray by totally wrong principles undermining even the most ingeniously built mental constructions, the native has a remarkable but shifty luck, which will be determined more clearly by other threads in the pattern. His body, as well as his knowledge, can be warped by some blemish, or his health can be sapped by some illness. Medicine and the like seem congenial callings.

29° Pisces

A drab mind, a limp will, impractical ideas, though not devoid of exactitude and care of details; a disciplined and rigorously methodic nature. The native obviously can be of great use in subordinate positions, whereas if left to himself he soon will lose courage, become listless and misanthropic, and drift aimlessly.

The danger of shipwreck is also materially present; or else the native may, be forced to wander at random and to feel desperately lonely in the very midst of human throngs.

30° Pisces

An overstressed sense of self with all attendant virtues and defects. A pride easily perverted into haughtiness, into encroachment upon the rights of one's neighbor, but never into mannerism. Great ambitions, strong desires, fiery passions, but a clear conscience; a deep righteousness is the really outstanding feature of the influence.

Will power and courage will shine in adversity and will enable the native to redress the ugliest situations and to get out of the most vicious scrapes. But the native's overbearingness will be hideous, his mind will be sharp and critical, but not nimble, and will tend toward haggling and quibbling. There is some gift for teaching and a certain freakishness.

Examples: Tamerlane (Timur Lenk), emperor of the Mongols (Moon's degree); Louis Deibler, executioner (degree of Pluto, ruler of the Ascendant).